Wonders

Grades 2–3
Practice and Assessment

FOUNDATIONAL SKILLS

Mc
Graw
Hill
Education

mheducation.com/prek-12

Send all inquiries to:
McGraw-Hill Education
8787 Orion Place
Columbus, OH 43240

ISBN: 978-0-02-129948-5
MHID: 0-02-129948-X

Printed in the United States of America.

9 10 11 12 RHR 18 17 16   C

CONTENTS

Phonemic Awareness

Phonics

Lesson 2: Short *a*

Lesson 3: Short *i*

Lesson 4: Short *o*

CONTENTS

CONTENTS

CONTENTS

Structural Analysis

CONTENTS

Name _____

Say the name of each picture. Say the beginning sound in both words. Draw a line to the picture on the right whose name begins with the same sound.

1.

2.

3.

4.

5.

6.

Name _____

Say the name of each picture. Draw a circle around the two pictures in each row whose names begin with the same sound.

1.

2.

3.

4.

5.

6.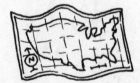

Name _____

Say the name of each picture. Say the ending sound in both words. Draw a line to the picture on the right whose name ends with the same sound.

1.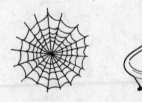

2.

3.

4.

5.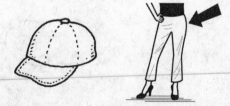

6.

Name _____

Say the name of each picture. Draw a circle around the two pictures in each row whose name ends with the same sound.

1.

2.

3.

4.

5.

6.

Name _____

Say the name of each picture. Say the middle sound in both words. Draw a line to the picture on the right whose name has the same middle sound.

1.

2.

3.

4.

5.
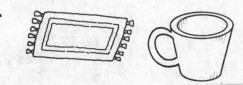 

6.

Name _____

Say the name of each picture. Draw a circle around the two pictures in each row whose name has the same middle sound.

1.

2.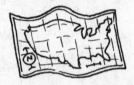

3.

4.

5.

6.

Name _____

**Say each picture name. Say the beginning sounds.
Circle the picture whose name has the same
beginning sound as the first picture in the row.**

1.			
2.			
3.			
4.			
5.			
6.			

Name _____

Say each picture name. Say the beginning sounds.
Circle the picture whose name has the same
beginning sound as the first picture in the row.

Name _____

**Say each picture name. Say the ending sounds.
Circle the picture whose name has the same ending
sound as the first picture in the row.**

1.			
2.			
3.			
4.			
5.			
6.			

Name _____

Say each picture name. Say the ending sounds. Circle the picture whose name has the same ending sound as the first picture in the row.

1.			
2.			
3.			
4.			
5.			
6.			

Name _____

**Say each picture name. Say the middle sounds.
Circle the picture whose name has the same middle
sound as the first picture in the row.**

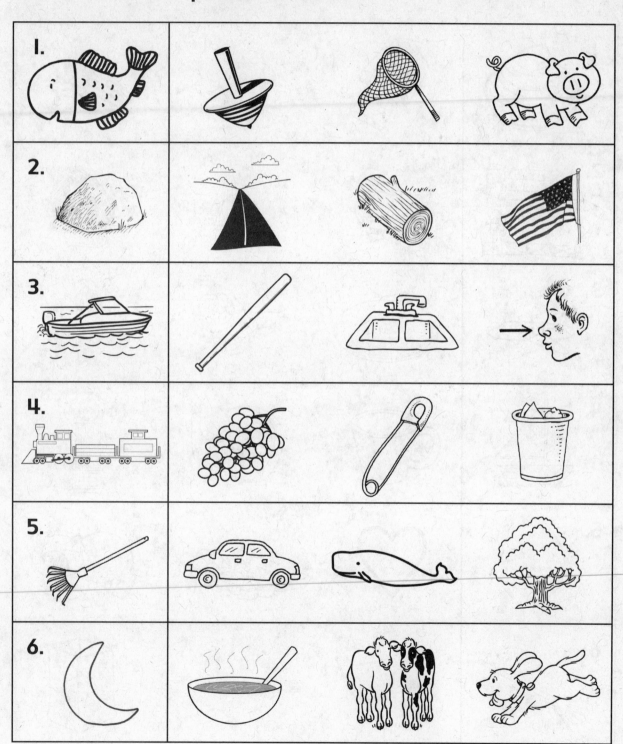

Name _____

Say each picture name. Say the middle sounds.
Circle the picture whose name has the same middle
sound as the first picture in the row.

1.			
2.			
3			
4.			
5.			
6.			

Name _____

Listen as your teacher reads the directions.

1.

2.

3.

4.

5.

Teacher Directions: Say the following sounds. Have students blend the sounds to say each word and then circle the picture that shows it. 1. /e/ /g/; 2. /ā/ /p/; 3. /h/ /ā/; 4. /sh/ /ü/; 5. /n/ /ē/

Name _____

Listen as your teacher reads the directions.

1.

2.

3.

4.

5.

Teacher Directions: Say the following sounds. Have students blend the sounds to say each word and then circle the picture that shows it. I. /ī/ /s/; 2. /t/ /oi/; 3. /p/ /ī/; 4. /b/ /ē/; 5. /p/ /ô/

Name _____

Listen as your teacher reads the directions.

1.

2.

3.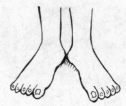

4.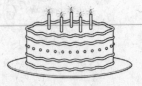

5.

Teacher Directions: Say the following sounds. Have students blend the sounds to say each word and then circle the picture that shows it. 1. /k/ /a/ /t/; 2. /n/ /ō/ /z/; 3. /hw/ /ā/ /l/; 4. /f/ /ē/ /t/; 5. /k/ /oi/ /n/

Name _____

Listen as your teacher reads the directions.

1.

2.

3.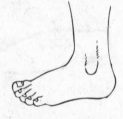

4.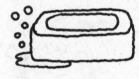

5.

Teacher Directions: Say the following sounds. Have students blend the sounds to say each word and then circle the picture that shows it. I. /kw/ /ē/ /n/; 2. /h/ /ī/ /v/; 3. /f/ /i/ /sh/; 4. /s/ /ō/ /p/; 5. /n/ /u/ /t/

Name _____

Listen as your teacher reads the directions.

I.

2.

3.

4.

5.

Teacher Directions: Say the following sounds. Have students blend the sounds to say each word and then circle the picture that shows it. I. /s/ /t/ /är/; 2. /t/ /r/ /u/ /k/; 3. /s/ /t/ /r/ /i/ /ng/; 4. /k/ /l/ /ou/ /n/; 5. /b/ /r/ /ā/ /d/

Name _____

Listen as your teacher reads the directions.

1.

2.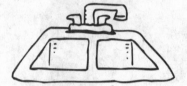

3.

4.

5.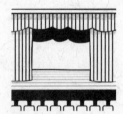

Teacher Directions: Say the following sounds. Have students blend the sounds to say each word and then circle the picture that shows it. 1. /th/ /r/ /ō/ /n/; 2. /sh/ /r/ /i/ /m/ /p/; 3. /b/ /r/ /e/ /d/; 4. /k/ /r/ /ou/ /n/; 5. /s/ /t/ /ā/ /j/

Name _____

Listen as your teacher reads the directions.

1.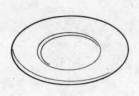

2.

3.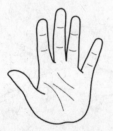

4.

5.

Teacher Directions: Say the following sounds. Have students blend the sounds to say each word and then circle the picture that shows it. I. /p/ /l/ /ā/ /t/; 2. /d/ /r/ /u/ /m/; 3. /h/ /a/ /n/ /d/; 4. /s/ /p/ /o/ /t/; 5. /s/ /t/ /a/ /m/ /p/

Name _____

Listen as your teacher reads the directions.

1.

2.

3.

4.

5.

Teacher Directions: Say the following sounds. Have students blend the sounds to say each word and then circle the picture that shows it. 1. /s/ /l/ /e/ /d/; 2. /s/ /t/ /r/ /ī/ /p/ /s/; 3. /b/ /r/ /a/ /n/ /ch/; 4. /p/ /l/ /a/ /n/ /t/; 5. /f/ /r/ /e/ /n/ /d/ /s/

Name _____

Listen as your teacher reads the directions.

1.

2.

3.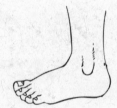

4.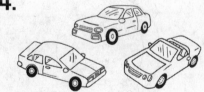

5.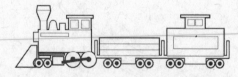

Teacher Directions: Say the following sounds. Have students blend the sounds to say each word and then circle the picture that shows it. I. /t/ /w/ /i/ /s/ /t/; 2. /b/ /e/ /n/ /ch/; 3. /f/ /r/ /ü/ /t/; 4. /s/ /t/ /är/ /z/; 5. /t/ /w/ /i/ /n/ /z/

Name _____

Listen as your teacher reads the directions.

1.

2.

3.

4.

5.

Teacher Directions: Say the following sounds. Have students blend the sounds to say each word and then circle the picture that shows it. 1. /s/ /k/ /r/ /ü/ /z/; 2. /t/ /w/ /e/ /l/ /v/; 3. /s/ /t/ /r/ /ô/ /n/ /g/; 4. /k/ /r/ /u/ /m/ /s/; 5. /s/ /t/ /ôr/ /k/

Name _____

Say the picture name. Then say the sounds in the
word, one at a time. Place one marker in each
box for each sound in the word. Write the number
of sounds on the line.

1.

_____

2.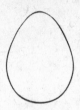

_____

3.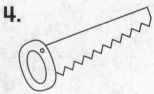

_____

4.

_____

5.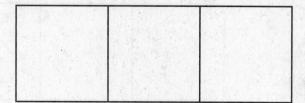

_____

6.

_____

Name _____

Say the picture name. Then say the sounds in the word, one at a time. Place one marker in each box for each sound in the word. Write the number of sounds on the line.

1.

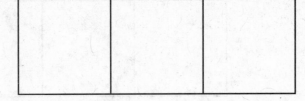 _____

2.

 _____

3.

 _____

4.

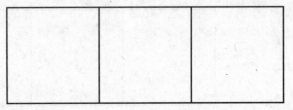 _____

5.

_____

6.

_____

Name _____

Say the picture name. Then say the sounds in the word, one at a time. Place one marker in each box for each sound you hear. Write the number of sounds.

1.

     _____

2.

     _____

3.

     _____

4.

     _____

5.

     _____

6.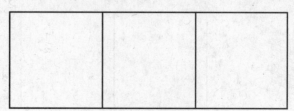

     _____

Name _____

Say the picture name. Then say the sounds in the word, one at a time. Place one marker in each box for each sound you hear. Write the number of sounds.

1.

_____

2.

_____

3.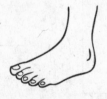

_____

4.

_____

5.

_____

6.

_____

Name _____

Say the picture name. Then say the sounds in the word, one at a time. Place one marker in each box for each sound you hear. Write the number of sounds.

1.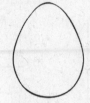

_____

2.

_____

3.

_____

4.

_____

5.

_____

6.

_____

Name _____

Say the picture name. Then say the sounds in the word, one at a time. Place one marker in each box for each sound you hear. Write the number of sounds.

1.
_____

2.
_____

3.
_____

4.
_____

5.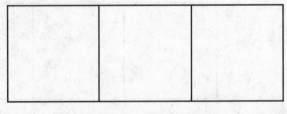
_____

6.
_____

Name _____

Say the picture name. Then say the sounds in the word, one at a time. Place one marker in each box for each sound in the word. Write the number of sounds in the word on the line.

1. _____

2. _____

3. _____

4. _____

5. _____

6. _____

Name _____

Say the picture name. Then say the sounds in the word, one at a time. Place one marker in each box for each sound in the word. Write the number of sounds in the word on the line.

1.
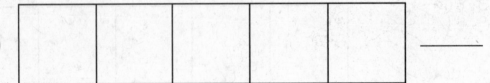
_____

2.

_____

3.

_____

4.
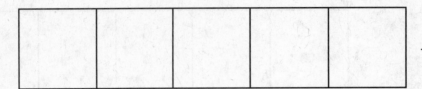
_____

5.

_____

6.
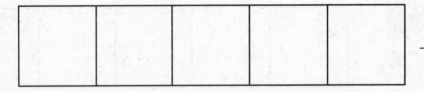

_____

Name _____

Say the picture name. Then say the sounds in the word, one at a time. Place one marker in each box for each sound in the word. Write the number of sounds in the word on the line.

1. | | | | | | _____

2. | | | | | | _____

3. | | | | | | _____

4. | | | | | | _____

5. | | | | | | _____

6. | | | | | | _____

Name _____

Say the picture name. Then say the sounds in the
word, one at a time. Place one marker in each
box for each sound in the word. Write the number
of sounds in the word on the line.

1.   _____

2. 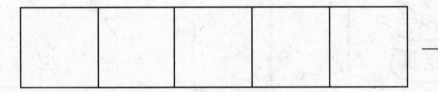 _____

3.  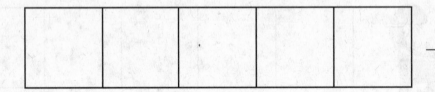 _____

4. 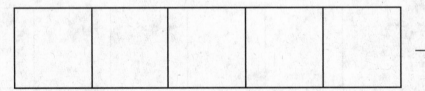 _____

5. 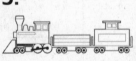 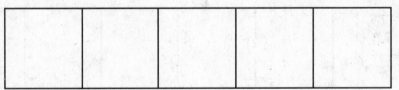 _____

6.  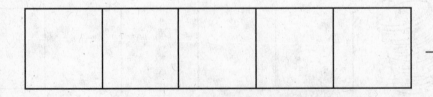 _____

Name _____

Say the picture name. Then say the sounds in the word, one at a time. Place one marker in each box for each sound you hear in the word. Write the number of sounds in the word on the line.

1. _____

2. _____

3. _____

4. _____

5. _____

6. _____

Name _____

Say the picture name. Then say the sounds in the word, one at a time. Place one marker in each box for each sound you hear in the word. Write the number of sounds in the word on the line.

1. 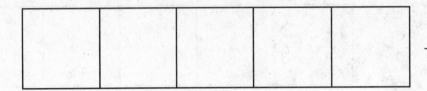 _____

2.  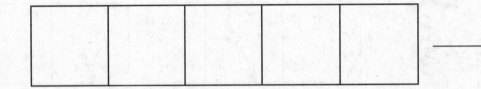 _____

3. 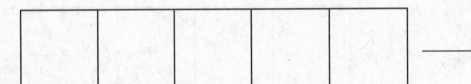 _____

4. 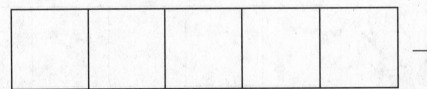 _____

5.  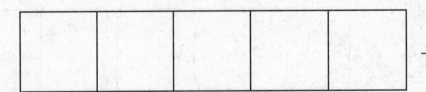 _____

6. 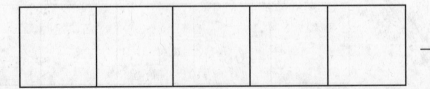 _____

Name _____

Look at each picture. Say the name of each picture out loud. Say the beginning sounds. Place an X on picture whose name has a different beginning sound.

I.

2.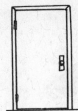

3.

4.

5.

Name _____

Look at each picture. Say the name of each picture out loud. Say the beginning sounds. Place an X on picture whose name has a different beginning sound.

1.

2.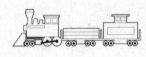

3.

4.

5.

Name _____

Look at each picture. Say the name of each picture out loud. Say the ending sounds. Place an X on picture whose name has a different ending sound.

1.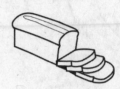

2.

3.

4.

5.

Name _____

Look at each picture. Say the name of each picture out loud. Say the ending sounds. Place an X on picture whose name has a different ending sound.

1.

2.

3.

4.

5.

Name _____

Look at each picture. Say the name of each picture out loud. Say the middle sounds. Place an X on picture whose name has a different middle sound.

1.

2.

3.

4.

5.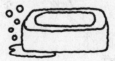

Name _____

Look at each picture. Say the name of each picture out loud. Say the middle sounds. Place an X on picture whose name has a different middle sound.

I.

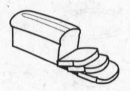  

2.

3.

4.

  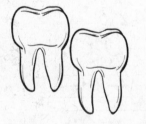

5.

  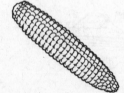

Name _____

Listen as your teacher reads the directions.

Teacher Directions: Say the first picture name: *hog*. Say the sound /l/. Change the /h/ in *hog* to /l/ and say the new word. Then circle the picture that shows it. Repeat with the following: 2. *can*: change /k/ to /v/; 3. *ram*: change /r/ to /h/; 4. *cake*: change /k/ to /r/; 5. *park*: change /p/ to /sh/.

Name _____

Listen as your teacher reads the directions.

Teacher Directions: Say the first picture name: *jar.* Change the /j/ in *jar* to /k/ and say the new word. Then circle the picture that shows it. Repeat with the following: 2. *pen*: change /p/ to /t/; 3. *gills*: change /g/ to /h/; 4. *bug*: change /b/ to /r/; 5. *bone*: change /b/ to /f/.

Name _____

Listen as your teacher reads the directions.

1.

2.

3.

4.

5.

Teacher Directions: Say the first picture name: *cat*. Change the /t/ in *cat* to /p/ and say the new word. Then circle the picture that shows it. Repeat with the following: 2. *rose*: change /z/ to /d/; 3. *map*: change /p/ to /n/; 4. *pig*: change /g/ to /n/; 5. *clown*: change /n/ to /d/.

Name _____

Listen as your teacher reads the directions.

1.

2.

3.

4.

5.

Teacher Directions: Say the first picture name: *mouse*. Change the /s/ in *mouse* to /th/ and say the new word. Then circle the picture that shows it. Repeat with the following: 2. *braid*: change /d/ to /n/; 3. *bus*: change /s/ to /g/; 4. *cage*: change /j/ to /k/; 5. *art*: change /t/ to /m/.

Name _____

Listen as your teacher reads the directions.

1.

2.

3.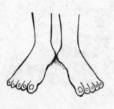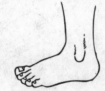

4.

5.

Teacher Directions: Say the first picture name: *mop*. Change the /o/ in *mop* to /a/ and say the new word. Then circle the picture that shows it. Repeat with the following: 2. *pen*: change /e/ to /a/; 3. *feet*: change /ē/ to /ù/; 4. *meal*: change /ē/ to /ā/; 5. *gate*: change /ā/ to /ō/.

Name _____

Listen as your teacher reads the directions.

1.

2.

3.

4.

5.

Teacher Directions: Say the first picture name: *log*. Change the /o/ in *log* to /e/ and say the new word. Then circle the picture that shows it. Repeat with the following: 2. *tip*: change /i/ to /ī/; 3. *sick*: change /i/ to /o/; 4. *moose*: change /ü/ to /ou/; 5. *beak*: change /ē/ to /ů/.

Name ____

Listen as your teacher reads the directions.

1.

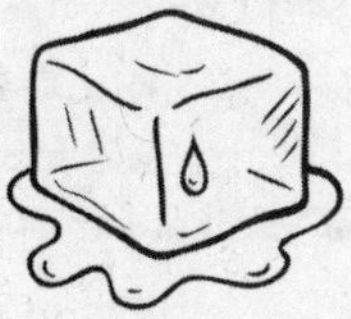
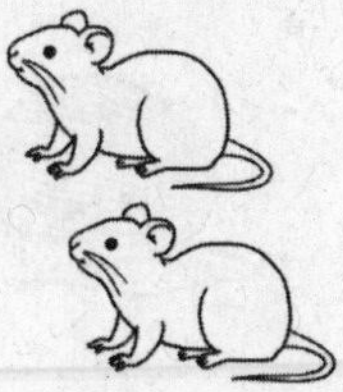
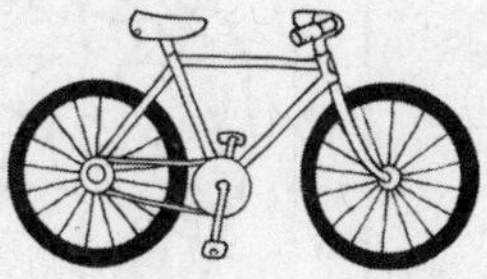

2.

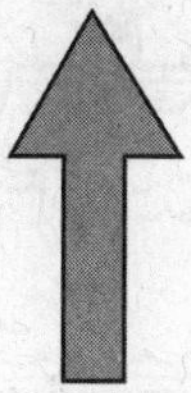
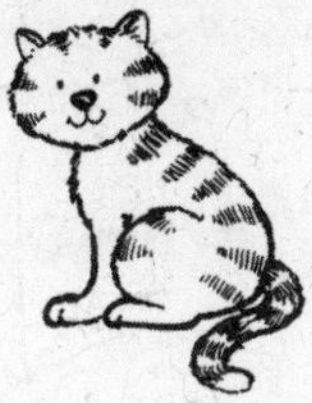
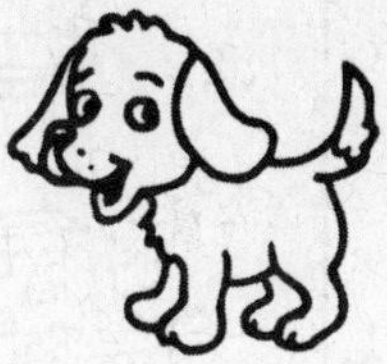

3.

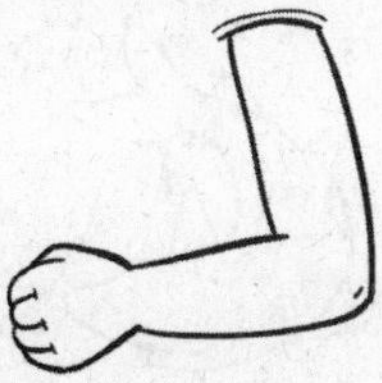
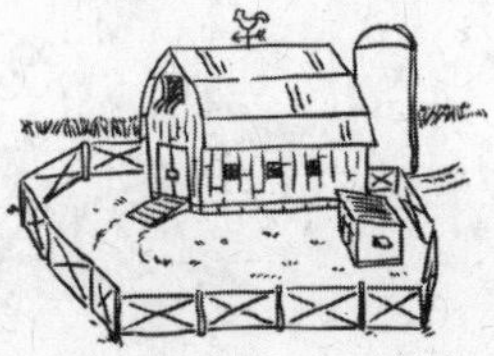
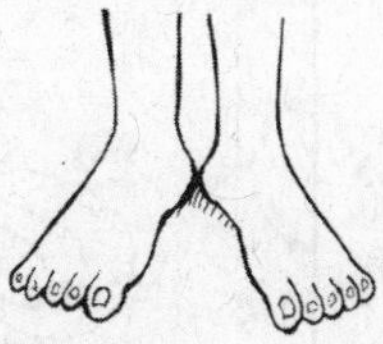

4.

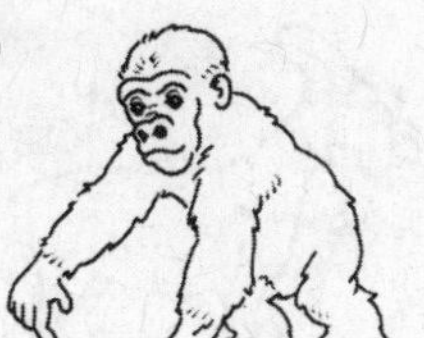
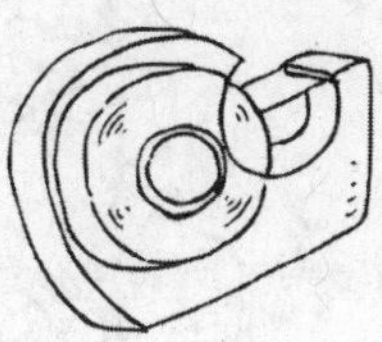
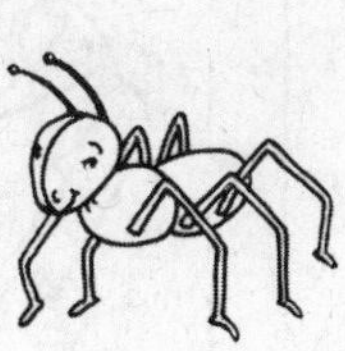

5.

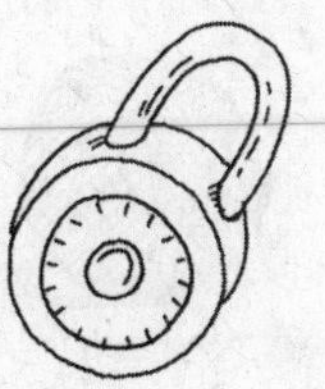
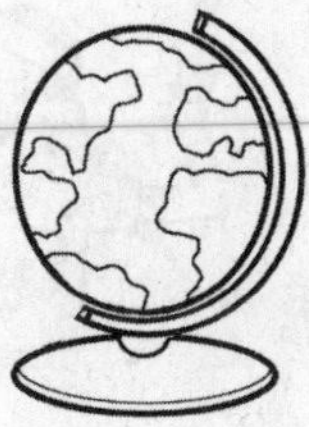
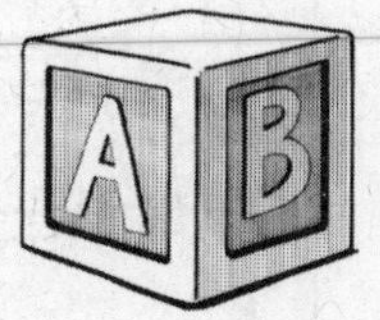

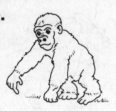

Teacher Directions: Say the first picture name (*ice*). Say the sound /m/. Add /m/ to the beginning of *ice* and say the new word. Then circle the picture that shows it. Repeat with the following: 2. /p/, *up*; 3. /f/, *arm*; 4. /t/, *ape*; 5. /b/, *lock*.

Name _____

Listen as your teacher reads the directions.

1.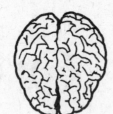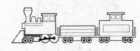

2.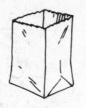

3.

4.

5.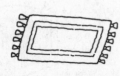

Teacher Directions: Say the first picture name (*rain*). Say the sound /t/. Add /t/ to the beginning of *rain* and say the new word. Then circle the picture that shows it. Repeat with the following: 2. /s/, *tool*; 3. /sh/, *ark*; 4. /k/, *oat*; 5. /th/, *row*.

Name _____

Listen as your teacher reads the directions.

1.

2.

3.

4.

5.

Teacher Directions: Say the first picture name (*toe*). Say the sound /d/. Add /d/ to the end of *toe* and say the new word. Then circle the picture that shows it. Repeat with the following: 2. *tea*, /m/; 3. *sea*, /t/; 4. *row*, /z/; 5. *cow*, /ch/.

Name _____

Listen as your teacher reads the directions.

1.

2.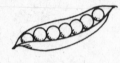

3.

4.

5.

Teacher Directions: Say the first picture name (*lamb*). Say the sound /p/. Add /p/ to the end of *lamb* and say the new word. Then circle the picture that shows it. Repeat with the following: 2. *pea*, /ch/; 3. *boy*, /l/; 4. *ram*, /p/; 5. *play*, /n/.

Name _____

Say the picture name. Take away the first sound and say the new word. Circle the picture that shows it.

1.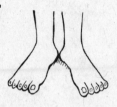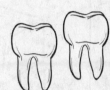

2.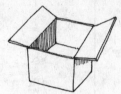

3.

4.

5.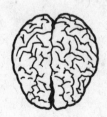

Name _____

Say the picture name. Take away the first sound and say the new word. Circle the picture that shows it.

1.

2.

3.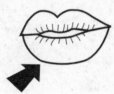

4.

5.

Name _____

Say the picture name. Take away the ending sound and say the new word. Circle the picture that shows it.

1.

2.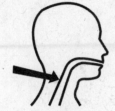

3.

4.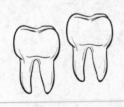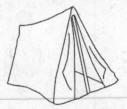

5.

Name _____

Say the picture name. Take away the ending sound and say the new word. Circle the picture that shows it.

1.  2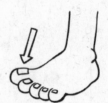

2.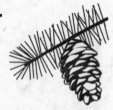

3.

4.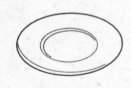

5.

Name _____

Say the name of each picture below. Draw a line matching the pictures that have their first and last sounds reversed.

1.

2.

3.

4.

5.

Name _____

Say the name of the first picture in each row. Circle the picture that stands for the new word formed when the first and last sounds are reversed.

1.

2.

3.

4.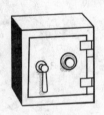

5.

Name _____

The letter **a** can stand for the short **a** sound.

h**a**t

A. Read both words. Circle the word that has the short **a** sound.

1. pen   pad   2. big   bad

3. rag   rub   4. yell   yam

B. Write the letters that complete the name of each picture.

1.    b _____

2.   m _____

3.    c _____

4.   p _____

5.    f _____

Name _____

> The letter *a* can stand for the short *a* sound.
>
> c<u>a</u>n

Circle the word that names each picture. Then write the word on the line.

1.

_____

mat   mad   rack

2.

_____

pad   bat   cat

3.

_____

map   van   jam

4.

_____

back   pan   man

5.

_____

tag   ax   an

6.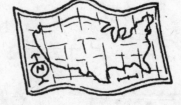

_____

map   man   yam

Name _____

Sam and Mac

9 | Sam has a cat. We call the cat "Mac."

18 | Sam has a cap. A cap is a hat.

24 | Mac the Cat has a cap!

30 | Mac the Cat ran a lap!

36 | Mac has a mat for cats.

46 | Mac has a nap on the mat. Sam pats Mac.

52 | Sam has ham. Mac has jam.

59 | Sam and Mac like jam and ham.

1. Circle all the words that have the short *a* sound.

2. Complete the sentences.

Mac the Cat has a _____!

Mac has a nap on the _____.

Name _____

> The letter *i* can stand for the short *i* sound.
>
> p<u>i</u>g

A. Look at each picture. Write the picture name on the line.

> pin   six   lip   mitt

I. _____

2. _____

3. _____

4. 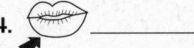 _____

B. Write the words with the short *i* sound on the line.

I. pit   cat   _____

2. fin   fan   _____

3. bat   bib   _____

Name _____

> The letter *i* can stand for the short *i* sound.
>
> p*i*n

Finish each word ladder. Change only one letter at a time.

1. Go from *pit* to *sip*.

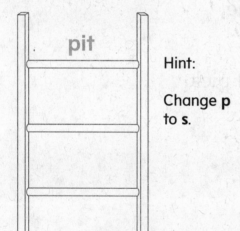

Hint:

Change **p** to **s**.

2. Go from *dim* to *kid*.

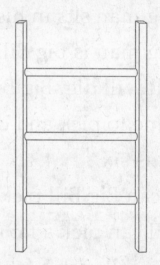

3. Go from *fig* to *pin*.

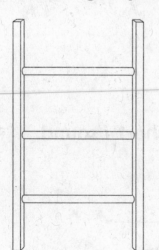

4. Go from *did* to *wig*.

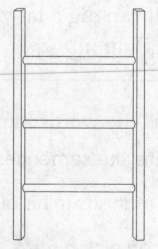

Name _____

Big Bill

8	The big man sits in his big rig.
14	The big man is Big Bill.
22	Big Bill will dig. Big Bill will pick.
29	Is it time to pick and dig?
34	It is. It is six.
39	What can Big Bill pick?
46	Big Bill can pick a fat fig.
55	Did Big Bill pick a fat fig? He did.
60	What can Big Bill dig?
67	Big Bill can dig a fat yam.
76	Did Big Bill dig a fat yam? He did.

1. **Circle all the words that contain the short _i_ sound.**

2. **Complete the sentences.**

The big man sits in his big _____.

Big Bill can pick a fat _____.

Name _____

> The letter *o* can stand for the short *o* sound.
>
> p<u>o</u>t m<u>o</u>p

A. Use a word from the box to complete each sentence.

> rock   on   not   hot

1. Don the Cat sits _____ top of the mat.

2. Tom can pick up the _____.

3. The pot is _____.

4. Sam can _____ hop over the log.

B. Circle the word with the short o sound. Then write the word.

1. ox   soap   _____

2. cat   dog   _____

3. hat   box   _____

Name _____

The letter *o* can stand for the short *o* sound.

d<u>o</u>g

Look at each picture. Write the missing letter or letters to finish the picture name.

1. l ___ ck

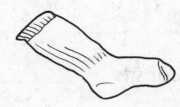

2. ___ ___ ck

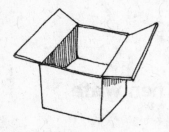

3. b ___ x

4. f ___ x

5. j ___ g

6. l ___ ___ ___

Name _____

Fox, Ox, and Hog

5	Bob and Rob are pals.
20	Bob is an ox and Rob is a fox. Rob has a job for Bob.
29	A big rock fell on top of his sack.
40	Can Bob help Rob tip a rock off of his sack?
50	Is it a job for an ox and a fox?
58	Bob and Rob can not tip the rock.
63	Don the Hog pops in.
72	Can Don help Bob and Rob tip the rock?
82	Yes Don can! Don, Bob, and Rob tip the rock.
94	It is a job for a hog, an ox, and a fox.

1. Circle all the words that contain the short *o* sound.

2. Complete the sentences.

Rob is a _____.

At the end, Bob, Rob, and Don _____.

Name _____

> The letter *e* can stand for the short *e* sound.
>
> b**e**d

A. Write a word from the box that rhymes with each word below. Then circle the letter that stands for the short *e* sound in each word you write on the line.

> fell   red   pen   yes   leg   wet

1. fed _____   2. egg _____

3. mess _____   4. sell _____

5. ten _____   6. let _____

B. Circle the word that names each picture. Then write the word on the line.

1.    hat   hen   ten   _____

2.   net   hat   pin   _____

3.    weed   wet   web   _____

Name _____

The short **e** sound can be spelled with the letter **e** as in **n<u>e</u>t**.

n<u>e</u>t

Circle the word that has the short e sound. Write the word. Then find the word in the puzzle.

1.   pen   pan   pin   _____

2.   pet   pick   pack   _____

3.   nut   nap   net   _____

4.   bag   bell   bill   _____

5.   bed   bib   bat   _____

o	p	s	e	b	a
s	p	e	t	e	p
p	t	g	e	l	f
e	h	d	c	l	n
n	k	a	l	f	e
b	e	d	y	d	t

Name _____

Deb the Vet

7	Deb is a vet. Deb helps pets.
13	She helps pets to get well.
19	Meg has a big red dog.
30	Rex the dog has a bad leg. Deb can help Rex.
40	Nick has a pet fox. Wes is his pet fox.
48	Nick can tell his pet is not well.
54	Deb will help Wes get well.
62	Pam has ten pigs. Six pigs are sick.
68	Deb met the six sick pigs.
75	She will help the pigs get well.

I. Circle all the words that contain the short *e* sound.

2. Complete the sentences.

Rex the dog has a bad _____.

The pet fox is named _____.

Name _____

> The letter **u** can stand for the short **u** sound you hear in the word **cub**.
>
> c<u>u</u>b

A. Look at each picture. Circle the word that names the picture. Write the word.

1. 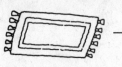 _____

rag   rug

2. _____

duck   dock

3. _____

jug   jog

4. _____

pop   pup

B. Write the missing words to complete the sentences.

> mug   bus   sun   run

5. The _____ is up.

6. His pet can _____.

7. His _____ is hot.

8. Get on the _____!

Name _____

Listen to the sound in the middle of the words **s<u>u</u>n** and **c<u>u</u>p**.
The letter **_u_** stands for the short **_u_** sound.

m<u>u</u>d

Finish each word ladder. Change only one letter at a time.

I. Go from **fun** to **sum**.

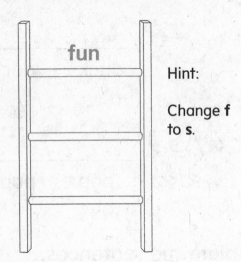

fun

Hint:

Change **f**
to **s**.

2. Go from **tug** to **hub**.

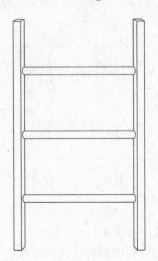

3. Go from **hug** to **run**.

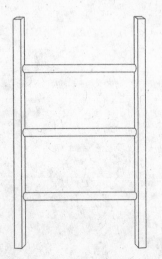

4. Go from **jut** to **rug**.

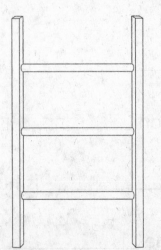

Name _____

Bud the Pup!

9   Russ and his pup, Bud, sit on a log.

20   The Sun is hot. It is not fun. It is dull.

30   Russ will get up and go back. But not Bud!

40   Bud can see a big bug buzz over the mud.

50   Russ can see Bud look at the bug. "Bud, no!"

61   Russ can tug at Bud, but Bud will get his bug!

69   Russ can see his pup hop in muck.

80   "Yuck, Bud!" The wet pup can see his bug buzz away.

1. Circle all the words that contain the short *u* sound.

2. Complete the sentences.

Bud will get his _____.

Bud will hop in the _____.

Name _____

c**a**t	l**i**p	j**e**t	t**o**p	s**u**n

Read the word. Circle the picture that it names.

1. hill

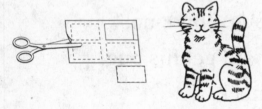

2. vet

3. cut

4. fan

5. fox

6. bat

7. dig

8. rug

Name _____

 m**a**p   m**i**tt   p**e**n   l**o**ck    b**u**g

Write *a, i, e, o,* or *u* to complete each picture name.

1. p ____ p

2. d ____ ck

3. p ____ ls

4. z ____ p

5. n ____ ck

6. ____ p

7. t ____ n

8. j ____ g

9. k ____ ck

Name _____

Cal Gets Fed

6   Tess has to get Cal fed.

16   Cal has not had a lick of food in days!

28   Tess will mix up six eggs with a fat cut of ham.

38   Cal tells Tess, "Yuck! Eggs on ham will not hit

40   the spot."

51   So Tess makes Cal a big pot of figs in jam.

56   Cal hugs his pal Tess.

67   Cal yells, "Quick, Tess! Mix more pots of figs in jam!"

76   Cal has his fill thanks to his bud Tess.

1. Circle all the words that contain the short *a* or short *i* sound. **Underline** all the words that contain the short *o*, short *e*, or short *u* sound.

2. Complete the sentences.

Tess has to get Cal _____.

Tess makes Cal a big pot of _____.

Name _____

Some words begin with a blend of sounds. Listen to the beginning sounds in the words *clam* and *flag.* You can hear the sound for each letter in the blend.

<u>cl</u>am   <u>fl</u>ag

Say each picture name. Write the two letters that stand for the sounds you hear at the beginning of each picture name.

cl   fl   gl   pl   bl   sl

1.  _____   2.  _____

3. _____   4. _____

5. _____   6.  _____

7.  _____   8.  _____

Name _____

> Some words begin with a blend of sounds. Listen to the beginning sounds in the words *sled* and *glass*. You can hear the sound for each letter in the blend.
>
> <u>sl</u>ed   <u>gl</u>ass

A. Read both words. Circle the word with the blend.

1. bat   black

2. fan   flat

3. click   cot

4. sat   slit

B. Fill in the letter or letters to finish each picture name.

1.  _____ ap

2.  cl _____ ss

3. _____ ug

4. _____ ock

5. cl _____

6. 1 + 1 = 2 _____ us

Name _____

Miss Glen Has a Class

9	Miss Glen has a class. Miss Glen writes plans.
15	She will set up for class.
22	Miss Glen will set up a clock.
29	Miss Glen will set up a flag.
35	Miss Glen will set up blocks.
41	Miss Glen will set out clips.
52	Miss Glen will set out rugs. So, no kid will slip.
60	Miss Glen is done. Miss Glen eats plums.
68	Miss Glen is glad. Miss Glen will clap!

1. Circle all the words that have *l*-blends.

2. Complete the sentences.

Miss Glen writes _____.

Miss Glen eats _____.

Name _____

Some words begin with a **blend** of sounds. Listen to the beginning sounds in the words <u>cr</u>ab and <u>fr</u>og. You can hear the sound for each letter in the blend.

<u>cr</u>ab   <u>fr</u>og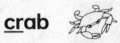

A. Look at each picture. Write the picture name on the line.

| grin | brick | crib | grill | drip | crack |

1. _____

2. _____

3. _____

4. _____

5.  _____

6. _____

B. Choose the word that completes each sentence. Then write the word on the line.

| drums | track | frog | drops |

1. Dan ran on the _____.

2. Ben has a pet _____.

3. Gus plays the _____.

4. Bob _____ his cap.

Name _____

Some words begin with a **blend** of sounds. Listen to the beginning sounds in the words _drip_ and _grass_. You can hear the sound for each letter in the blend.

<u>d</u>rip  <u>g</u>rass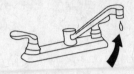

A. Write the missing letters to finish the picture name.

1. _____ um

2. _____ ab

3. _____ uck

4.  _____ ill

B. Finish each word ladder. Change only one letter at a time.

1. Go from **crop** to **trip**.

2. Go from **crib** to **gram**.

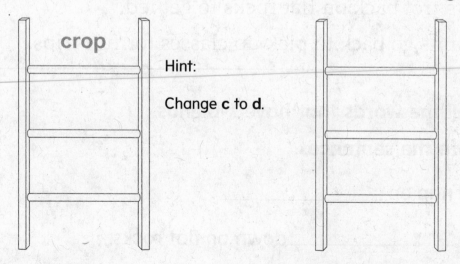

crop

Hint:

Change **c** to **d**.

Name _____

Trams Pass Big Cats

9	Trams run up hills on tracks at the zoo.
17	The trams pass plots where big cats sit.
26	Tan rocks on cliffs crack in the hot Sun.
38	Big cats nap on the grass, but flick mud at black bugs.
45	Big cats drop down on flat rocks.
52	Cats run up hills to the trams.
62	People grip the cab if big cats run in packs.
75	They grin, but do not like it if big cats pass the trams.
85	Big cats trot back on flat rocks to get fed.
96	The trams go back to pick up classes for fun trips.

I. Circle all the words that have *r*-blends.

2. Complete the sentences.

Big cats nap on _____.

Big cats _____ down on flat rocks.

Name _____

> Some words begin with a **blend** of sounds. Listen to the
> beginning sounds in the words **_skip_** and **_stem_**. You can hear
> the sound for each letter in the blend.
>
> **skip**   **stem**

**A. Look at each picture. Circle the word that names
the picture. Write the word.**

1.  _____   swim   sit

2.  _____   snack   stack

**B. Circle the word that completes each sentence.
Then write the word on the line.**

3. His dog will _____ the pot.
   sniff   sit   sick

4. The club put on a _____.
   sack   skit   six

5. The bug bit his _____.
   skin   sun   sock

6. I will hit the ball with a _____.
   sat   stick   six

Name _____

> Listen to the beginning sounds in the words _**sm**ell_ and _**sp**ill_.
> You can hear the sound for each letter in the **blend**.
>
> **sm**ell   **sp**ill

A. Look at each picture. Write the missing blend to finish each picture name.

st	sp	sn	sk	sm	sl

1. 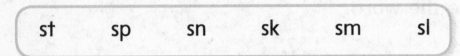 ____ ____ iff

2.  ____ ____ ip

3.  ____ ____ ack

4. 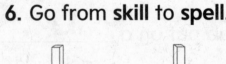 ____ ____ ot

B. Finish each word ladder. Change one letter at a time.

5. Go from **slam** to **swim**.

6. Go from **skill** to **spell**.

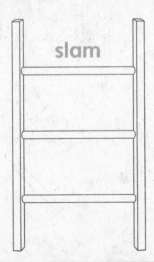

slam

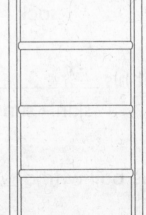

Name _____

Stick Bugs

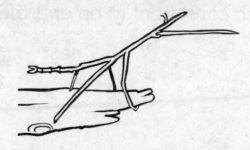

8	Can you spot a bug on this stick?
17	It is a trick! The stick is a bug!
24	Stick bugs look like sticks and stems.
30	Stick bugs will snack on grass.
36	Stick bugs will drop skin off.
42	This lets stick bugs get big.
46	Stick bugs can hiss.
53	Stick bugs can spit glop at bugs.
65	If stick bug glop hits a bug, the bug can not see.
71	Plus, stick bug glop smells bad!
80	Stick bugs can snap off legs to get away.

I. Circle all the words that have *s*-blends.

2. Complete the sentences.

Stick bug glop _____ bad.

Stick bugs can _____ off legs.

Name _____

Some words end with a **blend** of sounds. Listen to the ending sounds in the words *mask* and *nest*. You can hear the sound for each consonant in an **end blend**.

ma<u>sk</u>    ne<u>st</u>

A. Underline the ending blend in each word.

rust   dusk   slink   bump

grasp   brand   quest   sent

B. Circle each word from above in the puzzle.
Look for end blends to help you.

b	q	a	o	y	d	r
r	r	u	s	t	s	u	l
a	e	z	p	e	s	b
n	s	l	i	n	k	u
d	t	c	k	t	h	m
f	x	g	r	a	s	p

Name _____

Some words end with a **blend** of sounds. Listen to the ending sounds in the words *plant* and *lamp*. You can hear the sound for each consonant in an **end blend**.

pla<u>nt</u>

la<u>mp</u>

Say each picture name. Write the end blend that stands for the sounds you hear at the end of each picture name.

| st | nk | mp | nd | sk | nt | sp |

1.  te _____

2. sta _____

3. 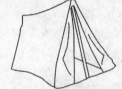 de _____

4. sku _____

5.  po _____

6. ne _____

7. 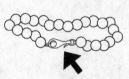 cla _____

8.  pla _____

Name _____

Skunks

7	Skunks are as big as pet cats.
12	Skunks can nest by ponds.
20	Skunks can dig dens in the damp sand.
25	Skunks nest in the dens.
32	Some skunks nest in logs and stumps.
37	Skunks eat plants and nuts.
42	Skunks rest in the Sun.
46	Skunks hunt at dusk.
52	Skunks hunt bugs and duck eggs.
57	Some skunks even hunt frogs!
67	Skunks can run and jump. But skunks are not fast.
75	Skunks can blast a mist. Skunk mist stinks!

I. Circle all the words that contain an end blend.

2. Complete the sentences.

Skunks can dig dens in the _____.

Skunks can blast a _____.

Name _____

The long *a* sound you hear in *cake* can be spelled with *a_e*.

c<u>a</u>k<u>e</u>

A. Read the words in the box. Circle the words that have the long *a* sound.

tape	plane	glass	rake
cape	bread	ape	back

B. Use a word from the box above to name each picture below. Write each word on the line.

 1. _____

 2. _____

 3. _____

 4. _____

 5. _____

Name _____

> The long ***a*** sound you hear in ***rake*** can be spelled with ***a_e***.
>
> r<u>a</u>k<u>e</u>

**A. Circle the word in each row with the long *a*
sound. Then underline the letters that stand for
the long *a* sound.**

1. bask   ball   back   base

2. rack   read   rate   rat

3. wake   ask   ant   ax

4. tack   tick   take   tax

5. fad   feed   fade   fit

B. Find the long *a* words from above in the puzzle.

i	h	u	d	f	s
o	o	d	y	a	z
b	j	w	y	d	w
a	t	a	k	e	a
s	e	w	n	e	k
e	r	a	t	e	e

Name _____

Jake Has a Pet Snake

10   Jake has a pet snake. His snake's name is Blake.

21   Most pet snakes are tame and safe. Blake is tame, too.

28   Jake's pal is Kate. Kate hates snakes!

40   "This is a big snake. Will it escape?" Jake tells Kate it

42   is safe.

53   Kate asks, "What does it eat?" Jake says it just eats

55   little things.

66   Kate is brave. She taps on the glass. Blake the snake

68   is awake!

79   Kate and Jake take off the lid. Kate looks at Jake.

84   Blake makes a funny hiss.

88   That is Jake's snake!

1. Circle all the words that contain the long *a* sound.

2. Complete the sentences.

Jake has a pet _____.

Jake tells Kate that the snake is _____.

Name _____

The long *i* sound you hear in **nine** can be spelled with *i_e*.

n<u>i</u>n<u>e</u>

A. Look at each picture. Circle the word that names each picture. Write the word.

1. _____

   kite   kit

2. _____

   shin   shine

3. _____

   grime   grim

4. _____

   ride   rid

B. Read the words in the box. Circle each word in the puzzle.

bike	crime	drive	mine

e	c	s	t	m
d	r	i	v	e
b	i	k	e	a
i	m	i	n	e
t	e	r	p	r

Name _____

The long *i* sound you hear in **ride** can be spelled with **i_e**.

r**<u>i</u>d<u>e</u>**

Look at each picture. Use the letter tiles to write each picture name.

	1. ◯ ◯ ◯ ◯
i e n	2. ◯ ◯ ◯ ◯
m d t	3. ◯ ◯ ◯ ◯
	4. ◯ ◯ ◯ ◯

Name _____

Dive into the Waves

11   If you get time, stand by the tide. Watch the gulls

15 dive in the waves.

25   Gulls dive to get clams. Gulls glide over waves. Gulls

29 spot clams and dive.

42   Gulls can skim on top of waves and dip in the tide to

45 get a prize.

55   Gulls must dive to get fish, crabs, and clams. Gulls

66 will take live clams, rise up, and drop the clams. Clams

78 will hit rocks and crack. If gulls can crack a clam, gulls

84 can dine on the clams inside.

I. Circle all the words that have the long *i* sound.

2. Complete the sentences.

Gulls _____ to get fish, crabs, and clams.

Gulls take _____ clams and drop them.

Name _____

The long *o* sound you hear in **hose** can be spelled with **o_e**.

h<u>o</u>se

A. Look at each picture. Circle the word that names the picture. Write the word.

1.  _____
robe   rob   rub

2.  _____
con   cone   clap

3.  _____
lot   glob   globe

4. _____
note   nut   not

5.  _____
slop   slope   stop

6. _____
lob   lobe   log

B. Go back and underline the letters that stand for the long *o* sound in the answers above.

Name _____

> The long **o** sound you hear in **_rose_** can be spelled with **_o_e_**.
>
> **r<u>o</u>s<u>e</u>**

A. Underline the letters that stand for the long _o_ sound in the words below.

rope   bone   nose   rode   Rome   stove

B. Choose a word from Part A to complete each sentence. Write the word on the line.

1. Her dog hid its _____.

2. Bev and Roz went on a quick trip to _____.

3. Gran's big pot on the _____ is hot!

4. Clive can smell a rose with his _____.

5. Bill _____ his new red bike.

6. Nell and Dave like to jump _____.

Name _____

Rose's Scones

7	Rose Nome was at home in bed.
14	Rose woke up at nine. Rose groped
23	for her big red robe and put it on.
29	Rose smiled. Time for lime scones
32	and grape jam!
43	Rose gaped at her big stone stove. Rose dove past the
53	wide stone sink. Rose poked her nose inside the stove
57	and sniffed. Rose froze.
66	At last, Rose spoke: "WHO stole my lime scones?!"
77	Rose saw a note on the stove. Rose read the note:
78	*Rose,*
84	*We owe you ten lime scones.*
88	*Please send grape jam!*
92	*— Gram and Gramp Nome*

1. Circle all the words that have the long *o* sound.

2. Complete the sentences.

Rose groped for her big red _____.

Rose saw a note on the _____.

Name _____

The long *u* sound you hear in **cube** can be spelled with ***u_e***.

c<u>u</u>b<u>e</u>

**A. Circle the word that completes each sentence.
Then write the word on the line.**

1. Ann's dog is _____.

   cut   cute

2. A box is like a _____.

   cube   cub

3. I can _____ my pots and pans.

   us   use

4. Cass can sled down a hill on a _____.

   tub   tube

5. _____ is a time in summer.

   June jug

6. Jeb plays the _____ in his band.

   flutter flute

**B. Go back and underline the letters that stand for
the long *u* sound in the answers above.**

Name _____

> The long *u* sound you hear in ***mule*** can be spelled with ***u_e***.
>
> m<u>u</u>l<u>e</u>

A. Read both words. Circle the word that has long *u*.

1. fun   fume

2. run   rude

3. refuse   fuss

4. mutt   mute

B. Finish each word ladder. Change only one letter at a time.

1. Go from **fume** to **muse**.   2. Go from **mule** to **lute**.

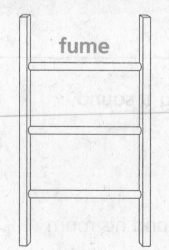

fume

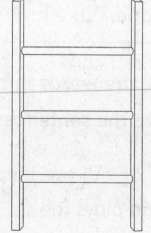

Name _____

I Like June

15	My name is Luke. I like June. It is hot in June. I like it
30	when it is hot. I can sit on the grass. I can swim in the
38	lake. I can play on a sand dune.
50	I like June. I play with my cute dog. His name is
57	Duke. I think Duke likes June, too!
70	I like June. Mom, Dad, and I play in a band. My dad
82	plays the flute. My mom plays the lute. And I sing a
89	tune. I sing a tune to June.
97	I like June. I like June a lot.

I. Circle all the words that have the long *u* sound.

2. Complete the sentences.

It is hot in _____.

Luke's dad plays the _____ and his mom

plays the _____.

Name _____

> The long *a* sound can be spelled *a_e*. The long *i* sound can be spelled *i_e*. The long *o* sound can be spelled *o_e*. The long *u* sound can be spelled *u_e*.

c<u>a</u>p<u>e</u>	h<u>i</u>d<u>e</u>	p<u>o</u>l<u>e</u>	t<u>u</u>b<u>e</u>

Say each picture name. Write the letters that stand for the long vowel sound of its name. The first one is done for you.

I. <u>o_e</u>	2. ____	3. ____

4. ____	5. ____	6. ____

7. ____	8. ____	9. ____

Name _____

The long *a* sound can be spelled *a_e*. The long *i* sound can be spelled *i_e*. The long *o* sound can be spelled *o_e*. The long *u* sound can be spelled *u_e*.

game	hive	rope	cute

Look at each picture. Write *a, i, o,* or *u* to complete the word that names it.

1. b ____ ke

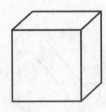

2. m ____ ne

3. t ____ ne

4. h ____ se

5. c ____ be

6. h ____ ke

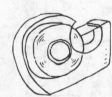

7. t ____ pe

8. n ____ ne

9. h ____ le

Name _____

Jade Stone

10   Jade stone has been used for centuries. Jade is a

21   prized stone in China. It is like gold in the West.

31   Brave Chinese men dug in unsafe mines, or big pits,

42   to find jade stones. Jade is green like grass. Men in

54   China got big slabs of jade stone in mines and cut bits

63   to make fine jewelry. Men made glazed jade tubes

76   and flat jade disks that had holes on top as art. Men in

85   China used jade stone in vase making as well.

96   Chinese culture still takes pride in its jade. Jade is a

98   fine stone.

1. Circle all the words that have a long vowel sound spelled with a final e.

2. Complete the sentences.

Jade is a prized _____.

Jade is green _____ grass.

Name _____

Sometimes the letter **c** stands for the **s** sound, as in **fa̱c̲e**.
The letter **g** can stand for the **j** sound, as in **gel**.
The letters **dge** can stand for the **j** sound, as in **fri̱d̲g̲e**.

face 　　　　gel 　　　　fridge

A. Fill in the blank with the word that completes each sentence.

I. Can I get a pack of gum for ten _____?
   a. cents　　　　　　**b.** cans

2. Sam likes _____ ball.
   a. dog　　　　　　　**b.** dodge

3. Grace makes rice with _____.
   a. spice　　　　　　**b.** stack

4. My mom has a big _____ in her ring.
   a. gum　　　　　　　**b.** gem

5. Madge has a _____ on her leg.
   a. black　　　　　　**b.** brace

B. Circle the letters that stand for the soft c, g, and -dge sounds in each answer above.

Name _____

Sometimes the letter **c** stands for the **s** sound, as in <u>c</u>ent.
The letter **g** can stand for the **j** sound, as in **gem**.
The letters **dge** can stand for the **j** sound, as in **smu<u>dge</u>**.

<u>c</u>ent   gem   smu<u>dge</u>

A. Circle the word that completes the sentence. Write the word on the line.

1. His cab is on the _____.

   cage   bridge   game

2. My dad made _____ for lunch.

   rice   grace   fence

3. He has five mice in a _____.

   cage   rice   ice

4. Pam is _____.

   face   rice   nice

B. Circle the words from above in the puzzle.

f	n	c	a	g	e	z
b	r	i	d	g	e	r
p	h	t	n	x	a	i
n	i	c	e	p	t	c
p	c	y	o	e	h	e

Name _____

Lance Can Dance

8	Madge likes to dance. Madge dances and prances
16	with grace. Madge dances with her pal Lance.
27	Lance is the same age as Madge. But Lance can not
37	dance. Lance kicks his legs and flops on the stage.
45	"It is like dancing on ice!" Lance yells.
52	Madge hopes Lance can dance on stage.
61	Madge spins past Lance, but Lance can not spin.
70	Madge slides past Lance, but Lance can not slide.
80	But Madge will not judge him. Madge pledges to get
90	him to dance. They dance together in a trance. Lance
97	takes his place and makes a spin.
105	"Nice spin, Lance! We may have a chance!"

1. Circle words with the soft *c* and soft *g* sound.

2. Complete the sentences.

Madge and Lance like to _____.

Lance takes his _____ and makes a spin.

Name _____

> **Digraphs** are groups of letters that stand for a single sound. The letters *sh*, *th*, and *ng* are digraphs.
>
> <u>fish</u>   <u>th</u>ink   ri<u>ng</u>

A. Use a word from the box to complete each sentence.

math	brings	sang	wish	bath

1. Chad makes his dog take a _____.

2. Seth thanks Sam for the "get well" _____.

3. Shane _____ cash to shop.

4. The class has a _____ test.

5. Tish _____ in the play.

B. Circle the word that names the picture. Underline the digraphs *th*, *sh*, or *-ng*.

1.  wing   wig

2. 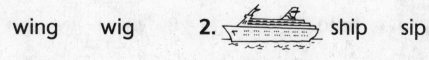 ship   sip

3.  path   pat

4. 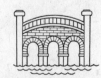 big   bridge

Name _____

Digraphs are groups of letters that stand for a single sound.
The letters *sh*, *th*, and *ng* are digraphs.

ship    bath   swing

Look at each picture. Write the digraph *sh*, *th*, or *ng*
to finish the picture name.

I.  fi _____   2.  ba _____

3. ri _____   4.  fa _____

5. tra _____   6.  pa _____

7.  brea _____   8.  swi _____

Name _____

Smash and Dash!

10	It is time for the Smash and Dash baseball game!
16	The Hedgehogs think, "We shall win!"
23	The Bone Dogs think, "We shall win!"
33	Seth Dog is up at bat. Shane Hedgehog slings the
45	ball. Seth Dog swings. Seth Dog crushes it! It is a home
52	run! Seth Dog dashes around the bases.
61	Now the Hedgehogs are up at bat. Can Bing
69	Hedgehog make a run with his thick bat?
80	Beth Dog zings the ball. Bing swings! It is a hit!
91	Bing rushes from base to base! Can he make it home?
101	Yes! He has made it! What a game this is!

I. Circle the words with digraphs *th, sh,* and *ng*.

2. Complete the sentences.

Seth Dog _____ around the bases.

Bing _____ from base to base!

Name _____

Digraphs are groups of letters that stand for a single sound.
The letters *ch, -tch, wh,* and *ph* are digraphs.

| <u>ch</u>in | cru<u>tch</u> | <u>wh</u>ale | <u>ph</u>one |

A. Circle the word that names each picture. Then write the word on the line.

1.	whip	2.	shack	3.	which
	while		check		itch
	wipe		chick		chip
	_____		_____		_____

4.	laugh	5.	catch	6.	chap
	graph		cats		shop
	grape		latch		chop
	_____		_____		_____

B. Circle the digraph *ch, tch, wh,* or *ph* in each answer above.

Name _____

> **Digraphs** are groups of letters that stand for a single sound.
> The letters *ch*, *-tch*, *wh*, and *ph* are digraphs.
>
> <u>ch</u>ick   ca<u>tch</u>   <u>wh</u>ale   gra<u>ph</u>
>
>      

Look at each picture. Write the missing letters to finish the picture name.

ch	tch	wh	ph

1. _____ ip

2. ✔ _____ eck

3.  cru _____

4. _____ one

5. _____ op

6. swi _____

7. Ste _____

8.  _____ ale

Name _____

Finches

9   Male finches make homes, which are nests, up on

18 branches. They grasp such things as sticks and thatch

29 in their bills. Thatch is made up of grass and stems.

39   Finches then use these sticks and thatch to make a

52 cup in the nest. The cup is a place for their eggs. Finch

64 eggs hatch in the nest. Finch eggs are close in size to

65 dimes.

75   Finch chicks live in the nest. Finches chomp on bugs

80 and things that they catch.

89   Finches can make nice pets in homes. Finches can

96 sing well. People like when finches sing.

1. Circle the words with digraphs *ch, tch,* or *wh.*

2. Complete the sentences.

Finches grasp such things as sticks and _____.

Finches make homes on _____.

Name _____

> **Blends** are groups of letters that work together.
> Some three-letter blends are *str, scr, spr, spl, shr, thr*.
>
> <u>str</u>ing   <u>scr</u>atch

A. Circle the picture that matches the three-letter blend. Then write the word on the line.

1.   _____ one

2.   _____ imp

3.  _____ int

B. Circle the word that names the picture. Underline the three-letter blend in the word.

1. stripe   check

2. splash   shell

3. swing   shrub

4. whale   spring

Name _____

Blends are groups of letters that work together.
Some three-letter blends are *str, scr, spr, spl, shr, thr*.

<u>str</u>ap   <u>spr</u>ing

Write the missing three-letter blend to finish the picture name.

1. _____ ash

2.  _____ etch

3. _____ ing

4. _____ it

5. _____ ink

6.  _____ ike

Name _____

Spring Changes

7   Springtime brings change to land. Ice splits.

16   It makes lakes throb with fresh water. Striped fish

26   thrash and splash. They jump and plop with a "splat!"

36   Plants spring up around the lake. They thrive in the

46   Sun. A spruce with big branches stretches up and up.

54   Rabbits with black splotches snack on plants. They

56   thrive, too.

67   But then, a fox gets ready to strike! It chases the

74   rabbits. The rabbits sprint with big strides.

85   They hide in a thick shrub. They get away with no

86   scratches.

96   It is a thrill to gaze at. Springtime is splendid.

I. Circle the words with three-letter blends.

2. Complete the sentences.

The _____ has big branches.

The rabbits sprint with big _____.

Name _____

> The letters ***ai*** and ***ay*** can stand for the long ***a*** sound.
>
> **r<u>ai</u>n**   **pl<u>ay</u>**

A. Use a word from the box to complete each sentence. Then circle the letters that stand for the long *a* sound.

> train   day   wait   pay   mail

1. The _____ runs on the track.

2. We had to _____ for the snack.

3. She had to _____ a letter to her dad.

4. I will _____ at the bus stop.

5. Which _____ are you going home?

B. Write the word with the long *a* sound on the line.

1. cat   train   _____

2. snail   rose   _____

Name _____

The letters *ai* and *ay* can stand for the long *a* sound.

tr<u>ai</u>n    cl<u>ay</u>

Finish each word ladder. Change or add only one letter at a time.

1. Go from **rain** to **mail**.

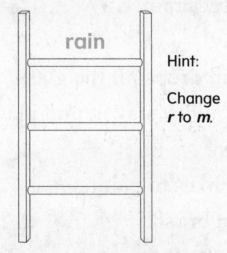

rain

Hint:

Change
r to *m*.

2. Go from **pay** to **clay**.

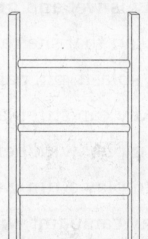

3. Go from **brain** to **trail**.

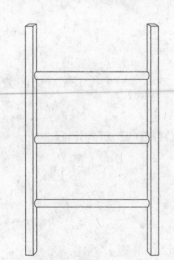

4. Go from **way** to **stay**.

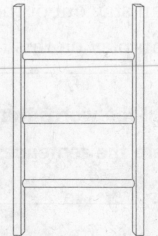

Name _____

Kay in the Rain

9	The day is wet and gray. Kay sees rain.
17	Kay is sad that she can not play.
27	Splish, splash, pit, pat, tap. Rain drops hit the glass.
39	Wait, Kay can still play! Kay can just stay in and play.
46	Kay can play with her red train.
56	Kay can play a fun game. Kay likes to paint.
64	Yes, Kay can paint with a paint brush.
73	Kay can find lots of fun things to do.
79	Kay can find ways to play.
86	Kay can stay out of the rain.
94	Kay can play on this fun, gray day.

---

1. Circle all the words that contain the long _a_ sound.

2. Complete the sentences.

   Kay sees _____.

   Kay can still _____.

Name _____

Some words have a long *i* sound. Listen to the vowel sound in the words *pie* and *night*. The letters ***i, igh, ie,*** or ***y*** can stand for this sound.

p<u>ie</u>   **n<u>igh</u>t**

skies   might   wild   pried   find   by

A. Read each word below. Find a word from the box that rhymes. Write the word.

1. why _____   **2.** tries _____

3. light _____   **4.** mild _____

5. cried _____   **6.** mind _____

B. Circle the picture that matches the word.
Underline the letters that stand for the long *i* sound.

1.

sky

2.

flight

3.

tie

4.

child

Name _____

> Some words have a long *i* sound. Listen to the vowel sound in the words *fry* and *rind*. The letters *i, igh, ie,* or *y* can stand for this sound.
>
> sky   rind

A. Look at the pictures. Use the letter tiles to write the name of each picture.

| c | d | f | r | l | y |

1. _____   2. _____

3. _____   4. _____

B. Look at the pictures. Finish the word that names each picture by filling in *i, ie,* or *igh*.

 1. w _____ nd    2. p _____

 3. fr _____ t    4. n _____ t

Name _____

Sights at Night

11	Dwight takes photos of the night sky. It is his job
23	to spy in the sky. At night, Dwight can find the best
33	sights. When it is nighttime, Dwight tries to spy high
45	in the sky. Dwight might get a fine shot this night! The
49	sky is just right!
58	Dwight unties his tripod and places it upright. He
68	looks up. The moon and stars shine bright and high.
77	Dwight snaps five shots. The camera flash is bright.
88	The light from the flash makes the foxes hide in fright.
98	Why, it is quite a sight! He snaps ten shots.
109	It is time for Dwight to drive home. The photo is
111	just right!

1. Circle all the words with long *i*.

2. Complete the sentences.

Dwight takes photos of _____.

At night, Dwight can find the best _____.

Name _____

Some words have a long **o** sound. Listen to the vowel sound in the words _cold, snow, goat,_ and _toe_. The letters **o, ow, oa,** or **oe** can stand for this sound.

c<u>o</u>ld   **sn<u>ow</u>**   **g<u>oa</u>t**   **t<u>oe</u>**

Choose a word to complete each sentence. Write the word on the line.

1. I have five _____.
     toes   toast   top

2. Our class will _____ pumpkin plants.
     go   grow   got

3. I put on a coat to play in the _____.
     snow   soap   soon

4. I don't know if this boat will _____.
     fat   float   foam

5. My pet is big and _____.
     so   slow   doe

Name _____

> Some words have a long **o** sound. Listen to the vowel sound in the words *roll, bowl, soap,* and *doe.* The letters **o, ow, oa,** or **oe** can stand for this sound.
>
> r<u>o</u>ll   b<u>ow</u>l   s<u>oa</u>p   d<u>oe</u>
>
>

B. Name the pictures. Then write the missing letters o, ow, oa, or **oe to complete each word.**

1.    c ____ t

2.   t ____

3.    t ____ d

4.    t ____ st

5.   b ____ t

6.    thr ____

7.    r ____ d

8.    sn ____

Name _____

Let it Snow!

10   Joan throws on a coat. The coat will protect her,

21 so Joan will not get soaked. Joan goes up the road.

30 What is this? It's not rain. It is snow!

36   "Whoa! Snow in May? No way!"

45   Joan's classmate, Moe, loans her a hat and mittens.

55 Joan picks up some snow and throws it. Moe shakes

65 off the snow. He chases Joan. Moe throws snow. Joan

71 laughs. Joan's face begins to glow!

83   Joan and Moe go up the road. Joan stops for a break.

91   "Moe, I like to play in the snow!"

101 Joan and Moe sing "Let it snow, let it snow!"

1. Circle the words that have long _o_.

2. Complete the sentences.

Joan throws on a _____.

Moe and Joan like to throw _____.

Name _____

> Some words have a long *e* sound. Listen to the vowel sound in the words *he* and *bee*. The letters *e, ee, ea,* or *e_e* can stand for this sound.
>
> **he**   **b<u>ee</u>**   **l<u>ea</u>f**   **Eve**
>

A. Underline the letters that stand for the long *e* sound in the words below.

flee   she   sea   sweep

fleet   flea   be   sleep

B. Choose a word to complete each sentence. Write the word on the line.

I. The bird stuck its _____ in the water.
          bee   beak   bait

2. We ate green _____ for dinner.
          pails   peeks   peas

3. The kitten got stuck in the _____.
          tea   tree   tap

4. _____ is ten years old.
    See   Show   She

5. I love to play at the _____.
          bike   bean   beach

Name _____

Some words have a long **e** sound. Listen to the vowel sound in the words *leaf* and *Eve*. The letters **e, ee, ea,** or **e_e** can stand for this sound.

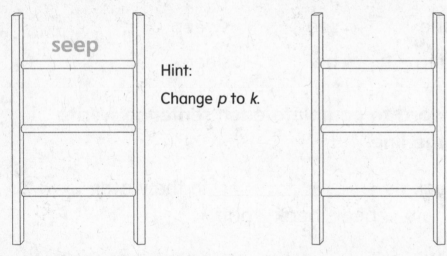

h<u>e</u>   b<u>ee</u>   l<u>ea</u>f   <u>E</u>ve

A. Finish each word ladder. Change or add only one letter at a time.

1. Go from **seep** to **peek**.

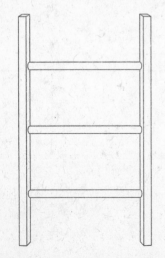

seep

Hint:

Change *p* to *k*.

2. Go from **bead** to **meat**.

3. Go from **seam** to **stream**.

4. Go from **sheet** to **sleep**.

Name _____

The Seal

13   It is time to feed Eve the seal. Eve eats fish for each

23   meal. She leaps up and leans. She gets a fish!

34   Pete will teach Eve. He will train Eve to leap and

46   play. Each time she does a feat, she gets a treat! Pete

56   teaches Eve each day. She leaps up. She smiles and

59   flashes her teeth.

72   Eve is on the seal team. The seals act in a big show.

82   Each seal does at least three tricks. Then Pete feeds

88   each seal. Eve gets three treats!

101 Eve is lean and clean. She has to be seen! Eve is the

113 lead seal. She is indeed the queen. Kids like to see Eve

116 steal the show!

1. Circle all the words with long *e*.

2. Complete the sentences.

Eve eats fish for each _____.

Eve is lean and _____.

Name _____

> Some words end with a long *e* sound. Listen to the ending sound in the words *baby* and *valley*. The letters *y* or *ey* can stand for this sound.
>
> **baby** **val<u>ley</u>**

A. Circle the word that completes each sentence. Then write the word on the line.

1. Ricky has three dimes and one _____.

       pony   penny   pond

2. I can unlock it with my _____.

       key   study   lily

3. We are so _____ this week.

    tabby   jockey   happy

4. Kathy can play ice _____.

    hobby   hockey   hanky

5. My pet _____ is named Fluffy.

    bunny   best   donkey

B. Go back and circle the letters that stand for the long *e* sound in the answers you wrote above.

Name _____

Some words end with a long **e** sound. Listen to the ending sound in the words bun**ny** and hock**ey**. The letters **y** or **ey** can stand for this sound.

bun**ny**   hock**ey**

Look at each picture. Write _y_ or _ey_ to complete the picture name.

1.  pon _____	2.  bab _____
3.  vall _____	4. **60** sixt _____
5.  pupp _____	6. k _____
7. penn _____	8.  stick _____

Name _____

Abby and Mickey

4	Abby and Mickey went
9	camping last week after their
14	hockey game. They tried to
20	find a sunny spot in Mickey's
25	leafy backyard. "This will be
32	funny — camping in the city," Abby said.
40	"Yes, but this sunlight is fading," Mickey replied.
50	"Let's make the tent." Abby and Mickey found a little
60	spot to place their tent on. The green leaves beneath
64	the tent were icy.
73	Abby and Mickey wanted to sleep beneath the glassy
82	sky. But the winds made the night really chilly.
88	"It's so windy out!" Mickey cried.
98	"This is silly. Let's go inside the tent," Abby said.
107	"It's lucky that our sleeping bags are so cozy."

---

1. Circle all the words with long *e* spelled *y, ey*.

2. Complete the sentences.

Abby and Mickey went camping after_____.

Their sleeping bags were _____.

Name _____

> The long *u* sound can be spelled with the letters *u_e, ew, ue,* or *u* as in the words *cube, few, music,* and *cue.*
>
> cube   music

A. Underline the letters that stand for the long *u* sound in the words below.

music	skew	rescue	mute
refuse	value	unit	spew

B. Circle each word from above in the puzzle below.

i	x	a	y	r	d	g	o
v	a	l	u	e	b	f	y
w	o	s	t	s	p	e	w
m	u	s	i	c	z	s	b
u	s	k	i	u	n	i	t
t	k	e	j	e	h	m	n
e	x	w	r	y	k	p	n
q	r	e	f	u	s	e	h

Name _____

The long *u* sound can be spelled with the letters, *u_e, ew, ue,* or *u,* as in the words *cute, few, unit,* and *rescue.*

c<u>u</u>te   resc<u>ue</u>

Look at each picture. Write the missing letters to finish the picture name.

| 1. 

c __ b __ | 2. 

men __ | 3. 

f __ __ l |
| 4. 

m __ sic | 5. 

m __ __ | 6. 

m __ l __ |

Name _____

Mules

11	Lots of people get confused and think that a mule is
23	a donkey. That is not right. A mule is a cross between
35	a horse and a donkey. Mules can be big, but they are
37	not huge.
47	Humans put lots of value in mules because mules are
57	so strong. Mules can be used in yanking plows. Mules
67	can help humans raise crops. So, lots of humans use
73	mules in lots of helpful ways.
83	What can mules use as fuel? Mules eat grain, like
94	bran and wheat. Mules eat less than horses. If a mule
105	works for too long, it will stop and refuse to work.
113	Mules tell humans when they need to rest!

I. Circle all the words with long _u_.

2. Complete the sentences.

Mules can be big, but they are not _____.

Mules help _____ to raise crops.

Name _____

When the letters **er**, **or**, **ir**, or **ur** work together, they stand for the sounds you hear in *fern*, *world*, *dirt*, and *curl*. It is an *r*-controlled vowel sound.

w<u>or</u>ld

f<u>er</u>n

d<u>ir</u>t

c<u>ur</u>l

A. Underline the letters in each word that stand for the same *r*-controlled vowel sound you hear in the word *shirt*.

verb   curb   worth   bird

B. Fill in the blank with the word that has the same *r*-controlled vowel sound as the word *dirt*.

I. My friend is _____.

   a. Herb   **b.** Tom

2. I fell and _____ my knee.

   a. hit   **b.** hurt

3. He has the hose to _____ water.

   a. spray   **b.** squirt

4. My cat has gray _____.

   a. eyes   **b.** fur

Name _____

When the letters **er**, **or**, **ir**, or **ur** work together, they stand for the sounds you hear in *germ*, *worth*, *shirt*, and *purse*. It is an *r*-controlled vowel sound.

herd  **work**  **purse**   **shirt**

Look at each picture. Circle the word that names the picture. Write the word.

1. _____
   burn   bun

4.  _____
   name   nurse

2.  _____
   skirt   skip

5.  _____
   work   woke

3.  _____
   perch   peach

6. _____
   stop   stir

Name _____

Worms Work!

11	A worm is not just a meal for birds. Worms work!
20	Learn about the worms that lurk in the turf.
31	But first, a note on dirt. Dead plants fall. Other plants
43	fall on top of them. The plants press on top of plants
54	under them. As the sun adds heat, plants will rot and
57	turn into dirt.
68	That is when worms go to work. Worms eat germs in
78	dirt. These germs can hurt plants. When a worm eats
90	germs in dirt, it sucks in dirt. Then the worm will pass
100	this dirt through its guts. Worms bring the best deep
111	dirt up to plants on top. When worms turn dirt, plants
120	thrive. Worms churn the turf to make dirt work!

I. Circle all the words that contain the *r*-controlled vowel sound you hear in the word *shirt* spelled *er, ir, ur, or*.

2. Complete the sentence.

Worms eat _____ in _____.

Name _____

The letters **ar** stand for the sounds you hear in *farm*.

f<u>ar</u>m

Read each word below. Choose the words in the box that rhyme with the word. Write the words.

| star | stop | jar | fan | car | crop |

1. far _____ _____ _____

| rub | plop | dart | black | start | art |

2. part _____ _____ _____

| bark | brag | clerk | park | perk | dark |

3. mark _____ _____ _____

| far | at | farm | jam | charm | harm |

4. arm _____ _____ _____

Name _____

The letters **ar** stand for the sounds you hear in *shark*.

sh**ar**k

Look at each picture. Use the letters to write each picture name.

	1. 
s a t r j	2. 
	3. 
	4. 
a m k r b c	5. 
	6. 

Name _____

The Harmless Farm Stand

10 | June and her mom drove home. They had spent all

22 | day in the car and June could not wait to get back.

33 | Her class play's first night was close, and June did not

38 | know her part that well.

50 | As her mom drove the car past a farm, June could see

61 | a small stand near a field. "Farm Fresh," June read on

74 | the side. Cakes and tarts sat in rows. June did not say a

84 | word, in hopes that her mom would not see it.

94 | No such luck. "A farm stand!" her mom burst out.

106 | "Such a cute place. And they sell art in their barn! We

116 | must stop, just for a bit. No harm in that!"

1. Circle the words with the *r*-controlled *ar* sounds.

2. Complete the sentences.

June did not know her _____ well.

June's mom wanted to stop at the _____.

Name _____

> The letters **or, oar, ore** can stand for the *r*-controlled vowel sounds you hear in *fork, board,* and *store.*
>
> f**or**k   b**oar**d   st**ore**

A. Circle the word that names each picture. Then write the word on the line.

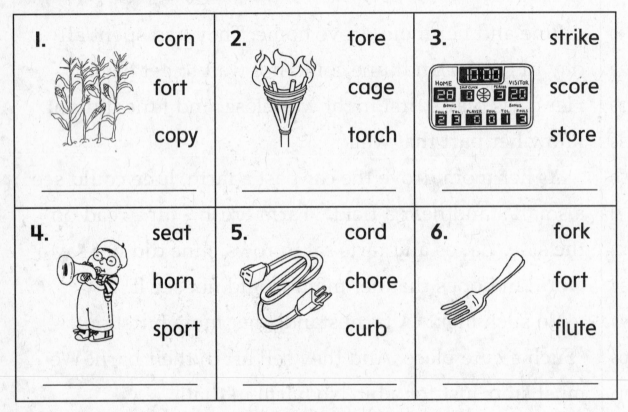

| 1. corn / fort / copy | 2. tore / cage / torch | 3. strike / score / store |
| 4. seat / horn / sport | 5. cord / chore / curb | 6. fork / fort / flute |

B. Read each word. Write a word from the box that rhymes.

| shorn | stork | roar | porch | cord |

1. oar _____   2. torch _____

Name _____

> The letters *or, oar, ore* can stand for the *r*-controlled vowel sounds you hear in *tore, roar,* and *corn.*
>
> **c<u>or</u>n**   **r<u>oar</u>**   **t<u>ore</u>**

A. Write *or, oar, ore,* or *our* to complete each picture name.

1.   th _____ n

2.    b _____

3.   c _____ n

4.    sh _____

B. Finish each word ladder. Change only one letter at a time.

1. Go from **corn** to **fork**.

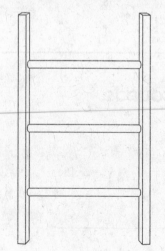

2. Go from **fort** to **sore**.

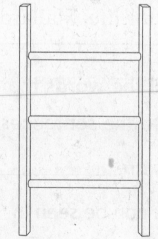

Name _____

Mallards Soar

6 | A mallard is a duck. You

12 | may find them by your home.

18 | These ducks can be seen in

23 | North America. There are more

29 | mallards than any kind of duck.

34 | Mallards live in wetlands, or

45 | by shores. These ducks live in the North before it gets

53 | cold. Then they leave for a warm place.

63 | Mallards soar in the sky. Mallards fly from place to

72 | place. While mallards fly, one mallard escorts, or leads,

74 | the rest.

84 | The male has green feathers. The female is tan with

96 | white spots. It is normal for a male and female to stay

103 | together for life. Mallards are neat ducks.

1. **Circle all the words that have the *or* sounds.**

2. **Complete the sentences.**

Mallards are _____.

Mallards can be seen in _____.

Name _____

> Some words have the sounds you hear at the ends of the words *deer, here*, and *smear*. The letters *eer, ere*, and *ear* can stand for this sound.
>
> d<u>eer</u>r   sm<u>ear</u>

A. Use a word from the box to complete each sentence.

> jeer   clears   fear   cheer   hears

1. Lance _____ birds singing.

2. Noreen _____ the desk at night.

3. It is not nice to _____ at strangers.

4. I _____ bats.

5. Kids _____ for the winning team.

B. Circle the word that matches the picture and write it on the line.

1. _____

   ear   eat   tear

2. _____

   speak   shirt   spear

3. _____

   tear   tent   team

4. _____

   bed   beard   bead

Name _____

Some words have the sounds you hear at the ends of the words *cheer* and *rear*. The letters **eer, ere**, and **ear** can stand for this sound.

cheer   **rear**

Finish the word ladders. Change one letter at a time.

1. Go from **near** to **deer**.

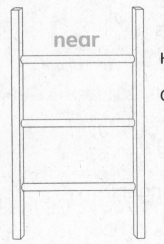

Hint:

Change *n* to *d*.

2. Go from **steer** to **cheer**.

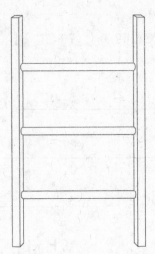

3. Go from **hear** to **sheer**.

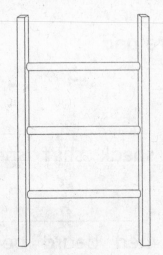

4. Go from **dear** to **veer**.

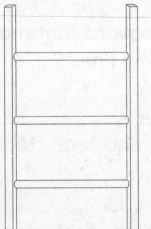

Name _____

Fun at Camp

2   Dear Dad,

13   We want to thank you for sending us to camp this

25   year. There is not a thing to fear. The camp is near

37   fields and lakes. We see deer in the fields here. We see

49   fish in the clear lake. The leader at camp takes us on

61   hikes. She steers us to see neat sights. We get our gear

74   and hike up the path. When we get to the top, we peer

86   at the tops of trees. We clear stones and sticks and set

100   up camp. We set up tents and make a fire. It is so fun

109   to sit by the fire and sing and cheer.

112   —Jan and Ben

1. Circle all the words that have the *ear* sounds.

2. Write the answer to each question.

Who wrote the letter? _____

What do the campers see in the field? _____

Name _____

> When the letters ***are, air, ear, ere*** work together, they can stand for the sounds you hear in *mare*, *hair*, *bear*, and *where*. It is an *r*-controlled vowel sound.
>
> m<u>are</u>   h<u>air</u>

**A. Find the words that complete the sentences.
Write the word on the line.**

chair	rare	wear
pear	share	fair

1. Kim sits in a _____.

2. Mike snacks on a _____.

3. Mel and Ray _____ their toys.

4. It is _____ to find a bear.

5. We _____ hats when it is cold.

6. Meg spots a pig at the _____.

Name _____

When the letters **are, air, ear, ere** work together, they can stand for the sounds you hear in **care, chair, bear,** and **there**. It is an *r*-controlled vowel sound.

b**ear**   th**ere**

A. Look at each picture. Circle the word that names the picture. Write the word.

1.   _____
   cheat   bear   chair

2.   _____
   her   hair   heat

3.    _____
   fair   feet   fear

4.   _____
   tear   tire   tea

5.    _____
   went   wear   week

6.   _____
   peach   pet   pear

B. Go back and underline the letters that stand for the vowel sound you hear in the word *air* in each answer above.

Name _____

Bears

7   Let's be aware of the kinds of

12   bears! The United States has

17   brown bears, black bears, grizzly

23   bears and polar bears. All bears

28   are mammals with thick hair.

38   The black bear is the most common bear. Black bears

50   can be 5 to 6 feet and 200–600 pounds. Brown bears

60   can grow bigger than black bears. They can reach 800

72   or 900 pounds. The biggest bear is the polar bear. It can

82   reach 900 to 1,600 pounds! It is the most rare.

93   We need to protect bears. If we care about wild bears,

103 we cannot feed them. Beware of bears caring for cubs

114 or hunting for food. Be prepared—they can give you a

125 scare! The more we know, the better off we will be.

1. Circle the words that have the same sounds as the word *air*.

2. Complete the sentences.

The most common bear is the _____.

Beware of bears that are caring for _____.

Name _____

The long **a** sound can be spelled **a**, **ea**, **eigh**, **ei**, or **ey**, as in **lady**, **break**, **sleigh**, **veil**, and **prey**.

br<u>ea</u>k   **sl<u>eigh</u>**   **v<u>ei</u>l**   **pr<u>ey</u>**

A. Underline the letters that stand for the long a sound in the words below.

neigh   great   obey   steak   baby

hey   they   raven   eight   weight

B. Now find the words in the puzzle below.

f	o	w	n	e	i	g	h	d	b
q	p	e	i	g	h	t	f	l	a
k	p	h	m	w	e	k	q	a	b
o	b	f	n	x	y	d	j	k	y
b	b	r	r	a	v	e	n	f	i
e	r	s	v	a	d	x	w	t	f
y	h	t	g	r	e	a	t	f	s
t	h	e	y	w	e	i	g	h	t
m	j	a	z	m	f	t	p	l	h
e	i	k	m	c	y	p	f	j	d

Name _____

The long *a* sound can be spelled *a, ea, eigh, ei,* or *ey*.
As in *lady, break, sleigh, veil,* and *prey*.

br<u>ea</u>k

sl<u>eigh</u>

v<u>ei</u>l

pr<u>ey</u>

A. Choose the word with the long *a* sound to complete the sentence. Write the word on the line.

1. My brother and sister are older than me.

   _____ are both in high school.

   this   them   they

2. Tomorrow is my birthday. I am going to

   be _____ years old.

   eight   eat   six

3. I will use a scale to _____ these pennies.

   wet   weigh   heat

4. I called over to my friend, "_____ can
   you come over here?"   Hey   Hat   This

5. It is good to _____ your teacher in class.

   help   obey   teach

B. Go back and circle the letters that stand for the long *a* sound in the answers above.

Name _____

Wetlands: Great Places

6   Have you ever seen wetlands at

14 daybreak? It is a great thing to see.

20   Wetlands can be home for lots

25 of animals: Birds like osprey,

29 blackbirds, storks, and kites;

36 mammals like otters, panthers, and bobcats; and

45 critters like gators, frogs and snakes. They all make

55 their home in wetlands. Wetlands are like a haven for

57 living things.

67   Lots of great plants can be seen in wetlands. The

78 grey and green of cypress trees are hard to miss. Pond

86 pines, ferns, and moss can be seen too.

96   Wetlands can keep us safe. If you and your neighbors

105 live near the seashore, wetlands may help lessen floods

114 from storms. That is why wetlands are so great!

I. Circle the words with long *a*: *a, ea, eigh, ei, ey*.

2. Complete the sentences.

Wetlands can be home for lots of _____.

The cypress trees are _____ and green.

Name _____

Some consonant pairs have a silent letter. The letters **kn** stand for the **n** sound. The letters **gn** stand for the **n** sound. The letters **wr** stand for the **r** sound. The letters **mb** stand for the **m** sound. The letters **sc** stand for the **s** sound.

k<u>n</u>it   **<u>g</u>nome**   **<u>w</u>rist**   **thu<u>mb</u>**   **<u>sc</u>ent**

A. Underline the word that names each picture. Then write the word on the line.

1. knot not know	**2.** inch wrench wrist	**3.** lamp limb lamb
4. scent seen scene	**5** knife knee nite	**6.** gap gnat nap

B. Circle the letter pair that includes a silent consonant in the words above.

Name _____

Some consonant pairs have a silent letter. The letters **kn** stand for the **n** sound. The letters **gn** stand for the **n** sound. The letters **wr** stand for the **r** sound. The letters **mb** stand for the **m** sound. The letters **sc** stand for the **s** sound.

knee   **gnat**   **wrench**   **lamb**   **scene**

Look at each picture. Write the missing letters to finish the picture name.

| wr | kn | gn | mb | sc |

1. _____ ight	2. _____ ap
3. thu _____	4. si _____
5. _____ ent	6.  _____ ot
7. _____ ome	8. co _____

Name _____

Wren the Knight

7	Once upon a time, there lived a
12	tiny, brave knight named Wren.
20	Wren was the size of a thumb. He
28	lived in a box made of knotty pine.
37	It sat on the limb of a tall tree.
45	Wren was much tinier than the other knights.
57	One day, Wren heard a knock at his door. He did not
67	reply. He only gnashed his teeth. "Open up! I know
76	you're there." Wren opened the door and dropped to
82	his knee. It was Queen Noreen!
92	"Get up, kind sir," Queen Noreen said. "Do not make
103	a scene. Please come live with me in my castle."
115	Wren made a sign and hung it on his pine box. He
124	wrote: "WREN IS NOT AT HOME!" Then Wren left
134	with Queen Noreen, riding on her wrist the whole way.

I. Circle the words with silent letters: *wr, kn, gn, mb, sc.*

2. Complete the sentences.

Wren was the size of a _____.

One day, Wren heard a _____ at his door.

Name _____

Some consonant pairs contain a silent letter. In the letter pairs *lf, lk, bt*, the first letter is silent, as in the words *calf, yolk,* and *debt*. In the letter pairs *mn, rh, st*, the second letter is silent, as in the words *column, rhyme,* and *fasten*.

calf yolk column

A. Underline the consonant pair that contains a silent letter in each word below.

rhyme   debt   column   half   folk   fasten

B. Circle each word in the puzzle.

f	o	l	k	r	c	x
a	a	l	u	n	o	y
s	z	s	h	a	l	f
t	u	y	i	c	u	w
e	s	r	h	y	m	e
n	d	e	b	t	n	v

Name _____

Some consonant pairs contain a silent letter. In the letter pairs *lf, lk, bt,* the first letter is silent, as in the words *half, folk,* and *debt. In the letter pairs mn, rh, st,* the second letter is silent, as in the words *column, rhino,* and *listen.*

rh<u>ino</u>   li<u>st</u>en

Write the missing letters to complete each picture name.

rh	mn	lf	lk	st

1.  ca _____	2.  colu _____	3.  li _____ en
4.  yo _____	5.  ha _____	6.  _____ ino

Name _____

Folk Music

6	Do you like listening to rock
13	and roll, jazz, or hip hop? If
21	so, then you owe a debt to folk
26	music. Those kinds of music
30	started as folk music.
41	Folk music is known as roots music as well. A few
52	kinds of folk music are blues, Cajun, and jug bands. So
61	folk music can be really happy or really solemn.
70	People who write folk music use rhymes in telling
77	tales. They will sing hymns as well.
87	Bands that play music that is <u>not</u> folk music might
98	still use folk music. They might take half of their notes
108	and rhythms from one kind of folk music and half
118	from another kind. They mix them and make a fresh
130	kind of music. Folk music is where so much music is born.

1. Circle the words with silent letters: *rh, bt, mn, lk, lf.*

2. Complete the sentences.

Folk music can be really happy or _____.

People that write folk music use _____.

Name _____

Sometimes the letters *ou* and *ow* can stand for the vowel sound you hear in the words *house* and *cow*.

h<u>ou</u>se   c<u>ow</u>

A. Circle the word that names each picture. Then write the word on the line.

I. 	clown claim coal _____	2. 	ground grin groan _____	3. 	moat moth mouth _____

B. Choose the words from the box that completes each sentence. Then write the words on the lines.

| clouds | count | house | south | town |

4. How many _____ will Jill see in the sky?

5. Jim paints a wall of his new _____.

6. In the Fall, birds fly _____.

7. Meg can _____ to ten.

8. We take a trip to the book store in _____.

Name _____

Sometimes the letters **ou** and **ow** can stand for the vowel sound you hear in the words **shout** and **clown**.

sh<u>ou</u>t   cl<u>ow</u>n

Look at each picture. Use the letter tiles to write each picture name.

o u w c c d e h n r s	1.  ⬭ ⬭ ⬭ ⬭ ⬭
	2. ⬭ ⬭ ⬭ ⬭
	3.  ⬭ ⬭ ⬭ ⬭ ⬭
	4.  ⬭ ⬭ ⬭ ⬭
	5.  ⬭ ⬭ ⬭ ⬭ ⬭

Name _____

An Owl Prowls the Sky

11   Night falls. A mouse hears a sound that fills it with

19 dread. *HOOT!* An owl prowls the night sky!

32   An owl can hunt in two ways. First, it can perch in a

44 tree and wait. Then, when it sees a meal, it drops down

56 to strike. An owl can also hunt while in flight. It flies

65 close to the ground, scouting for the night's prize.

75   An owl can hear very faint sounds. An owl's ruff,

85 the two soft disks around the eyes, leads sound waves

99 to the owl's ears as it flies. An owl hears so well that it

108 can hunt when there is no light at all!

118   Owls make no sound as they fly. The owl's wings

129 have a shape that lets air slip by without sound. The

135 mouse will not hear it strike!

I. Circle the words with the vowel sound you hear in *cow.*

2. Complete the sentence.

An owl can hunt _____ light to see.

Name _____

The letters *oi* and *oy* can stand for the vowel sound you hear in the words *oil* and *boy*.

o<u>i</u>l   b<u>oy</u>

Circle the word that names each picture. Then write the word on the line.

1.	sole	2.	cone	3.	voice
	soil		cane		vote
	sale		coin		vase
	___		___		___
4.	job	5.	boat	6.	toys
	joy		boil		toes
	jug		bow		toss
	___		___		___

Name _____

> The letters *oi* and *oy* can stand for the sound you hear in the words *boil* and *joy*.
>
> b<u>oi</u>l j<u>oy</u>

Look at each picture. Write the letters *oy* or *oi* to complete the picture name.

I.  ch _____ ce	2.  b _____	3.  n _____ se
4.  br _____ l	5.  p _____ nt	6. enj _____

Name _____

No Noise Picnic

6   Joyce and Troy packed a lunch

12   for a long afternoon picnic in

17   the backyard. They planned on

22   spending time away from the

24   noise inside.

29   Troy made some hard boiled

40   eggs. He also joined nuts and dried fruit to make a

49   trail mix. Joyce made some sandwiches that they could

50   enjoy.

59   Troy said, "We could wrap the sandwiches in foil.

68   That will help them not spoil in our knapsacks."

78   They walked to the point they were looking for. It

89   was a place in the yard where they could avoid noise.

98   "There are no voices here, that's for sure," Troy

99   shouted.

1. Circle all the words that contain *oi* or *oy* sounds.

2. Complete the sentences.

Troy made some hard _____ eggs.

We could wrap the sandwiches in _____.

Name _____

> The letters *oo*, *ou*, or *u* can stand for the vowel sound you hear in the words **wood**, **should**, and **put**.
>
> w<u>oo</u>d

Look at each picture. Write the picture name on the line.

| foot | push | hook | bush | book | hood |

| 1.

 _____ | 2.

 _____ | 3.

 _____ |
| 4.

 _____ | 5.

 _____ | 6.

 _____ |

Name _____

> The letters **oo, ou,** or **u** can stand for the vowel sound you hear in the words **book, could,** and **bull**.
>
> b<u>oo</u>k b<u>u</u>ll

A. Read both words. Circle the word that has the vowel sound you hear in *could*.

1. prize   pull

2. slime   would

3. spoil   crook

4. shook   game

5. put   paint

B. Write *oo,* or *u* to complete each picture name.

 1. br _____ k   2. b _____ sh

 3. w _____ d   4. c _____ k

 5. b _____ ll

Name _____

Book Nook

7   I like to go to this bookstore.

13 Its name is "Book Nook." It

20 is SO neat! You will think so,

27 too. First, I pull open the door.

33 Then I set foot inside. Wow!

40 I can look at books about lots

53 of things. I can look at books on wool. I can look at

65 books on bulls. I can look at books on cooking. The last

78 time I was looking at a book about dogs. I did like it,

92 so I paid for it and took it home. The book was full of

102 neat things about dogs. At Book Nook they sell things

105 to eat, too.

116   Would you like to find neat books? You should go to

119 the Book Nook!

---

1. Circle the words that have the vowel sound you hear in *book*.

2. Complete the sentences.

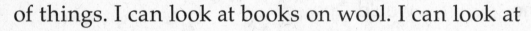

The bookstore's name is _____.

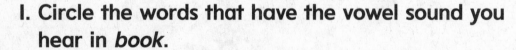

The book was _____ of neat things about dogs.

Name _____

> The letters *oo, u, u_e, ew, ue, ui* can stand for the vowel sound you hear in *broom, flu, tune, new, blue,* and *suit*.
>
> **broom**   **tune**

A. Look at each picture. Circle the word that names the picture. Write the word.

1.  _____

   flute   fork   fin

2. _____

   port   pool   pot

3. _____

   fruit   feet   fog

4. _____

   scrape   stew   screw

5. _____

   glow   glue   glass

6. _____

   tuna   tape   tub

B. Go back and underline the letters that stand for the vowel sound you hear in the word *new* in the answers above.

Name _____

The letters *oo, u, u_e, ew, ue, ui* can stand for the vowel sound you hear in *moon, July, flute, drew, blue,* and *fruit*.

m**oo**n	J**u**ly	fl**u**t**e**	dr**ew**	bl**ue**	fr**ui**t
					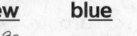

A. Write *oo, u, u_e, ew, ue,* or *ui* to complete each picture name.

1.   t ____ th

2.   st ____

3.   s ____ t

4.   gl ____

B. Finish each word ladder. Change only one letter at a time.

1. Go from **spoon** to **swoop**.   2. Go from **June** to **tube**.

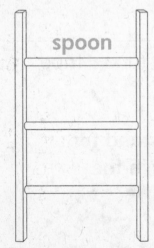

spoon

Hint:

Change **p** to **w**.

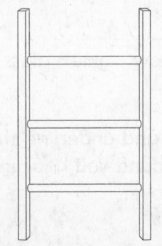

Name _____

Loons

9	A loon is a kind of bird that has
15	a nice sounding coo. Loons can
22	be found all over the place. Five
29	kinds of loon can be found in
31	North America.
41	Loons are good divers. They find food in lakes and
51	pools. They zoom down from the sky and dive into
61	lakes to scoop up fish. They can even zoom around
66	under water and pursue fish.
76	Loons roost in nests close to water. The truth is,
88	loons are more suited to water. So, they go on land just
91	to lay eggs.
102	Loons lay eggs in May or June. When the eggs hatch,
112	loons must feed their brood. The new chicks are fed
123	small bits of food. Soon, the chicks can dive for food.

1. Circle the words that have the vowel sound you hear in *spoon*.

2. Complete the sentences.

Loons _____ in nests close to water.

The _____ chicks are fed small bits of food.

Name _____

The letters **aw**, **au**, **a**, and **al** can stand for the vowel sound you hear in the words **paw**, **haul**, **ball**, and **walk**.

p<u>aw</u>	h<u>au</u>l	b<u>a</u>ll	w<u>al</u>k

A. Circle the word that completes each sentence. Then write the word on the line.

1. Paul cuts wood with a _____.

    sat   saw   sauce

2. She wears a _____ in the cold.

    claw   crawl   shawl

3. Judy throws a blue _____.

    ball   tall   hall

4. Pat is too _____ to go on the ride.

    talk   small   smell

B. Circle the picture that matches the word. Underline the letters that stand for the vowel sound.

1.

    paw

2.

    lawn

3.

    walk

Name _____

The letters **aw**, **au**, **a**, and **al** can stand for the vowel sound you hear in the words **yawn**, **launch**, **tall**, and **talk**.

y<u>aw</u>n   l<u>au</u>nch   t<u>a</u>ll   t<u>al</u>k

A. Look at each picture. Write aw, al, or au to complete each picture name.

1. cr _____ l

2. footb _____ ll

3. s _____ ce

4. j _____

5. m _____ ll

6. w _____ k

B. Use the tiles to write each picture name.

b   d   l   l   r   w   a

1. _____

2. _____

3. _____

Name _____

A Walk in the Grasslands

5   Grasslands can be found all
10 over the world. Grasslands do
16 not get the amount of rainfall
22 needed for a forest to grow.
29 Still, it is not always dry in
37 grasslands. Because of this, grass can grow there.
46   All kinds of animals can be found in grasslands.
55 In the North American grasslands, you might hear a
67 coyote call out, or see a deer walk up. In Africa, you
79 might see a rhino open its jaws with a yawn. In South
89 America, you might see a bush dog hauling its pups.
97   When rain falls on grasslands, up spring flowers
107 both small and tall. Because grassland soil is so deep
118 and rich, a lot of things grow well there. So, grasslands
127 can be useful for animals, but also for humans!

1. **Circle all the words that have the vowel sound you hear in** *ball.*

2. **Write the answer to each question.**

Grasslands can be found _____.

Grasslands can be useful for _____.

Name _____

The letters *augh* stand for the vowel sound you hear in *caught*. The letters *ough* stand for the vowel sound you hear in *thought*.

c<u>augh</u>t   th<u>ough</u>t

A. Underline the letters that stand for the vowel sound you heard in *caught* and *thought*.

fought   brought   ought   naught

daughter   sought   taught   thought

B. Circle each word from above in the puzzle.

b	r	o	u	g	h	t	t	t	s
z	v	r	n	c	u	d	a	u	u
x	n	v	q	o	n	a	u	r	g
o	g	j	o	s	a	u	g	f	u
m	s	l	j	o	u	g	h	o	d
r	m	i	o	u	g	h	t	u	p
t	h	o	u	g	h	t	j	g	o
p	t	w	z	h	t	e	r	h	k
o	u	g	h	t	z	r	h	t	p

Name _____

> The letters **ough** stand for the vowel sound you hear in
> **bought**. The letters **augh** stand for the vowel sound you
> hear in *taught*.
>
> b<u>ough</u>t   t<u>augh</u>t

A. Circle the word that completes each sentence. Write the word on the line.

1. I _____ that the clock was slow.
throat   thought   tooth

2. The old man's _____ was very beautiful.
        daughter   dark   down

3. We _____ to clean the dishes.
        other   ought   ox

4. The cat and dog always _____.
                fourth   fun   fought

5. The boy _____ the baseball.
        caught   catch   coach

B. Go back and underline the letters that stand for the vowel sound you hear in *bought* and *taught* in each answer above.

Benjamin Franklin, A Thoughtful American

4   Some call Benjamin Franklin

9   "The First American." He fought

16   for America's right to be free. He

22   was known for careful thought. He

28   sought to learn about the world.

37   Ben Franklin was born in 1706. When he was

48   12 years old, he taught himself to read and write well.

60   At the age of 15, he wrote letters to a newspaper. He

71   gave tips. The letters were a hit! Ben liked to invent

78   things. He invented a battery and bifocals.

90   Ben had a wife and two kids: a son and a daughter.

101   When he was older, he started a school that taught kids

111   about the things he cared about. He thought that all

120   kids ought to learn as much as they can!

1. Circle all the words with *augh* or *ough*.

2. Complete the sentences.

Ben Franklin sought to learn _____.

Ben had a son and a _____.

Name _____

> The short **e** sound can be spelled **ea**, as in ***thread***. The short **u** sound can be spelled **ou**, as in ***touch***. The short **i** sound can be spelled **y**, as in ***gym***.
>
> thr**ea**d   t**ou**ch   g**y**m

A. Underline the letters that stand for the vowel sound in each word.

double   spread   wealth   myth

feather   touch   head   breath

B. Circle the word that names each picture. Then write the word on the line.

1.
   _____   breed   bread

2.
   _____   young   food

3.
   _____   head   heed

4.
   _____   tiny   gym

Name _____

> The short **e** sound can be spelled **ea**, as in **bread**. The short **u** sound can be spelled **ou**, as in **double**. The short **i** sound can be spelled **y**, as in **crystal**.
>
> br**ea**d   d**ou**ble   crystal

A. Read both words. Circle the word that has the short vowel sound.

1. dead   deed

2. fly   gym

3. touch   tune

4. sweet   sweat

B. Read each word. Find a word from the box that rhymes. Write the word on the line.

> myth   tread   young   double

1. rung _____

2. bubble _____

3. bed _____

4. with _____

Name _____

Getting Healthy

7 | All people should try to be healthy.

12 | Getting healthy means doing things

18 | that are good for the body.

26 | One thing that can be done to stay

37 | healthy is to eat better. You should not flood your body

46 | with junk food and snacks. Instead, eat vegetables and

55 | fruit. Eat home cooked meals instead of eating out.

65 | Another thing that can be done to stay healthy is

73 | exercise. Young people in this country are getting

82 | healthy by moving around more. You can go running

96 | or play a sport. Adults might go to a gym and run on a

97 | treadmill.

109 | We can all try to be healthy. Let's get out and get

110 | healthy!

1. Circle the words with short *e* spelled *ea*, short *i* spelled *y*, or short *u* spelled *ou*.

2. Complete the sentences.

All people should try to be _____.

Adults might go to a _____.

Name _____

> Digraphs are groups of letters that stand for a single sound. The digraphs **ss** and **ch** can stand for the sound you hear in the middle of *mission* and *brochure*. The digraph **gh** can stand for the sound at the end of the word *laugh*.
>
> mission   brochure    laugh

Choose the word that completes the sentence. Then write the word on the line.

| chef   issue   mission   rough   tissue |

1. The doctor is on a _____ to help others.

2. We got the new _____ of the news paper in the mail.

3. The sand paper is _____.

4. I need a _____ after I sneeze.

5. The _____ used beets and beef.

Name _____

Digraphs are groups of letters that stand for a single sound. The digraphs **ss** and **ch** can stand for the sound you hear in the middle of *ti**ss**ue* and the beginning of *<u>ch</u>ef*. The letters **gh** can stand for the sound at the end of the word *tou<u>gh</u>*.

ti<u>ss</u>ue tou<u>gh</u>  <u>ch</u>ef

Unscramble the tiles. Write each picture name on the line.

1. ⬭r⬭ ⬭h⬭ ⬭g⬭ ⬭u⬭ ⬭o⬭ _____

2. ⬭g⬭ ⬭h⬭ ⬭l⬭ ⬭u⬭ ⬭a⬭ _____

3. ⬭s⬭ ⬭s⬭ ⬭u⬭ ⬭e⬭ ⬭i⬭ ⬭t⬭ _____

4.  ⬭s⬭ ⬭t⬭ ⬭m⬭ ⬭u⬭ ⬭c⬭ ⬭h⬭ _____
⬭e⬭ ⬭a⬭

Name _____

Temple Grandin and the Hug Machine

5   Temple Grandin had autism. Some

11 days were tough. The feeling of

17 pressure reassured her, but she did

23 not like to hug other people.

33   When Temple grew up, she liked to help animals. She

45 found a better way to feed pigs with a trough. She also

56 wanted to help kids. She made it her mission to create

65 a machine that helped kids with autism. The machine

75 was called the Hug Machine. It has two boards with

87 thick, soft pads. A box on the end makes sure it gives

97 enough pressure. A kid lies between the pads. It gives

103 the feeling of having a hug.

113   Now kids can get hugs from a machine. A session

122 helps treat them. With this machine, Temple shows her

125 compassion for kids.

1. Circle the words that have /f/ and /sh/ sounds.

2. Write the answer to each question.

Temple Grandin helped pigs by _____.

Temple Grandin made _____.

Name _____

A **closed syllable** ends with a consonant. It has a short vowel sound. Some words contain two closed syllables. Listen to the word *sunset*. You can hear that each syllable ends with a consonant.

su__nse__t

A. Put the two closed syllables together to form a word that matches the picture. Then write the word on the line.

1. pen   cil   _____

2. pup   pet   _____

3. bas   ket   _____

4. den   tist   _____

B. Complete each sentence using a word from above.

1. The waste _____ is filled with trash.

2. I write with a _____.

Name _____

> A **closed syllable** ends with a consonant. It has a short vowel sound. Some words contain two closed syllables. Listen to the word *ribbon*. You can hear that each syllable ends with a consonant.
>
> **ri_bb_on**

A. Read each word. Draw a line to divide each word into syllables. Then write the syllables on the lines.

1. kitten _____ _____

2. insect _____ _____

3. contest _____ _____

4. muffin _____ _____

B. Complete each sentence using a word from above.

1. My team came in last place in the _____.

2. She has a _____ for a pet.

Name _____

A Pilgrim Ship

6 When the pilgrims sailed to find

14 new land, they were at sea for sixty

20 days. Their ship, the Mayflower, had

27 more than a hundred people on it.

38 At the start there was a small vessel that rode with

48 the Mayflower. But that tiny ship had to return home

60 due to sudden storms and a leak in the bottom. So the

69 pilgrims packed all the items on just one ship.

79 A list told the pilgrims what they might need, such

87 as food, clothing, tools, and household items. The

96 pilgrims found that they could not land where they

105 wanted. So they chose a different place and called

114 it Plymouth. With help from the native people, the

122 pilgrims made it through a long hard winter.

I. Circle all the words that have two closed syllables.

2. Complete the sentences.

The small vessel had a leak in the _____.

The pilgrims made it through a long hard _____.

Name _____

Each syllable in a word has only one vowel sound. A **final e syllable** ends in a vowel, consonant, final **e**. The final **e** is silent. The vowel sound before it is long. In the word **athlete**, the syllable **lete** has the long **e** sound.

ath<u>lete</u>

A. Underline the final e syllable in each word.

perfume   reptile   excites   polite   inside   excuse

B. Circle each word in the puzzle. Look for the CVCe syllables to help you.

p	e	r	f	u	m	e	s	t
o	p	e	x	c	i	t	e	s
l	m	p	i	p	r	b	i	k
i	l	t	e	c	e	l	n	a
t	d	i	n	s	i	d	e	z
e	d	l	s	m	t	u	c	t
b	r	e	x	c	u	s	e	l

Name _____

Each syllable in a word has only one vowel sound. A **final e syllable** ends in a vowel, consonant, final **e**. The final **e** is silent. The vowel sound before it is long. In the word *tadpole*, the syllable *pole* has the long *o* sound.

ta<u>dpole</u>

A. Underline the final *e* syllables in the words below.

invite   mistake   female

inside   ninety   reptile

B. Choose a word from Part A that completes each sentence. Write that word on the line.

1. Meg made a _____ on her homework.

2. A snake is a _____.

3. My grandfather is _____ years old.

4. I will _____ you to my party.

5. Come _____. It is raining.

6. My cat is not a male cat. She is a _____ cat.

Name _____

Extreme Termites!

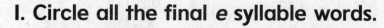

5   When you walk through the

9   African grasslands, you admire

16   a huge mound made of mud that

24   stretches to the sunrise. It is a home

29   for termites. Termite mounds can

39   be forty feet high! That is a two-story house.

47   How do termites build these mounds? They make

57   a mix of soil and saliva. Worker termites are extreme.

68   They work all day and never sleep. The inside of a

78   termite mound is a complex maze. It has many tunnels.

86   Some termite mounds contain enough termites to fill

95   seven pick-up trucks. Termite mounds have shafts that

105 control how hot or cold it gets inside. Most termites

115 do not go outside. They work under the ground. This

119 system helps them survive.

I. Circle all the final _e_ syllable words.

2. Write the answer to each question.

What are termite mounds made of? _____.

How long can termites work? _____.

Name _____

> Syllables that end with one vowel are called **open syllables**.
> The vowel sound is usually long. Listen to the first syllables in
> the words _**baby**_ and _**open**_. The syllables _ba_ and _o_ are **open**
> **syllables**.
>
> **ba**by **o**pen

**A. Fill in the blank with the word that completes
each sentence.**

> pony   robot   rodent   solo   spider

1. A mouse is a kind of _____.

2. Our _____ will perform tasks
   around the house.

3. The itsy bitsy _____ went up
   the water spout.

4. I think I will get a _____ for
   my birthday.

5. Now I will play my _____ for
   the crowd.

**B. Go back and circle the open syllable in each
answer above.**

Name _____

Syllables that end with one vowel are called **open syllables**. The vowel sound is long. Listen to the first syllables in the words _lady_ and _solo_. The syllables _la_ and _so_ are **open syllables**.

l<u>a</u>dy   s<u>o</u>lo

Look at each picture. Write the open syllable to finish the picture name.

1.	2.	3.

_____ nut	_____ sic	_____ zen

4.	5.	6.

_____ bra	_____ con	_____ bra

Name _____

Bison on the Open Plain

7	The bison is a great animal of
13	the American Plains. Bison are the
18	heaviest animals in North America!
25	But they are still very fast. One
34	moment, you see them standing still. The next moment,
39	they are across the plains!
48	Bison cannot digest their food the first time. They
59	must chew it twice! Bison are adapted to all types of
71	weather. They roll in the dirt in summer to stay cool. In
79	winter, bison's coats protect them from frozen weather.
90	Bison used to roam in great herds in the open plains.
101	Now only a tiny number of bison are left. This is
109	because humans hunted them for many years. Today,
117	most bison live in parks or on farms.

1. Circle all the words that contain open syllables.

2. Complete the sentences.

Bison cannot _____ their food the first time.

Now only a _____ number of bison are left.

Name _____

> Some words end in a consonant and *le, el,* or *al*. This is a final stable syllable. Listen to the ending sound in the words *candle* and *oval*. You can hear the final stable syllable at the end of each word.
>
> can**dle**   o**val**

A. Circle the word that names each picture. Then write the word on the line.

I.	petal	2.	jelly	3.	pail
	pail		juggle		all
	pet		jiggle		apple
	_____		_____		_____
4.	ten	5.	call	6.	mussel
	turtle		handle		music
	tiger		camel		mitten
	_____		_____		_____

B. Go back and circle the final stable syllable in each answer above.

Name _____

> Some words end in a consonant and *le, el,* or *al*. This is a final stable syllable. Listen to the ending sound in the words *camel* and *turtle*. You can hear the final stable syllable at the end of each word.
>
> camel    turtle

Look at each picture. Write the missing letters to finish the picture name.

| le   el   al |

1. muss _____	2. circ _____
3. roy _____	4. bubb _____
5. beet _____	6. glob _____
7. tab _____	8. nick _____

Name _____

The Plastic Bottle

6	Plastic bottles are a global problem.
13	Many plastic bottles end up as trash.
20	Plastic trash ends up in public parks,
27	lakes, and streams. There is a huge
38	circle of plastic trash in the ocean. That circle is more
42	than 300,000 square miles!
52	How can we deal with this problem? You might be
63	thinking, "But I am just a pupil. How can I help?"
74	There is one simple thing to do: Drink water from a
76	local source.
87	If you buy water in a plastic bottle, don't throw the
97	bottle away. Recycle it. In some states, you can return
107	an empty bottle for a nickel. When you travel, carry
119	water in a metal bottle. The less plastic we use, the less
125	harm we bring to our planet.

1. Circle all the words that have a final stable syllable.

2. Complete the sentences.

Plastic bottles are a _____ problem.

You can return an empty bottle for a _____.

Name _____

When two vowels appear together in a long word, they often stay in the same syllable. This is called a **vowel team syllable**. Listen to the vowel sounds in *cooking*. Sometimes a vowel and a consonant can stand for one vowel sound in the examples *ow* and *oy*. Listen to the vowel sounds in *bowtie*.

c<u>oo</u>king   b<u>ow</u>tie

A. Look at each picture. Write the picture name on the line.

toenail   raincoat   beaver   window   pillow

I. _____

2. _____

3. _____

4. _____

5. _____

B. Draw a line to divide the two syllables of each word you chose.

Name _____

When two vowels appear together in a long word, they often stay in the same syllables. This is called a **vowel team syllable**. Some words have a vowel team in only one syllable of the word. Listen to the vowel sounds in *hockey* and *mushroom*.

hock**ey**   mushr**oo**m

A. Write the missing letters to complete each picture name.

| ay | ea | ee | ey | oi | oo |

1. coff _____

2. birthd _____

3. classr _____ m

4.  p _____ nuts

B. Write the word that completes each sentence.

| yellow | freedom | oatmeal | enjoy |

1. He did _____ that good meal.

2. We have _____ for breakfast.

3. She put her _____ raincoat away.

Name _____

Healthy Eating

6   How can you make wise choices

12 about eating food? You must think

17 about foods that promote healthy

23 living. A balanced menu helps you

27 maintain a healthy weight.

36   MyPlate contains five food groups. These groups are

44 grains, proteins, dairy, fruits, vegetables. Try to drink

54 water. Avoid drinks that contain too much sugar. If you

64 can, drink water between mealtimes. Try to cut back on

74 foods high in sugar, fat, and salt. These foods include

84 hot dogs and cake. Eat fruits or grains at mealtimes.

92   Make plates with green, leafy foods like spinach.

97 Choose small plates or bowls.

105   Enjoy eating healthy food. And, always, wash your

108 hands before eating.

---

1. **Circle all the words that have vowel team syllables.**

2. **Complete the sentences.**

    You should avoid _____.

    You should eat fruits and grains _____.

Name _____

When a vowel or a pair of vowels is followed by the letter *r*, it changes the vowel sound. The vowels and the *r* stay in the same syllable. You can hear **r-controlled syllables** at the end of *flower* and the beginning of *artist*.

flow**er** **ar**tist

Circle the words with *r*-controlled syllables. Then find them in the puzzle below.

garnish   credit   outlaw

carton   market   rulebook

lady   forget   tardy

g	a	r	n	i	s	h
m	n	t	s	k	f	o
a	c	a	r	t	o	n
r	u	r	s	t	r	i
k	c	d	a	i	g	n
e	o	y	g	j	e	e
t	s	q	i	h	t	p

Name _____

> When a vowel or a pair of vowels is followed by the letter
> *r*, it changes the vowel sound. The vowels and the *r* stay in
> the same syllable. This is called an **r-controlled syllable**.
> You hear *r*-controlled syllables at the end of **_under_** and the
> beginning of **_circus_**.
>
> under   circus

**A. Connect the two syllables to make a word. Write
the word on a line.**

I. hor   net   _____

2. star   light   _____

3. num   ber   _____

4. per   fect   _____

5. gar   den   _____

**B. Look at the picture. Write the missing *r*-controlled
syllable.**

I. spi _____   **2.** 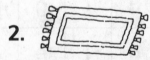 _____ pet

3.  ti _____

Name _____

Recycle Paper!

7   Many of the things we use every

13   day come from lumber, wood from

20   trees. Think of all the things you

27   use that are made from paper. Paper

34   is made from small bits of wood,

46   called pulp. The pulp is spread in a thin layer and is

55   covered with water. The pulp absorbs water, then water

65   drips away. Most all the things we purchase that are

71   made from paper can be recycled.

81   A huge number of pieces of paper are discarded each

91   year. They will take more room in landfills. We may

101 discard a milk carton in the trash. But, that carton

106 could be reused or recycled.

111 So, remember to recycle!

1. Circle all the words that have *r*-controlled syllables.

2. Write the answer to each question.

Wood pulp is _____.

What is lumber? _____

Name _____

> The ending **-s** can be added to a noun to tell about more than one thing like in **pans** and **bugs**.
>
> pan**s**    bug**s**

A. Circle the word that names each picture. Then write the word.

1.   mop   mops   _____

2.   rat   rats   _____

3.   fan   fans   _____

4.   pig   pigs   _____

5.   rug   rugs   _____

B. Read the sentence. Underline the word that tells about more than one thing. Write the word on the line.

1. Sam has cats. _____

2. The dogs can run. _____

3. Ben and Jan have six bats. _____

Name _____

> You can add the ending **-s** to a noun to tell about more than one like in **_rams_** and **_pins_**.
>
> ram<u>s</u>   pin<u>s</u>

**A. Add -s to each word to tell about more than one.
Then write the word.**

1. nap + s = _____

2. leg + s = _____

3. nut + s = _____

4. bib + s = _____

B. Read the sentence. Add -s to make the underlined word name more than one. Write the new word.

1. Six <u>pup</u> nap in the sun. _____

2. Mom put <u>egg</u> in the pan. _____

3. Pat had the <u>yam</u>. _____

4. Mom can fill ten <u>mug</u>. _____

Name _____

Fun Pals

8   Pug is a dog. Tab is a cat.

19   Flip is a duck. Pug and Tab and Flip are pals.

26   Pug has a gift for his pals.

35   "What is this gift in my bag?" asks Pug.

40   "Is it yams?" asks Tab.

46   Pug says it is not yams.

51   "Is it figs?" asks Flip.

58   But Pug says it is not figs.

65   "Is it pots of jam?" asks Tab.

74   But Pug says it is not pots of jam.

79   "It is nuts!" yells Pug.

1. Circle the words that end in -s and mean more than one.

2. Complete the sentences.

Pug is a _____ .

Pug has _____ for his pals.

Name _____

> When an action word follows a name or the words
> *he, she,* or *it,* add the ending *-s* to show action that
> is happening now.
>
> **I tag you.   She tag<u>s</u> me.   Dan tag<u>s</u> you.**

**Circle the word that completes each sentence.
Then write the word.**

1. He _____.
   jump   jumps

2. It _____.
   hops   hop

3. Russ _____ his bag.
   packs   pack

4. She _____.
   swim   swims

5. Pam _____.
   run   runs

6. It _____.
   sits   sit

Name _____

> When an action word follows a name or the words
> *he, she,* or *it,* add the ending *-s* to show action that
> is happening now.
>
> **I help.**   **She help<u>s</u>.**

**Add the *-s* ending to the word in bold. Write the
new word.**

1. I **fill** the box.   Nan _____ the box.

2. I **sell** a cup.   He _____ a cup.

3. I **pack** a bag.   Sis _____ a bag.

4. I **chop** a log.   Dad _____ a log.

5. I **jump** on a mat.   Ken _____ on a mat.

6. I **pick** up the cat.   Pam _____ up the cat.

7. I **hug** Mom.   Bob _____ Mom.

8. I **hop** on the bed.   It _____ on the bed.

9. I **play** with my pal.   Jan _____ with Mom.

Name _____

Frogs

10	This is a frog. It has spots on its back.
19	The frog sits. It sits in the hot sun.
28	The frog naps. It naps on a big log.
34	The frog dips in the pond.
42	The frog swims. It swims in a pond.
51	The frog jumps. It jumps up on its pad.
60	The frog hops. It hops on land. Plop, plop!
65	Frogs can do a lot.
78	If you see a frog, see if it hops or if it runs.

I. Circle all the words that end in -s that tell about an action that is happening now.

2. Complete the sentences.

The frog has _____ on its back.

This frog _____ on a log.

Name _____

When a noun ends in *-s, -ss, -sh, -ch,* or *-x,* add *-es* to tell about more than one.

glass<u>es</u>    fox<u>es</u>

A. Add *-es* to these words to name the pictures. Then write the new words.

1. box _____   _____

2. bus _____   _____

3. ax _____   _____

B. Read the sentence. Add *-es* to the underlined word to make it mean more than one. Write the new word.

1. Dad has two kinds of <u>glass</u>. _____

2. She had two <u>class</u> on the bus. _____

3. The pup gets in lots of <u>mess</u>. _____

4. Tom and Matt had two <u>ax</u>. _____

Name _____

Add the ending *-es* to form the plural of nouns that end in *-s, -ss, -sh, -ch,* or *-x.*

fox + <u>es</u> = <u>foxes</u>

A. Add -es to make each word name more than one. Then write the word.

1. dress + _____ = _____

2. bus + _____ = _____

3. fox + _____ = _____

4. box + _____ = _____

5. pass + _____ = _____

B. Read the sentence. Circle the word that means more than one. Write the word on the line.

1. The foxes ran in the pen. _____

2. Nan has passes for the pet show. _____

3. The glasses fit in the sink. _____

4. The children sat on the boxes. _____

Name _____

Six Foxes

13   A mom fox has six pups. Six red foxes sit in a den.

20   One pup jumps out. Six pups play.

26   The pups run. The pups jump.

35   Six foxes run and jump. Six foxes wag tails.

42   The foxes snip and snap for fun.

47   The foxes snack on bugs!

55   Foxes can dig. Foxes dig in the grass.

63   Six foxes run past the grasses and mosses.

71   Six foxes rest. They nap in the den.

I. Circle all the words that end in -es and mean more than one.

2. Complete the sentences.

The _____ sit in the den.

Six foxes run past the _____.

Name _____

Add **-es** to action words that end with **ch, sh, s,** or **x** to show that an action is taking place now.

I fix my hair.   **Mom fix<u>es</u> my hair.**   **Jan fix<u>es</u> her hair.**

Circle the word that completes each sentence.
Then write the word.

1. Ted _____ fast.
   mix   mixes

2. Dad _____ the bed.
   fix   fixes

3. Kim _____ a ball.
   toss   tosses

4. Sam _____ Mom.
   kiss   kisses

5. He _____ a lot.
   fuss   fusses

Name _____

> Add the ending *-es* to words ending in *ch, sh, s, x,* and *z* to make them tell about an action happening now.
>
> **I fix.**   **He fix<u>es</u>.**

Add the *-es* ending to the word in bold.

1. I **mess** up the bed.   Jan _____ up the bed.

2. I **toss** the ball.   Ken _____ the ball.

3. I **mix** the sand.   Sis _____ the sand.

4. I **fuss** a lot.   Ben _____ a lot.

5. A snake can **hiss**.   It _____ .

6. I **pass** a cup.   Dan _____ a cup.

7. I **kiss** Mom.   Sal _____ Mom.

8. I **pass** the plate.   Fran _____ the plate.

Name _____

Mom Fixes Yams

6 | Yams can be a quick snack.

13 | I will tell how Mom fixes yams.

22 | Dad gets six yams. Dad passes them to Mom.

32 | Mom cuts up six yams. Next Mom presses the yams.

38 | Then the yams are not wet.

45 | Mom mixes butter and sugar and nuts.

51 | Dad puts it on the yams.

62 | Mom pops the six cut up yams in a crock pot.

66 | The yams get hot.

74 | My big sis, Viv, wants a quick snack.

81 | Viv never fusses if Mom fixes yams.

1. Circle all the words that end in *-es* that tell about an action that is happening now.

2. Complete the sentences.

Viv never _____ if Mom fixes yams.

Mom _____ butter and sugar and nuts.

Name _____

A **closed syllable** is a word part that ends in a consonant and has one vowel. Closed syllables usually have a short vowel sound.

rab / bit   rabbit

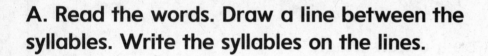

A. Read the words. Draw a line between the syllables. Write the syllables on the lines.

1. pup pet   _____ _____

2. mag net   _____ _____

3. pump kin   _____ _____

4. con test   _____ _____

B. Label each picture with a word from the box. Draw a line between the syllables.

| mitten   cactus   muffin   basket |

 1. _____

 2. _____

 3. _____

 4. _____

Name _____

> When a syllable ends in a consonant and has one vowel, the vowel sound is usually short. This is called a **closed syllable**.
>
> **mag / net**   **magnet**

A. Use a word from the box to complete each sentence. Then draw a line to divide the syllables in the word.

> napkin   helmet   insect   kitten

1. This tan _____ is my pet.

2. Mom cleaned up the spill with a _____.

3. See the _____ on the plant.

4. I wear a _____ when I ride my bike.

B. Blend the syllables to make a word. Write the word on the line.

1. sud   den _____

2. plas   tic _____

3. up   set _____

4. den   tist _____

Name _____

The Picnic Basket

5	"What is in this picnic
8	basket?" asks Kip.
15	"Is it jam?" asks Jan. "It is!"
18	Kip tells Jan.
22	"Milk?" asks Jan. "Yes!"
24	Kip says.
28	"Napkins?" asks Jan. "Yes!"
30	Kip says.
39	"A kitten?" asks Jan. "Not a kitten," says Kip.
48	"A pumpkin?" asks Jan. "Not a pumpkin," says Kip.
53	"A hundred muffins?" asks Jan.
60	"A hundred muffins cannot fit!" says Kip.
69	"Can six muffins fit in this basket?" Kip asks.
76	"Yes, six muffins can fit," Kip says.
84	"Six muffins will be just right," says Jan.

1. Circle all the two-syllable words that have a closed syllable.

2. Complete the sentences.

A _____ is not in the basket.

The basket has six _____ in it.

Name _____

The ending *-ed* can be added to an action word to show action that has already happened.

pack

packed

A. Circle the word that completes each sentence. Then write the word.

1. Dad _____ the lamp yesterday.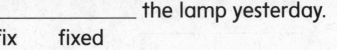
    fix   fixed

2. The cat _____ Ben.
    licked   lick

3. My dog _____ up on my lap.
    jumped   jump

4. Pam _____ her milk.
    spill   spilled

5. My mom _____ the egg.
    cracked   crack

B. Read the sentence. Circle the word that tells what someone or something did. Write the word.

1. Dan helped Kim. _____

2. Jan lifted a bag. _____

3. Ned yelled, "Stop!" _____

Name _____

You can add the ending *-ed* to some action words to tell about something that already happened.

jump    jumped

A. Add *-ed* to each word to tell about something that happened in the past. Write the word.

1. lift   +   ed   =   _____

2. smell   +   ed   =   _____

3. dress   +   ed   =   _____

4. fix   +   ed   =   _____

B. Read the sentence. Add *-ed* to make the underlined word tell about something that already happened.

1. Sam <u>spill</u> the milk.   _____

2. Tim <u>help</u> his pal.   _____

3. Lin <u>jump</u> on a mat.   _____

4. Dad <u>camp</u> in a tent.   _____

Name _____

Cracked!

11	Hen fixed up its nest. It packed the nest with twigs.
18	Hen pressed the twigs and mud together.
30	Then hen lifted its egg. It helped the egg into the nest.
35	Hen fluffed up its wings.
47	Hen sat on its egg in the nest. Hen sat and sat.
55	The egg cracked. It cracked just a bit.
66	Then it cracked a lot. Hen fussed.
73	It pecked at the egg. The egg pecked back at Hen.
75	Hen jumped!
81	The egg cracked and cracked. Crack!
86	A chick filled the nest.

1. Circle all the words that end in *-ed* that tell about an action that happened in the past.

2. Complete the sentences.

Hen _____ up its wings.

The egg _____ just a bit.

Name _____

> The *-ing* ending in an action word means that the action
> is happening now.
>
> smelling

**A. Use a word from the box to complete each
sentence. Then circle the *-ing* ending in each word.**

> snacking   lending   waxing   asking   helping

1. I am _____ this hat to Rex.

2. Jeff is _____ Mrs. Lin for help.

3. Ken is _____ Ben in class.

4. Pat is _____ on nuts.

5. Dad is _____ his red truck.

**B. Fill in the missing part to make the word in bold.
Write the word on the line.**

1. Sam is **packing** his bags.

   pack + _____ = _____

2. A duck is **nesting** in the pond.

   nest + _____ = _____

Name _____

> Add the ending *-ing* to an action word to tell what is happening now.
>
> melt + ing = melting

A. Add *-ing* to the words below to make new words. Write the new words on the lines.

1. dust _____   _____

2. mess _____   _____

3. pump _____   _____

4. lift _____   _____

5. box _____   _____

B. Use *-ing* to make the underlined word tell about an action that is happening now. Write the word on the line.

1. The pup is <u>jump</u> on the bed.   _____

2. Dad is <u>fix</u> a snack.   _____

3. Jon is <u>mend</u> his sock.   _____

4. Pam is <u>read</u> to her pal.   _____

Name _____

Helping

8	Jack the Hippo is standing in the pond.
16	Mack is standing on the back of Jack.
22	Jack has bugs on his back.
26	Mack is helping Jack.
35	Mack is pecking at bugs that land on Jack.
41	Jack is yelling, "Get that bug!"
49	Mack pecks and pecks and gets the bug.
57	Jack is resting. Mack is pecking at bugs.
66	Mack gets lots and lots of bugs to eat.
74	Mack is helping Jack. Jack is helping Mack.

I. Circle all the action words that have the *-ing* ending.

2. Complete the sentences.

Jake is _____ in the pond.

Mack is _____ at bugs on Jack.

Name _____

> A **possessive** is a word that tells who or what owns something. You can form a possessive by adding an apostrophe (') and *s*.
>
> Ned + 's = Ned's   Ned's hat

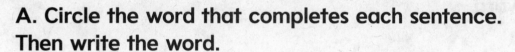

A. Circle the word that completes each sentence. Then write the word.

1. This is a _____ bell.

   bikes   bike's

2. This is the _____ dock.

   ships   ship's

3. This is _____ backpack.

   Jake's   Jakes'

4. This is _____ van.

   Moms   Mom's

5. This is the _____ shell.

   crab's   cra'bs

B. Read the sentence. Circle the word that is the possessive. Write the word on the line.

1. Jim's pet is big. _____

2. Tam's bike is red. _____

Name _____

> A **possessive** is a word that tells who or what owns something. You can form a possessive by adding an apostrophe (') and **s**.
>
> ### Fred + 's = Fred's

A. Add -'s to each word to make a possessive. Then write the word.

1. Matt + 's = _____

2. frog + 's = _____

3. Kate + 's = _____

4. mule + 's = _____

B. Complete the second sentence by writing the possessive form of the word in bold.

1. Matt gave the truck to **Nick**. It is _____ truck.

2. I gave this doll to **Pam**. It is _____ doll.

3. **Brad** had a red hat. The red hat is _____.

4. The **duck** has a worm. It is the _____ worm.

5. **Sam** played with his ball. It is _____ ball.

Name _____

Ben's Stove

6	Ben Franklin invented lots of things.
12	Ben invented things that helped people.
20	In Ben's time, homes were made of logs.
28	Homes had fireplaces. A fireplace was not safe.
38	It could catch fire. It let smoke inside a home.
46	Then Ben came up with a new stove.
53	His stove's sides kept the fire inside.
62	Homes with Ben's stoves were kept safe from fire.
69	Ben's stove let the smoke get outside.
76	Ben's stove kept homes nice and warm.

I. Circle all the words that end in -'s that means that something belongs to a person or thing.

2. Complete the sentences.

His _____ sides kept the fire inside.

_____ stove kept homes nice and warm.

Name _____

When an action word ends in silent **e,** drop the **e** before adding the endings **-ed** and **-ing.**

bake - e + ed = baked
bake - e + ing = baking

A. Read the sentences. Match each underlined word to its root word.

I. Mom <u>voted</u> at ten.

a. ride

2. Jon is <u>giving</u> a gift to Max.

b. poke

3. I <u>traced</u> my name on the pad.

c. give

4. I am <u>riding</u> the bus with Dad.

d. vote

5. The pup <u>poked</u> his nose at me.

e. trace

B. Read each sentence. Write the root word for the underlined word.

I. Jed is <u>hiking</u> in the hills. _____

2. Tam <u>named</u> her dog Rex. _____

3. Puff is <u>dozing</u> in the sun. _____

Name _____

Look at the word *whine*. It ends with the letter **e**. To add
-**ed** or -**ing,** first drop the **e**.

$$whi\underline{ne} - e + ed = whined$$
$$whi\underline{ne} - e + ing = whining$$

A. Add -*ed* **or** -*ing* **to the words below to make new
words. Write the new words on the lines.**

I. save   - _____ + ed = _____

2. slide   - _____ + ing = _____

3. drive   - _____ + ing = _____

4. skate   - _____ + ed = _____

5. grade   - _____ + ing = _____

**B. Use one of the new words you wrote to complete
each sentence.**

I. Mrs. Lane is _____ the tests.

2. Zeke _____ on the pond.

3. Jack is _____ the bus.

Name _____

Lake Life

7	This is the lake in the daytime.
11	The sun is shining.
15	A frog is waking.
22	A crane is wading past the frog.
29	A fish is racing past the crane.
38	A duck is having a bug for a snack.

46	This was the lake late in the day.
52	A frog dozed on a log.
58	A fish glided past the grasses.
65	A crane hiked back to his nest.
68	A duck slept.

1. Circle all the action words that have the *-ed* or *-ing* ending.

2. Complete the sentences.

At night, a frog _____ on a log.

Then, a fish _____ past the grasses.

Name _____

When you add **-ed** or **-ing** to a word that ends with a vowel and then one consonant, double the final consonant.

jog + g + ing = jogging   **Sam is jogging with Mom.**
step + p + ed = stepped   **Max stepped in a big hole.**

A. Circle the word that completes each sentence. Then write the word.

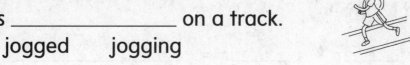

1. Dave is _____ on a track.
   jogged   jogging

2. The bus _____ to let kids pass.
   stopped   stopping

3. The frog _____ in the pond.
   hopping   hopped

4. Zack is _____ his hands.
   clapped   clapping

5. Meg _____ the glass of milk.
   tipping   tipped

B. Circle the words that have the correct ending. Write the words on the line.

1. slipped   sliped   _____

2. camped   campped   _____

Name _____

> When you add ***-ed*** or ***-ing*** to a word that ends with a vowel and then one consonant, double the final consonant.
>
> drip + p + ed = dripped   hug + g + ing + hugging

A. Add *-ed* to tell about an action that happened in the past. Fill in the parts to make the word in bold.

1. I **hugged** Mom.

   hug + _____ + _____ = _____

2. Fran **zipped** up her vest.

   zip + _____ + _____ = _____

3. The frog **hopped** up on a step.

   hop + _____ + _____ = _____

4. Jack **grabbed** the dog.

   grab + _____ + _____ = _____

B. Add *-ing* to tell about an action that is happening now. Fill in the parts to make the word in bold.

1. Viv is **running** on the track.

   run + _____ + _____ = _____

2. Dad is **cutting** a branch.

   cut + _____ + _____ = _____

Name _____

Swimming in a Lake

7	Last spring we went on a trip.
15	We hopped in a van. It was a
21	long drive. We napped on the
29	way. When I woke up, we were at
36	a big lake. Mom called, "Grab the
43	bags. Let's get unpacked and go swimming!"
54	Ben and I trotted up to a cabin. "This is nice,"
61	grinned Ben. Ben flopped on a bed.
71	Dad stepped in the cabin."I spotted a nice place for
72	swimming."
80	After swimming, we went shopping with Mom. Dad
92	went back and chopped logs. At night we sat at a camp
101	fire. Mom strummed a guitar. Ben and I hummed.

I. Circle the words ending in -*ed* or -*ing* with a double final consonant.

2. Complete the sentences.

Ben and I _____ up to the cabin.

"Let's get unpacked and go _____."

Name _____

> Some words can be split into two syllables. Sometimes one syllable has a consonant, a vowel, a consonant and a final *e*. Usually these syllables have a long vowel sound and the final *e* is silent.
>
> n<u>i</u>n<u>e</u>ty **90**

A. Write a CVCe word to name each picture. Draw a line between the syllables. Circle the CVCe syllable.

1.  _____

2. _____

3. _____

4. _____

B. Split these words into two syllables. Circle the CVCe syllable.

1. combine _____

2. impose _____

3. define _____

4. produce _____

Name _____

> Some words can be split into two syllables. Sometimes one syllable has a consonant, a vowel, a consonant and a final *e*. Usually these syllables have a long vowel sound and the final *e* is silent, like in **inflate**.
>
> infl<u>a</u>te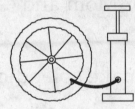

A. Underline the word with the CVCe syllable. Write each syllable of that word on a line. Circle the CVCe syllable.

1. lock alone _____ _____

2. racetrack rack _____ _____

3. pack pancake _____ _____

4. rent reptile _____ _____

B. Fill in a blank with a word from above that makes sense. Circle the CVCe syllable in the answer.

1. I ran around the _____.

2. The _____ got out of its cage.

3. I was scared when I was _____ in the big, dark house.

Name _____

Splendid Pancakes

6	Be nice. Get up at sunrise.
11	Make pancakes for Mom and
12	Dad.
18	Use these tips to make splendid
19	pancakes.
24	Combine flour, eggs, and milk.
34	Mix it up and put a bit in a pan.
40	Let it get nice and hot.
47	In a little while, flip the pancakes.
58	It is a mistake to let them sit a long time.
65	Then place the pancakes on a plate.
69	The pancakes are complete.
78	Tell Mom and Dad, it is time to eat!

1. **Circle all the words that have a long vowel sound with a silent *e*.**

2. **Complete the sentences.**

   In a little while, flip the _____.

   It is a _____ to let them sit a long time.

Name _____

> A **prefix** is a word part added to the beginning of a word to change its meaning.
> The prefix **un-** means "not".
> The prefix **re-** means "again."
> The prefix **dis-** means "opposite of."
>
> <u>re</u>act   <u>un</u>lock   <u>dis</u>place

A. Match each sentence to a word with a prefix. Use the underlined words to help you.

1. I will <u>use</u> the bag <u>again</u>.   **a.** unlocked

2. Ken will <u>fill</u> the fish tank <u>again</u>.   **b.** dislike

3. Leave the door <u>not</u> <u>locked</u>.   **c.** reuse

4. He is <u>not</u> <u>wise</u>.   **d.** refill

5. This is the <u>opposite of</u> <u>like</u>.   **e.** unwise

B. Read the sentences. Underline the words that have prefixes. Write the words on the line.

1. Jack will unpack his bag. _____

2. Mom will refill the glass with milk. _____

3. Ted dislikes mud. _____

Name _____

> **Prefixes** are word parts added to the beginning of words to change their meanings. The prefix *re-* means "again." The prefix *un-* means "not" and the prefix *dis-* means "the opposite of."
>
> <u>re</u>act   <u>un</u>lock   <u>dis</u>place

A. Find words with the prefixes *re-, un-,* and *dis-* in the word search.

1. _____

2. _____

3. _____

4. _____

5. _____

r	d	i	s	l	i	k	e
e	q	r	e	m	a	k	e
u	z	u	n	p	l	u	g
s	e	u	n	z	i	p	p
e	t	r	p	m	c	c	i

B. Fill in each blank with a word from above. Circle the prefixes in your answers.

1. Will you _____ my vest?

2. I will _____ my bed.

3. Dad will _____ his lunch bag.

4. I _____ milk.

5. Can you _____ the lamp?

Name _____

Mike's Bike

6	Mike is getting a new bike.
11	This bike will be big.
17	It will replace his old bike.
24	Mom, Dad, and Mike went to a
26	bike shop.
31	Mike saw lots of bikes.
39	Mike passed by white bikes. He disliked them.
46	Then Mike reacted with a big smile.
52	Mike spotted a nice red bike.
61	"Will you unlock this bike?" Mike asked the bike
63	shop owner.
71	"Yes. Take it for a ride," he grinned.
78	"But first I will refill the tires."
81	"Mike," said Dad.
92	"Put on this helmet. It is unsafe to ride without it."

1. Circle the words that contain prefixes.

2. Complete the sentences.

Mike _____ white bikes.

It is _____ to ride without a helmet.

Name _____

> A **suffix** is a word part at the end of a word. A suffix changes the meaning of the word.
>
> *-ful* means "full of"   hopeful = full of hope
> *-less* means "without"   hopeless = without hope

A. Read each sentence. Underline the word that has the suffix *-ful* or *-less*. Write the word on the line.

1. A rake is a useful thing. _____

2. A little pup is helpless. _____

3. The dishes are spotless. _____

4. We will not be wasteful. _____

B. Read the words. Circle the best meaning for each word.

1. dustless   full of dust   without dust

2. skillful   full of skill   without skill

3. trustful   full of trust   without trust

4. useless   full of use   without use

Name _____

> You can build a word by adding a **suffix** to the end. A suffix changes the meaning of the word.
>
> help + -ful = helpful   "full of help"
> help + -less = helpless   "without help"

A. Fill in the missing parts to make the word in bold print.

1. _____ + _____ = careless

2. _____ + _____ = restful

3. _____ + _____ = spotless

4. _____ + _____ = graceful

B. Add *-ful* or *-less* to make a new word for each meaning. Write the word on the line.

1. without rest   rest   + _____ = _____

2. full of hope   hope   + _____ = _____

3. without end   end   + _____ = _____

4. full of wishes   wish   + _____ = _____

Name _____

Useful and Helpful

6   An invention is a new thing

13   that is made. It can be useful

15   and helpful.

21   Let's take a look at some

25   useful and helpful things.

30   Do you like chatting? A

41   phone is useful and helpful. You can chat with a pal.

52   Are you skillful when riding a bike? A bike is useful

61   and helpful. You can ride to a pal's home.

71   Washing dishes can be a cheerless job. A dish washer

80   is useful and helpful in making your dishes spotless!

87   Can you name useful and helpful things?

95   Which useful and helpful thing is the best?

1. Circle the words that have suffixes.

2. Complete the sentences.

An invention can be _____ and _____.

A dish washer can make dishes _____.

Name _____

> A **compound word** is made up of two smaller words. Compound words have more than one syllable.
>
> ### back + pack = backpack

A. Circle the compound word. Then draw a line between the two smaller words. Write the compound word.

1. pancake   cake   _____

2. bagging   bagpipe   _____

3. wishbone   wished   _____

4. homes   homesick   _____

5. inside   ink   _____

B. Read the sentences. Underline the compound words. Write the words on the line.

1. The bathtub is filled with suds.   _____

2. Dad met him with a handshake.   _____

3. Mom likes to make pancakes.   _____

Name _____

A **compound word** is made up of two smaller words.
Compound words have more than one syllable.

hand + made = handmade

A. Find compound words in the wordsearch.

1. _____

2. _____

3. _____

4. _____

5. _____

s	p	r	i	n	g	t	i	m	e
s	a	n	d	b	o	x	t	q	n
b	e	d	s	i	d	e	p	g	v
w	i	n	d	m	i	l	l	v	p
c	u	p	c	a	k	e	f	e	v

B. Fill in each blank with a word from above to make a compound word. Then write the compound word.

1. Kids like to play in a _____ box.

   _____

2. A nice time of year is spring _____.

   _____

3. Ted has a clock by his bed _____.

   _____

4. Mom likes to make _____ cakes.

   _____

Name _____

Springtime

7   I went to camp in the springtime.

13   The camp was not close by.

19   Mom and Dad drove past a

23   windmill to get there.

31   I did lots of fun things at camp.

41   I woke up at sunrise. First I helped make pancakes.

54   Then I made my lunch. I put it in a backpack and I

65   hiked up to a hilltop. I snapped ten nice snapshots on

67   the hilltop.

76   Before sunset, I gathered pinecones. I used them to

79   make handmade gifts.

86   It was a trip of a lifetime.

95   But I did get a bit homesick at camp.

1. Circle all the compound words.

2. Complete the sentences.

First I helped make _____.

It was a trip of a _____.

Name _____

> A **contraction** is a word that is made from two words.
> An apostrophe (') replaces the letter or letters that
> are taken out.
>
> he is = he's   you are = you're
> she will = she'll   we have = we've

**A. Read the words. Draw a line to match each word
pair to its contraction.**

1. it is   a. you'll

2. we are   b. we're

3. you will   c. it's

4. they have   d. they've

**B. Read each contraction. Circle the correct word
pair for each contraction.**

1. she's   she will   she is

2. they're   they are   they have

3. we'll   we will   we are

4. I've   I will   I have

Name _____

> Form a **contraction** by joining two words together, such as *we* and *have*. Use an apostrophe (') in place of the letter or letters that are taken out.
>
> **we have ⟶ we + (') + ve = we've**

A. Fill in each blank to make the underlined contraction.

1. <u>You're</u> the best!   _____ + _____

2. <u>It's</u> fun.   _____ + _____

3. <u>We'll</u> win!   _____ + _____

4. <u>I've</u> got a bike.   _____ + _____

B. Read each sentence. Write the contraction for the underlined pair of words.

1. <u>She is</u> at the game.   _____

2. <u>We have</u> made a cake.   _____

3. <u>I will</u> help Mom.   _____

4. <u>They are</u> late.   _____

Name _____

They'll Neigh

7	Miss Kane's class went on a trip
10	to Jane's ranch.
15	Jane showed them the goat.
21	"This is Ben," Jane said. "He's
29	the best pet I've had! He eats grass.
37	He'll eat grass until I make him stop!"
46	Then she asked, "See my horses? They'll neigh when
58	it's time to eat a meal. They'll stamp their feet until I
67	feed them! They're big so they eat a lot."
78	When it was time to go, Miss Kane told Jane, "Thank
89	you. We've had fun! It's nice to be at a ranch!"
97	"You're welcome," said Jane. "I've had fun, too!"

1. Circle all the contractions in the story.

2. Complete the sentences.

_____ eat grass until I make him stop!

_____ big so they eat a lot.

Name _____

> When a syllable ends in a vowel, the vowel sound is usually long. This type of syllable is called an **open syllable**. The first syllable in *robot* is *ro*. The syllable *ro* is an open syllable and the sound of the vowel *o* is long.

A. Read each word. Then draw a line between the syllables. Write each syllable on the line.

1. cozy _____ _____

2. secret _____ _____

3. silent _____ _____

4. donut _____ _____

5. human _____ _____

B. Use the correct word from above to answer each riddle. Write the word on the line.

1. I make no noise. I am _____.

2. I am a round treat. I am a _____.

3. I am a person. I am a _____.

4. Do not tell. I am a _____.

5. I am soft and warm. I am _____.

Name _____

An **open syllable** is a syllable that ends in a vowel. It has a long vowel sound.

<u>mu</u> / sic   <u>be</u> / gin

A. Put the two syllables together to form a word that matches the picture. Write the word on the line.

1. ro   bot   _____

2. po   ny   _____

3. la   dy   _____

4. do   nut   _____

5. ba   con   _____

B. Circle the word in each pair that has an open first syllable. Write the word.

Example: o / pen   end / less   <u>open</u>

1. pi / lot   sun / ny   _____

2. ba / by   in / vite   _____

3. rab / bit   fe / male   _____

4. sit / ting   hu / man   _____

Name _____

The Pony

10   A pony is a tiny horse. It has a thick

19 mane and tail. A baby pony is called a

26 foal. It grows up in three years.

34   If you want a pony, you must take

37 care of it.

47   A pony likes wide, open spaces. A pony cannot be

54 lazy. It needs to run and play.

66   A pony needs to graze all day. It needs to always be

70 beside grass and hay.

81   A pony may sleep in a pen. Remind yourself to keep

84 this pen tidy.

95   A pony likes to be with other ponies. It also likes

108 to be with humans. A pony can make a fun pet. As a

117 bonus, a pony is fun for kids to ride!

1. Circle all the words with open syllables.

2. Complete the sentences.

A _____ pony is called a foal.

A pony likes wide, _____ spaces.

Name _____

> A **contraction** is a short form of two words. An **apostrophe**
> (') takes the place of the missing letters.
>
> $$\text{is} + \text{not} = \text{isn't}$$
>
> The apostrophe (') in *isn't* stands for the letter *o*.

A. Read the sentences. Circle each contraction. Fill in the blanks for the words that make up each contraction.

1. I can't find my hat. _____ <u>not</u>

2. Mom hasn't made the cake yet. <u>has</u> _____

3. We weren't in class today. _____ <u>not</u>

4. He wasn't feeling well. <u>was</u> _____

5. They haven't raked the leaves. _____ <u>not</u>

B. Write the contraction for the two words.

1. did + not = _____

2. are + not = _____

3. had + not = _____

Name _____

> Form a **contraction** with *not* by joining the two words together. Then use an **apostrophe (')** to take the place of *o* in *not*.
>
> has not   hasn—t + (') = hasn't

A. Read the sentences. Write a contraction for the underlined pair of words.

1. We <u>were not</u> awake.   _____

2. Mom <u>is not</u> going to the shop.   _____

3. We <u>have not</u> had rain for days.   _____

4. Gran and Gramps <u>are not</u> home.   _____

B. Fill in the blanks to make each contraction.

1. _____ + _____ = wasn't

2. _____ + _____ = doesn't

3. _____ + _____ = hasn't

4. _____ + _____ = didn't

Name _____

Pig Wouldn't Quit

7   One day Pig went for a ride.

13   "This isn't fun!" Pig cried. "I

20   didn't think this would be a bad

24   ride but it is!"

28   But Pig wouldn't quit.

40   "This isn't fun!" Pig said. "I can't make it up the hill!"

44   But Pig wouldn't quit.

54   "This isn't fun!" Pig said. "It's hot! This isn't good!"

58   But Pig wouldn't quit.

67   "This isn't fun!" Pig said. "This hasn't been nice!"

71   But Pig wouldn't quit.

81   Then Pig reached the hill top. He rode down. He

88   spotted a pond. Pig splashed and swam.

98   "This is fun!" Pig cried. "But I should ride home.

101   Pig wouldn't quit.

---

1. Circle all the contractions with *not*.

2. Complete the sentences.

Pig _____ having fun on his bike.

Pig _____ quit.

Name _____

> To add the ending **-es** or **-ed** to a word that ends with the letter **y**, first change the **y** to **i**.
>
> puppy – y + i + es = puppies   cry – y + i + ed = cried
>   cry – y + i + es = cries

A. Write the word that completes each sentence.

1. Beth picked some _____.
   daisys   daisies

2. Mom _____ the fish.
   fried   fryed

3. I have six _____.
   pennies   pennyes

4. Meg _____ to make her bed.
   tryed   tried

5. We went to three _____.
   cities   cityes

B. Circle the words that have the correct ending.
Write the words on the line.

1. ponyes   ponies   _____

2. spied   spyed   _____

3. cryes   cries   _____

Name _____

> To add the ending **-es** or **-ed** to a word that ends with the
> letter **_y_**, first change the **_y_** to **_i_**.
> **pony - y + i + es = ponies   try - y + i + es = tries**
> **try - y + i + ed = tried**

A. Fill in the missing parts to make the word.

1. _____ - _____ + _____ = stories

2. _____ - _____ + _____ = puppies

3. _____ - _____ + _____ = cried

4. _____ - _____ + _____ = tries

5. _____ - _____ + _____ = studied

B. Use **-es** to make the underlined words mean "more than one."

1. My teacher has many <u>duty</u>.   _____

2. We had two <u>party</u> this week.   _____

3. I like to read <u>story</u> before bed.   _____

4. Two <u>family</u> live close to me.   _____

5. My nana cares for two <u>baby</u>.   _____

Name _____

Bunnies

6	We know that puppies, kitties, and
12	even ponies can make nice pets.
18	Well, bunnies can make nice pets,
24	too. Bunnies are baby rabbits. These
31	babies are also called kits or kittens.
41	Bunnies can be kept as pets. But there are some
50	things you need to know. Can you hear bunnies?
57	Bunnies make little cries and humming sounds.
65	Bunnies make their homes in burrows. There may
74	be many families in one burrow. Bunnies eat plants,
83	berries, and even dry grass. Did you know bunnies
93	can't run? They can't! But bunnies can hop very fast!
103	Bunnies like to be carried and like to be petted.
108	Bunnies can make fun pets.

1. Circle all the words with *-ed* and *-es*.

2. Complete the sentences.

Bunnies make little _____ and

humming sounds.

Bunnies eat plants, _____, and dry grass.

Name _____

> The *-er* ending is added to the end of a word to compare
> two things. The *-est* ending is added to the end of a word to
> compare three or more things.
> **cold** + er = cold**er**   It is <u>cold**er**</u> today than yesterday.
> **cold** + est = cold**est**   Today is the <u>cold**est**</u> day of the year.

**A. Circle the word in each sentence that has the *-er*
or *-est* ending. Write the root word on the line.**

1. The sun is brighter this week than last week.

   _____

2. Mr. Tate has the greenest grass of anyone.

   _____

3. This cake is sweeter than that one. _____

4. This tree is the oldest one on our street.

   _____

**B. Write the root word and ending to make the
word in bold.**

1. _____ + _____ = neatest

2. _____ + _____ = wilder

3. _____ + _____ = dampest

4. _____ + _____ = longer

Name _____

> Add the ending *-er* to a word to compare two things. Add the ending *-est* to a word to compare three or more things.
>
> Pine Street is <u>longer</u> than Oak Street.　　add **-er** to **long**
> High Street is the <u>longest</u> street of all.　　add **-est** to **long**

A. Add *-er* or *-est* to each word to make new words. Write the words on the lines.

　　　　　　　　　　　Add *-er*　　　　　　　**Add *-est***

I. kind　　_____　　_____

2. strong　_____　　_____

3. cheap　_____　　_____

4. pink　　_____　　_____

5. tight　　_____　　_____

B. Write the correct form of the word in parentheses ( ) to complete each sentence.

I. My desk is (clean) _____ than Nate's desk.

2. That is the (deep) _____ lake in the state.

3. James is (old) _____ than me.

Name _____

Fast, Faster, Fastest

10   What are the ways we go places? Let's name three

23 ways that people travel—a bus, a train, and a jet. A bus

36 can take you places, but it is not the fastest way to go.

50 Is a train faster? Yes, a train is faster than a bus, but it

65 is not the fastest way to go. Is a jet faster? Yes, a jet is

78 faster than a bus. A jet is the fastest way to go places.

89 Jets can fly over the highest hills and the deepest seas.

100 Jets can fly much longer than they did in the past.

111 You can take off at sunrise and land long after the

114 sun has set.

1. Circle all the words with endings *-er* and *-est*.

2. Complete the sentences.

The _____ way to go places is the jet.

A bus is _____ than a train.

Name _____

> Some nouns change their spelling to name more than one.
>
> **man   men   child   children**
>
> Some words do not change their spelling to name more than one.
>
> **sheep   sheep**

A. Circle the correct word to complete the sentence. Write the word.

1. Jan has three pet _____.

    mouses   mice

2. I got two new _____ for my tank.

    fish   fishes

3. Big _____ are falling from the tree.

    leafs   leaves

4. I lost five _____ last year.

    teeth   tooths

5. There are twenty _____ in the race.

    woman   women

B. Read the sentence. Underline the word that names more than one thing. Write the word.

1. I saw three geese. _____

2. Many people came to the fair. _____

3. There were two deer in the park. _____

Name _____

> We add **-s** or **-es** to make some words mean more than one.
>
> > rug   rug**s**   box   box**es**
>
> Some nouns change their spelling to name more than one.
>
> > man   **men**   child   **children**
>
> Some words do not change their spelling to name more than one.
>
> > sheep   **sheep**

A. Make the noun name more than one. Write the word.

I. child   _____   **3.** loaf   _____

2. mouse   _____   **4.** tooth   _____

B. Read the sentence. Make the underlined word name more than one.

I. Six <u>ox</u> led the wagon.   _____

2. How many <u>man</u> landed on the moon?   _____

3. I like to get my <u>foot</u> wet.   _____

4. Most <u>wolf</u> live in the wild.   _____

Make Way for Geese

4 | The children of Springlake
11 | like their park. It has trees with
19 | leaves of all sizes. There is a big
25 | pond filled with fish. At dusk,
32 | you can even see deer grazing on
39 | the grass. There is one thing the
48 | children do not like. The geese! Geese are everywhere.
58 | There are geese in the sandbox and geese on the
67 | swings. Any time anyone looks down, they see geese!
80 | One day some men had an idea. They put up a fence. It
92 | was near the pond. The men put loaves of bread on the
103 | other side of the fence. The geese went after the bread.
114 | It worked! Now people drop off old loaves of bread as
124 | treats for the geese. The geese, the children, and the
129 | people of Springlake are happy.

1. Circle all the words with irregular plurals.

2. Complete the sentences.

At dusk you can see _____ grazing on grass.

Some _____ had an idea.

Name _____

> An **abbreviation** is a short way to write a longer word.
> An abbreviation begins with a capital letter and ends with
> a period.
>
> Mister = <u>Mr.</u>

**A. Draw a line to match each word with its
abbreviation.**

1. Doctor		**a.** Rd.
2. Avenue		**b.** St.
3. Road		**c.** Ave.
4. Street		**d.** Apt.
5. Apartment		**e.** Dr.

**B. Read the sentence. Circle that word that matches
the abbreviation.**

1. I rode my bike on Hill St.	Street	Road
2. Is Mr. Green home yet?	Miss	Mister
3. Did Dr. Tan stop by?	Doctor	Mister
4. They hiked up Mt. Tam.	Mister	Mount
5. We went to First Ave.	Avenue	Street

Name _____

> An **abbreviation** is a short way to write a longer word.
>
> Titles are often abbreviated. **Mr.** for **Mister**
> Places may also be abbreviated. **Ave.** for **Avenue**

A. Write the abbreviation for each word.

1. Street _____

2. Mister _____

3. Avenue _____

4. Doctor _____

5. Road _____

B. Write each title or place on the line using an abbreviation.

1. Doctor Smith _____

2. Seaside Avenue _____

3. Spring Road _____

4. Apartment 7A _____

5. Mount Olympus _____

Name _____

Dr. Dave Helps

9 Tim's dog, Rex, needed a checkup. Mrs. Scott drove

20 them to see Dr. Dave on First Ave. in Lake Hill.

32   "Rex likes to run and play," said Dr. Dave. "I hope he

37 has lots of space outside."

47   "He will soon," said Tim. "Next week we will move

60 to a farm on Oak Rd. Rex will like the farm a lot!"

72   "I know a man with a farm on Oak Rd.," said Dr.

83 Dave. "His name is Mr. Shore and his dog is Sam."

94   "I hope Rex and Sam will be good pals!" said Tim.

104   "You will have a friend, too," said Dr. Dave. "Mr.

110 Shore has a son named Jake!"

I. Circle all the abbreviations.

2. Complete the sentences.

Rex's vet is named _____ Dave.

Tim will move to a farm on _____.

Name _____

> When a vowel or pair of vowels is followed by the letter
> *r*, it changes the vowel sound. The vowels and the *r* stay
> together in the same syllable.

**A. Read each word. Draw a line between
the syllables.**

1. farmer   4. normal

2. surprise   5. perfect

3. circle   6. circus

**B. Read the words in each row. Underline the word
that has an *r*-controlled vowel syllable. Circle the
two letters that make the *r*-controlled vowel sound.**

1. people   really   prepare

2. forget   flowing   folded

3. slowly   sharpen   saving

4. harvest   homemade   helpful

5. moment   magic   market

6. bathtub   birthday   baseball

Name _____

> When a vowel or a pair of vowels is followed by the letter *r*, it changes the vowel sound. The vowels and the *r* stay in the same syllable.

A. Write the words from the word box that have the same *r*-controlled vowel as each of the words listed below. Then divide the words into syllables.

birthday	prepare	turkey	circus
forget	market	parcel	
normal	purple	careless	

1. cart _____ _____

2. fort _____ _____

3. curl _____ _____

4. dare _____ _____

5. stir _____ _____

B. Which word in each pair has an *r*-controlled syllable? Write the word. Divide it into syllables.

1. favor   funny   _____

2. testing   turkey   _____

3. cupcake   careless   _____

Name _____

A Birthday Surprise

7   Today is Martha's birthday. Martha's family planned

16 a birthday surprise. First, they gave Martha a purple

24 shirt with sparkles. Then they made her favorite

32 birthday lunch. Martha was having a nice day.

39   But then she heard her family murmuring.

48 "Later, we are going some place that has tigers,

53 horses, and performers," said Sister.

62   "Can you guess where we are going?" said Mother.

69   "Is it the circus?" asked Martha, grinning.

72   "Yes!" they cheered.

79   "This is a perfect birthday!" said Martha.

1. Circle all the words with *r*-controlled syllables.

2. Complete the sentences.

Martha got a _____ shirt.

_____ was having a nice day.

Name _____

> When a word ends in *-le, -el,* or *-al,* the consonant before it plus the ending form the last syllable.
>
> pud/**dle**   duf/**fel**   vo/**cal**

A. Draw a line to divide each word into syllables. Write each syllable on the line.

1. puzzle   _____   _____

2. purple   _____   _____

3. funnel   _____   _____

4. total   _____   _____

5. little   _____   _____

B. Use one of the words above to complete each sentence.

1. A pup is a _____ dog.

2. A grape can be white or _____.

3. A _____ is made up of lots of shapes.

Name _____

> When the letters -*le*, -*el*, or -*al* come at the end of a word with a consonant before them, the consonant + -*le*, -*el*, or -*al* form the last syllable.
>
> marble   mar/**ble**

A. Add a word part from the box to each word part below to make a word. Write the word part on the line. Then draw a line to the picture it names.

> dle   rel   ble   tal

1. ta _____   **a.**

2. can _____   **b.**

3. bar _____   **c.**

4. pe _____   **d.**

B. Draw a circle around the word that makes sense in each sentence.

1. A **bugle, bushel** is a kind of horn.

2. An **ankle, eagle** is a kind of bird.

3. A **bottle, beetle** is a kind of bug.

4. A **puzzle, pretzel** is a kind of game.

Name _____

A Snake Can Wiggle

13   A snake is a reptile. A turtle is a reptile, too. But a

24 snake does not have legs like a turtle. Snakes wiggle to

32 travel. Their muscles help them push and pull.

41   Snakes try to stay away from people. Snakes can

52 cause great harm if they bite. Poison in their teeth can

64 make you sick. Stay away from a coral snake. It is red,

72 yellow, and black. Its bite will hurt you.

81   Some snakes send a warning before they strike. A

93 rattlesnake will shake the rattle on its tail to tell you it

105 is there. That is your signal to get away fast. Then the

112 snake can wiggle away from you, too!

**I. Circle all the words with consonant + -le, -el, and
-al syllables.**

2. Complete the sentences.

Both snakes and _____ are reptiles.

A snake may shake its _____ as a warning.

Name _____

> Vowel teams with two vowels, such as **ea, ee, oa, au, ai,**
> and **oo** stay together in the same syllable. A vowel and a
> consonant, such as **ow, ay,** and **oy** can be a vowel team, too.

A. Circle the vowel team in each word. Draw a line to divide each word into syllables.

hoisting	leaving
cartoon	decay
maybe	noisy
seaside	raccoon
midday	spoiling
season	mushroom

B. Write each word above in the correct list below.

oi	ea	oo	ay
_____	_____	_____	_____
_____	_____	_____	_____
_____	_____	_____	_____

Name _____

> Look for vowel teams such as *oi, ea, oo*, and *ay* to help you read words with more than one syllable. The vowel teams stay together in the same syllable.
>
> Example: s**ea**t - belt = seatbelt

A. Put the two syllables together to make a word. Read the word. Write it on the line. Then circle the vowel team or teams in each word.

1. sea   weed   _____

2. half   way   _____

3. sea   son   _____

4. bal   loon   _____

5. join   ing   _____

B. Complete each sentence with a word you made. Circle the vowel teams.

1. I am _____ finished with my homework.

2. Winter is my favorite _____.

3. I got a big, red _____.

4. The beach was filled with _____.

5. My brother is _____ a baseball team.

Name _____

The Seaside

10   The summer season is a great time for visiting the

19   seaside. You can enjoy many things there. You may

29   wish to spend your days soaking up the sun. Or

39   maybe you might enjoy a long walk up and down

47   the coastline. You may find seashells and seaglass.

58   You may see lots of seaweed when the tide comes in.

69   Sometimes if you look far off in the sea, maybe you

80   will see a sailor on a steamship. The seaside is also

89   pretty at night. You can see moonbeams dancing across

99   the sea. The seaside is a wonderful place to be!

1. Circle all the words with vowel team syllables.

2. Complete the sentences.

You may see _____ when the tide comes in.

It's great to visit the seaside in the summer

_____ .

Name _____

> The *-er* ending is added to the end of a word to compare two nouns. The *-est* ending is added to the end of a word to compare more than two nouns. Some words need spelling changes first:
> - if a word ends in *y*, change the *y* to *i*: dr**y**   dr**ier**   dr**iest**
> - if a word ends in *e*, drop the *e*: lat**e**   lat**er**   lat**est**
> - if a word ends in a vowel and a consonant, double the final consonant: hot   ho**tter**   ho**ttest**

A. Add the *-est* ending to the word in parentheses.

1. I had a (lazy) day. _____

2. The (fat) pig will win the prize. _____

3. Bill had the (large) backpack. _____

4. Tina told the (funny) joke. _____

5. Pam is the (brave) person I know. _____

**B. Circle the word in each sentence that has the *-er*
or *-est* ending. Write the root word on the line.**

1. This is the easiest job of all. _____

2. Is this pumpkin bigger than that one? _____

3. This snack is healthier than that snack. _____

Name _____

> Add the suffix **-er** to a word to compare two nouns. Add
> the suffix **-est** to a word to compare more than two nouns.
> Pay attention to spelling changes.
>
> | | | |
> |---|---|---|
> | happ**y** | happ**ier** | happ**iest** |
> | bi**g** | bi**gger** | bi**ggest** |
> | fin**e** | fin**er** | fin**est** |

**A. Make new words by adding -er and -est to each
word. Write the new words on the lines.**

	Add **-er**	Add **-est**
1. nice	_____	_____
2. messy	_____	_____
3. thin	_____	_____
4. tiny	_____	_____
5. wise	_____	_____

**B. Write the correct form of the word in
parentheses ( ) to complete each sentence.**

1. Nan's bedroom is _____ than mine. (large)

2. This toothpaste will give you the _____
smile of all. (white)

3. Dad told a _____ joke than Mom. (funny)

Name _____

The Noisiest Kid

7   Nell and Jake wanted to play outside.

15   "I wish the rain would stop," said Nell.

24   "Me too," said Jake. "It is rainier than yesterday!"

32   "Remember how hot it was last summer?" asked

44 Nell. "It was hotter here than it was in Florida! It was

46 sunnier, too!"

56   "Let's pretend that today is the sunniest day of all

65 time," said Jake. "Let's tell what we will do."

75   "Yes!" said Nell. "I plan to climb the biggest tree."

86   "I plan to bang on my drum and march down the

97 street!" cried Jake. "I'll be the noisiest kid on Oak Lane!"

I. Circle all the words with comparative inflectional endings *-er, -est*.

2. Complete the sentences.

Nell plans to climb the _____ tree.

Jake wants to be the _____ kid.

Name _____

> A **syllable** is a word part. Words can have one or more **syllables**.
>
> bas + ket + ball = 3 syllables

A. Say each word. Write 2, 3, or 4 next to the word to tell how many syllables it has.

Example: sister   2

1. horizon   _____

2. number   _____

3. equipment   _____

4. impossible   _____

5. banana   _____

B. Fill in each blank with the word from above that best completes the sentence.

1. I like to eat a _____ with my lunch.

2. We watched the sun set on the _____.

3. It is not _____ to run a mile if you practice.

4. We saw lots of fire _____ at the firehouse.

5. The _____ ten is even.

Name _____

> A **syllable** is a word part. Words can have one or more **syllables**.
>
> care + less + ness = 3 syllables

A. Put the syllables together to form a word. Write the word on the line. Tell whether the first syllable is open, closed, or *r*-controlled.

1. re + cy + cle   _____ _____

2. im + i + tate   _____ _____

3. hor + i + zon   _____ _____

4. par + tic + i + pate   _____ _____

5. i + den + ti + cal   _____ _____

B. Divide each word into the correct number of syllables. The number of lines is a hint.

1. aroma   _____ ro _____

2. interrupt   _____ _____ **rupt**

3. energy   **en** _____ _____

4. capable   _____ **pa** _____

5. apologize   _____ **pol** _____ **gize**

Name _____

Recycle!

6   Everybody should recycle! Recycling is important

17 for a variety of reasons. It will help save our natural

27 resources, like trees. It is an excellent way to cut

35 down on pollution. Recycling glass and paper is

43 extremely popular. But many people are unaware of

52 other materials that can be recycled. Did you know

60 that foil, drink boxes, and even strawberry baskets

68 can be recycled? Many towns have special recycling

75 equipment. Big trucks collect and separate the

82 materials. Everybody should be motivated to recycle.

93 If everybody does his or her part, I am confident that

102 it will be a cleaner and more enjoyable world!

1. Circle all the words with three or more syllables.

2. Complete the sentences.

Drink boxes and _____ baskets get recycled.

Recycling will make a more _____ world.

Name _____

> A **plural possessive noun** shows ownership. To make most plural nouns possessive, add an apostrophe after the **s**.
>
> the hive that belongs to the bees = the bee**s'** hive

A. Fill in the blank in the second sentence by writing the plural possessive for the word in bold.

1. The oats belong to the **horses**. They are the

   _____ oats.

2. The books belong to the **teachers**. They are the

   _____ books.

3. The cars belong to the **drivers**. They are the

   _____ cars.

4. The pets belong to my **friends**. They are

   my _____ pets.

5. The fruit belong to the **monkeys**. They are the

   _____ fruit.

B. Circle the correct word in parentheses ( ) to complete each sentence.

1. The (pups', pups) bowls are empty.

2. The (books's, books') pages are all wet.

3. The (girls', girls) moms picked them up after the show.

Name _____

> **Plural possessive nouns** tell who or what owns or has something. Most plural possessive nouns end with an *s* and an apostrophe.
>
> the players that belong to the teams = the team**s'** players

A. Rewrite each phrase using a plural possessive noun.

I. the books that belong to the boys

_____

2. the petals that belong to the flowers

_____

3. the pots that belong to the cooks

_____

4. the supplies that belong to the students

_____

B. Fill in the blanks to form the plural and the plural possessive for each word.

	plural	plural possessive
I. tree	_____	_____
2. monkey	_____	_____
3. worm	_____	_____
4. doctor	_____	_____

Name _____

The Beavers' Lodge

6   Beavers are a kind of woodland

11   mammal. They use twigs and

18   mud to make a place to live

23   called a lodge. Beavers' lodges

28   can be found near streams,

33   ponds, and lakes. The animals'

43   teeth are strong. They use them to cut down trees.

53   Then the trees' branches are chewed to make the twigs

63   the beavers use for their lodges. The mud holds the

71   lodge together. When storms come, the beavers' homes

80   are sometimes damaged. The beavers may have to add

84   more mud and twigs.

92   Some beavers live in national parks. Beavers mostly

103   come out at night to eat and swim. The beavers' tails

111   begin slapping the water as they swim past.

---

1. Circle all the words that are plural possessives.

2. Complete the sentences.

_____ lodges are found near streams.

The _____ branches are chewed to
make twigs.

Name _____

> The prefix **pre-** means "before". The prefix **non-** means "not." The prefix **mis-** means "bad" or "wrong."
>
> **precook** = to cook before   **nonstick** = does not stick
> **mismatch** = a bad match

A. Read each pair of words. Circle the word that has a prefix. Write its meaning.

1. pretty   prepaid   _____

2. misprint   missile   _____

3. novel   nonstop   _____

4. pencil   preteen   _____

5. misuse   mitten   _____

B. Read each sentence and underline the word that contains a prefix. Circle the prefix. Then write the word on the line.

1. I chose a nonfiction book. _____

2. My mom will preview the show before we watch it.

   _____

3. Sam miscounted the coins. _____

4. We always use nontoxic paint. _____

5. Did you go to preschool? _____

Name _____

> The prefix *pre-* means "before." The prefix *non-* means "not." The prefix *mis-* means "bad" or "wrong."

A. Add the prefix to each base word. Read the word. Write it on the line. Then circle the prefix.

1. mis + lead _____

2. non + profit _____

3. pre + dawn _____

4. mis + inform _____

5. pre + test _____

B. Complete the word in each sentence with the right prefix in ( ).

1. I (pre, mis) _____spelled the word *flicker*.

2. My dad cooks with a (mis, non) _____stick pan.

3. We took a math (pre, mis) _____test.

4. My older sister is a (mis, pre) _____teen.

5. I have on two mittens that are (pre, mis) _____matched.

Name _____

A Real Mismatch?

6	Today was the day of the
11	spelling bee. I spent weeks
17	preparing. My dad gave me a
22	pretest and I misspelled quite
28	a few words. But I've been
32	practicing nonstop. My teacher
40	even gave me lists of words to practice.

51   I made it all the way to the semi-finals. The judge

55   gave me my word.

62   "The word is *nonreturnable*," said the judge.

74   I took a deep breath. I told myself to not mistrust my

76   gut. "Nonreturnable – *n, o, n, r, e, t, u, r, n, a, b, l, e.*"

89   I did it! I made it to the finals. I will compete against

100   a preteen. I hope it's not a real mismatch...for her!

I. Circle all the words with the prefixes *pre-*, *non-*, or *mis-*.

2. Complete the sentences.

I _____ quite a few words.

But I've been practicing _____.

Name _____

A **suffix** is a word part at the end of a word. Adding the suffix *-y* to the end of a word forms an adjective.

chill + **y** = **chilly**   It is a <u>chilly</u> day.

Adding the suffix *-ly* to the end of a word forms an adverb.

quick + **ly** = **quickly**   Matt <u>quickly</u> ran home.

A. Read each sentence. Underline the word that has the suffix *-y* or *-ly*. Write the word on the line and circle the suffix.

l. The rainy day made us change our plans.

_____

2. He eagerly washed the dishes. _____

3. We hungrily ate our lunch. _____

4. The mud on our shoes made a sloppy mess.

_____

B. Circle the suffix in each of the words below. Write the root or base word on the line. Watch out for spelling changes.

l. pushy _____   5. weakly _____

2. flaky _____   6. funny _____

3. lovely _____   7. smelly _____

4. lazily _____   8. breezy _____

Name _____

> You can build new words by adding suffixes -**y** and -**ly**.
> cream + **y** = cream**y**
> spotless + **ly** = spotless**ly**

A. Fill in the missing parts to form the new words with suffixes -*y* and -*ly*.

1. _____ + _____ = restlessly

2. hopeful + ly = _____

3. kind + _____ = kindly

4. _____ + _____ = quickly

5. dream + y = _____

6. chat + _____ = chatty

B. Circle the word with the suffix -*y* or -*ly* in each sentence. Write the base word and the suffix on the lines below.

1. The knight bravely fought the dragon.

_____   _____

2. We looked out at the snowy day.

_____   _____

3. Mom cheerfully made the cupcakes.

_____   _____

Name _____

They Go Bravely

11   An astronaut is trained to explore space. It is not an

21 easy job that people can learn quickly. Men and women

29 spend lots of hours carefully learning important skills

38 before they are prepared to travel into space. They

49 must learn how to safely walk in places with little or

59 no gravity. They often train in pools of water where

66 they can float weightlessly. Astronauts wear special

76 suits that have tanks filled with air and masks that

86 safely cover their faces. Astronauts must be brave to go

95 places where others have not gone before. Maybe one

105 day space travel will be easy for all of us!

I. Circle all the words that have the suffixes -y or -ly.

2. Complete the sentences.

Astronauts learn to _____ walk in space.

One day space travel will be _____.

Name _____

> A **suffix** is a word part added to the end of a word. A suffix changes the meaning of the word. The suffix *-ness* means "state of." The suffix *-able* means "can be." The suffix *-ment* means "action" or "process." The suffix *-ous* means "possessing the qualities of."

A. Read each sentence and underline the word that contains a suffix. Write the word on the line and circle the suffix.

1. I did 25 sit-ups for the fitness test. _____

2. The old lamp is still usable. _____

3. The party was very enjoyable. _____

4. I showed my excitement by cheering. _____

5. A famous author visited our library. _____

B. Write each word on the line. Draw a line between the base word and the suffix.

1. kindness _____

2. movement _____

3. fixable _____

4. famous _____

5. brightness _____

Name _____

> The **suffix** *-ness* means "state of." The suffix *-able* means
> "can be." The suffix *-ment* means "action" or "process."
> The suffix *-ous* means "possessing the qualities of."

**A. Add the suffix to each base word. Read the word.
Write it on the line. Then circle the suffix.**

1. bright + ness _____

2. teach + able _____

3. move + ment _____

4. joy + ous _____

5. crazy + ness _____

6. adore + able _____

7. appoint + ment _____

8. envy + ous _____

**B. Write two sentences about something you like
to do. Use the word *joyous* in one sentence. Use the
word *movement* in the other.**

1. _____

2. _____

Name _____

A Key to Happiness

5   Many people say staying active

11   makes them happy. The key is

17   finding the right exercise for you.

22   Have you ever felt weariness?

27   Have you ever felt sadness?

40   Try going for a jog or a run. It can be very enjoyable.

40   Running can improve your fitness. It can help with

57   other movements, too. Running can add excitement to

67   your day. But remember to stay safe. Don't run when

77   darkness sets in. That can be dangerous. Here are tips

85   for running. Start out slowly. Ask for encouragement

92   from family. Write down your achievements. Running

100 can be one of your keys to happiness!

1. Circle all the words with the suffixes *-ness, -able,* *-ment,* or *-ous*.

2. Complete the sentences.

Running can improve your _____.

Running when _____ sets in can be dangerous.

Name _____

Speed Drill I

Practice reading the high-frequency words. Tell your teacher when you are ready to be timed.

here	big	make	in	red
to	see	I	for	a
can	run	not	me	look
see	here	can	big	make
a	look	for	I	red
me	not	run	to	in

Name _____

Speed Drill 2

Practice reading the high-frequency words. Tell your teacher when you are ready to be timed.

up	come	the	you	it
is	blue	and	funny	one
we	said	my	find	two
blue	funny	it	my	the
said	we	you	two	is
one	find	come	up	and

Name _____

Speed Drill 3

Practice reading the high-frequency words. Tell your teacher when you are ready to be timed.

play	came	get	jump	that
no	go	away	help	ran
yellow	three	where	he	at
away	help	jump	go	he
came	three	no	ran	where
that	yellow	at	play	get

Name _____

Speed Drill 4

Practice reading the high-frequency words. Tell your teacher when you are ready to be timed.

down	but	little	all	good
be	now	our	saw	do
have	on	they	like	was
now	they	good	our	be
do	all	but	down	on
little	like	have	was	saw

Name _____

Speed Drill 5

Practice reading the high-frequency words. Tell your teacher when you are ready to be timed.

black	into	am	well	ride
who	too	new	she	are
so	this	will	eat	white
well	new	she	black	so
white	am	ride	will	into
are	who	this	too	eat

Name _____

Speed Drill 6

Practice reading the high-frequency words. Tell your teacher when you are ready to be timed.

brown	an	yes	must	four
there	pretty	went	out	did
ate	by	say	please	let
yes	four	an	let	pretty
did	brown	ate	by	must
please	say	out	there	went

Name _____

Speed Drill 7

Practice reading the high-frequency words. Tell your teacher when you are ready to be timed.

under	what	every	going	any
ask	fly	soon	him	give
take	has	want	as	with
soon	any	ask	has	under
every	take	give	him	as
going	want	fly	with	what

Name _____

Speed Drill 8

Practice reading the high-frequency words. Tell your teacher when you are ready to be timed.

know	then	again	how	from
her	were	open	some	his
had	after	just	put	of
again	put	had	then	open
some	his	from	her	just
of	know	after	were	how

Name _____

Speed Drill 9

Practice reading the high-frequency words. Tell your teacher when you are ready to be timed.

best	could	when	thank	live
around	call	gave	stop	over
five	made	may	them	once
call	best	five	when	gave
stop	live	thank	once	made
over	may	could	around	them

Name _____

Speed Drill 10

Practice reading the high-frequency words. Tell your teacher when you are ready to be timed.

sit	work	always	cold	both
many	think	walk	us	old
round	fast	been	or	tell
work	old	tell	round	fast
walk	or	think	sit	many
cold	been	us	both	always

Name _____

Speed Drill II

Practice reading the high-frequency words. Tell your teacher when you are ready to be timed.

why	wash	these	your	buy
before	wish	would	sleep	does
first	read	off	found	upon
these	your	sleep	off	first
read	upon	wish	wash	would
does	why	your	buy	before

Name _____

Speed Drill 12

Practice reading the high-frequency words. Tell your teacher when you are ready to be timed.

pull	goes	back	which	day
those	very	write	also	cut
use	sing	its	green	right
day	those	very	cut	its
green	use	also	right	goes
sing	back	which	write	pull

Name _____

Speed Drill 13

Practice reading the high-frequency words. Tell your teacher when you are ready to be timed.

done	got	called	pick	man
time	different	keep	ten	bring
way	carry	hot	if	full
bring	ten	got	keep	if
about	time	done	man	way
hot	pick	full	same	carry
called	same	about	different	bring

Name _____

Speed Drill 14

Practice reading the high-frequency words. Tell your teacher when you are ready to be timed.

such	try	through	another	fall
more	part	word	better	water
used	clean	own	long	small
own	hurt	used	draw	word
try	small	clean	part	better
more	fall	long	such	water
through	draw	hurt	another	own

Name _____

Speed Drill 15

Practice reading the high-frequency words. Tell your teacher when you are ready to be timed.

grow	hold	light	shall	drink
number	other	even	than	start
because	warm	place	kind	most
warm	today	hold	drink	kind
shall	because	far	other	light
start	most	than	place	grow
even	today	number	far	because

Name _____

Speed Drill 16

Practice reading the high-frequency words. Tell your teacher when you are ready to be timed.

eight	each	myself	seven	much
their	six	people	never	laugh
years	things	only	show	don't
each	myself	never	six	their
only	laugh	don't	much	together
show	seven	eight	things	years
people	together	their	never	laugh

Name _____

Decoding Strategy Chart

Step 1	Look for word parts (prefixes) at the beginning of the word.
Step 2	Look for word parts (suffixes) at the end of the word.
Step 3	In the base word, look for familiar spelling patterns. Think about the six syllable-spelling patterns you have learned.
Step 4	Sound out and blend together the word parts.
Step 5	Say the word parts fast. Adjust your pronunciation as needed. Ask yourself, "Is this a word I have heard before?" Then read the word in the sentence and ask, "Does it make sense in this sentence?"

Name _____

Progress Chart

Beginning Date: _____   **Ending Date:** _____

Book/Passage: _____

Number of Words Correctly Read in One Minute: _____

Words Correct Per Minute	0	1	2	3	4	5
200						
190						
180						
170						
160						
150						
140						
130						
120						
110						
100						
90						
80						
70						
60						
50						
40						
30						
20						
10						

Number of Trials

Name _____

2005 Oral Reading Fluency Data (Hasbrouck & Tindal)

Grade	Percentile	Fall WCPM*	Winter WCPM*	Spring WCPM*	Avg. Weekly Improvement**
1	90		81	111	1.9
	75		47	82	2.2
	50		23	53	1.9
	25		12	28	1.0
	10		6	15	0.6
2	90	106	125	142	1.1
	75	79	100	117	1.2
	50	51	72	89	1.2
	25	25	42	61	1.1
	10	11	18	31	0.6
3	90	128	146	162	1.1
	75	99	120	137	1.2
	50	71	92	107	1.1
	25	44	62	78	1.1
	10	21	36	48	0.8
4	90	145	166	180	1.1
	75	119	139	152	1.0
	50	94	112	123	0.9
	25	68	87	98	0.9
	10	45	61	72	0.8
5	90	166	182	194	0.9
	75	139	156	168	0.9
	50	110	127	139	0.9
	25	85	99	109	0.8
	10	61	74	83	0.7
6	90	177	195	204	0.8
	75	153	167	177	0.8
	50	127	140	150	0.7
	25	98	111	122	0.8
	10	68	82	93	0.8

*WCPM = Words Correct Per Minute   **Average words per week growth

Foundational Skills Assessment

CONTENTS

FOUNDATIONAL SKILLS ASSESSMENT

Phonological and Phonemic Awareness

Letter Naming and Sight Words

Phonics and Structural Analysis

Oral Reading Fluency Assessment

Phonological and Phonemic Awareness

Phonological and Phonemic Awareness

Overview

Research has shown that deficits in phonological and phonemic awareness may be at the root of many difficulties in reading and spelling. For this reason, early assessment is important. By administering this assessment, you can objectively estimate a student's level of phonological and phonemic awareness. The assessment also can help to identify those students whose difficulty in the acquisition of reading and spelling skills may be due to a lack of phonological and phonemic awareness. The results will give you a good idea of where to focus your *McGraw-Hill Reading WonderWorks* instruction.

Phonological and Phonemic Awareness Subtests

The Phonological and Phonemic Awareness Assessment consists of these subtests:

Phonological Awareness Subtests (Grade K–early Grade 1)

1. Recognize Rhyming Words
2. Produce Rhyming Words
3. Segment and Count Syllables
4. Blend Syllables
5. Blend and Segment Onsets and Rimes

Phonemic Awareness Subtests (Grades K–3)

1. Count Phonemes
2. Isolate and Pronounce Phonemes
3. Match Phonemes
4. Blend Phonemes to Produce Words
5. Segment Words into Phonemes
6. Delete Phonemes to Make New Words
7. Add Phonemes to Make New Words
8. Substitute Phonemes to Make New Words
9. Represent Phonemes with Letters
10. Distinguish Long from Short Vowels

Phonological and Phonemic Awareness

How to Use the Assessment

It is recommended that you administer the subtests on an individual basis. Students are led through the tasks by the teacher. Most of the subtests are conducted orally, with the teacher recording the student's responses on a record sheet. A few have a student page on which students indicate their answers by circling pictures or writing letters. Students unfamiliar with these types of tasks should receive practice in completing such tasks prior to administration of this assessment.

The subtests progress in difficulty according to the developmental sequence in which these skills are generally learned. Some of the subtests have multiple sections, and these sections are also sequenced by difficulty. If a student is unable to complete the first section of a subtest, do not go on to the second section. If a student is unable to complete two subtests, it is best to stop the assessment at that point.

How to Interpret the Results

The ability to identify individual sounds in words and match sounds in different words is a key indicator of a student's decoding ability. Students' results in this assessment can point you to deficits in phonological and phonemic awareness (and the need for further instruction), or the results may show that students are ready to handle connected text.

Generally, students who do well on the phonological and phonemic awareness assessment are progressing well and have a good foundation for learning to read and spell. If a student does not do well on any part of the test, reassess the student to determine where the difficulty lies.

Phonemic awareness and phonics instruction go hand-in-hand. Phonemic awareness is a precursor to reading but also develops as students learn to read. Students who are able to hear the individual phonemes in words are ready for phonics instruction. By the time students are decoding words easily, they no longer need to be assessed in phonemic awareness skills.

Recognize Rhyming Words

This phonological awareness test assesses a student's ability to recognize words that rhyme. Say a word. Have the student circle the picture that names a word that rhymes.

Instructions for Administering the Assessment

Make a copy of the test page for each child. For Test 1, say the following directions to the child. Follow this same script for each test that follows, substituting the appropriate words from the test; rhyming words appear in **bold** before each answer.

1. *Look at Number 1* (point to the number). *Listen carefully as I say a word:* pet. *Now listen to these answer choices:* cap, net, bus. *Which word rhymes with* pet? *Circle the picture of the word that rhymes with* pet.

2. *Look at Number 2* (point to the number). *Listen carefully as I say a word:* van. *Now listen to these answer choices:* vase, fork, fan. *Which word rhymes with* van? *Circle the picture of the word that rhymes with* van.

3. *Look at Number 3* (point to the number). *Listen carefully as I say a word:* coat. *Now listen to these answer choices:* boat, hat, dog. *Which word rhymes with* coat? *Circle the picture of the word that rhymes with* coat.

4. *Look at Number 4* (point to the number). *Listen carefully as I say a word:* trunk. *Now listen to these answer choices:* drum, train, skunk. *Which word rhymes with* trunk? *Circle the picture of the word that rhymes with* trunk.

5. *Look at Number 5* (point to the number). *Listen carefully as I say a word:* gate. *Now listen to these answer choices:* goat, skate, fruit. *Which word rhymes with* gate? *Circle the picture of the word that rhymes with* gate.

Directions for Scoring

Give 1 point for each correct response. The highest score is 5.

Test 1, page A9
Answers: **1. pet:** net; **2. van:** fan; **3. coat:** boat; **4. trunk:** skunk; **5. gate:** skate

Test 2, page A10
Answers: **1. cat:** bat; **2. wig:** pig; **3. top:** mop; **4. pen:** hen; **5. hut:** nut

Test 3, page A11
Answers: **1. tag:** bag; **2. win:** fin; **3. fox:** box; **4. bell:** shell; **5. luck:** duck

Test 4, page A12
Answers: **1. man:** pan; **2. dish:** fish; **3. log:** frog; **4. meat:** feet; **5. rug:** bug

Test 5, page A13
Answers: **1. hair:** chair; **2. car:** star; **3. rest:** nest; **4. tool:** school; **5. rock:** sock

Test 6, page A14
Answers: **1. date:** plate; **2. drink:** sink; **3. crib:** bib; **4. hope:** rope; **5. red:** bed

Phonological Awareness

Name: _____ **Date:** _____

Recognize Rhyming Words, Test 1

1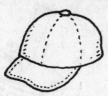

2

3

4

5

Score: _____ / 5

Name: _____ Date: _____

Recognize Rhyming Words, Test 2

1

2

3

4

5

Score: _____ / 5

Phonological Awareness

Name: _____ Date: _____

Recognize Rhyming Words, Test 3

1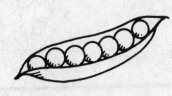

2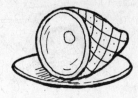

3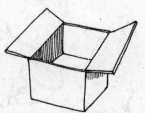

4

5

Score: _____ / 5

Name: _____ Date: _____

Recognize Rhyming Words, Test 4

1

2

3

4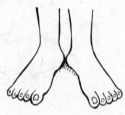

5

Score: _____ / 5

Name: _____ Date: _____

Recognize Rhyming Words, Test 5

1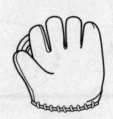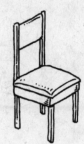

2

3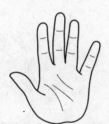

4

5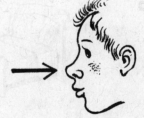

Score: _____ / 5

Name: _____ Date: _____

Recognize Rhyming Words, Test 6

1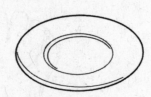

2

3

4

5

Score: _____ / 5

Phonological Awareness

Produce Rhyming Words

This phonological awareness test assesses a student's ability to produce his or her own rhymes. Say a word. Ask the student to say a rhyming word. Accept nonsense words that rhyme with the target word.

Instructions for Administering the Assessment

Make a copy of the record sheet for each child. Use the sheet to record the child's oral responses. Say these directions to the child:

I am going to say a word. I want you to tell me a word that rhymes with it. If you want, you can make up a word. Let's try one. Listen: big. *Tell me a word that rhymes with* dig. (Examples: big, fig, gig, hig, jig, kig, pig, wig, and so on.)

Directions for Scoring

Give 1 point for each correct response. The highest score is 5.

Test 1, page A16
Sample answers: **1.** not; **2.** club; **3.** bake; **4.** ride; **5.** pick

Test 2, page A17
Sample answers: **1.** pack; **2.** rub; **3.** pine; **4.** set; **5.** pole

Test 3, page A18
Sample answers: **1.** sip; **2.** pool; **3.** take; **4.** beam; **5.** fun

Test 4, page A19
Sample answers: **1.** tap; **2.** flu; **3.** sock; **4.** keep; **5.** will

Test 5, page A20
Sample answers: **1.** fed; **2.** tail; **3.** soap; **4.** wig; **5.** leg

Test 6, page A21
Sample answers: **1.** say; **2.** hug; **3.** feed; **4.** wire; **5.** hood

Phonological Awareness

Name: _____ Date: _____

Record Sheet, Test 1

Produce Rhyming Words

Tell me a word that rhymes with . . .

Word	Response
1. hot	_____
2. rub	_____
3. rake	_____
4. slide	_____
5. kick	_____

Score _____ / 5

Phonological Awareness

Name: _____ **Date:** _____

Record Sheet, Test 2

Produce Rhyming Words

Tell me a word that rhymes with . . .

	Word	Response
1.	back	_____
2.	cub	_____
3.	line	_____
4.	bet	_____
5.	hole	_____

Score _____ / 5

Phonological Awareness

Name: _____ **Date:** _____

Record Sheet, Test 3

Produce Rhyming Words

Tell me a word that rhymes with . . .

Word	**Response**
1. hip	_____
2. tool	_____
3. flake	_____
4. team	_____
5. run	_____

Score _____ / 5

Name: _____ Date: _____

Record Sheet, Test 4

Produce Rhyming Words

Tell me a word that rhymes with . . .

	Word	Response
1.	nap	_____
2.	blue	_____
3.	rock	_____
4.	jeep	_____
5.	hill	_____

Score _____ / 5

Phonological Awareness

Name: _____ **Date:** _____

Record Sheet, Test 5

Produce Rhyming Words

Tell me a word that rhymes with . . .

	Word	Response
1.	red	_____
2.	nail	_____
3.	hope	_____
4.	big	_____
5.	egg	_____

Score _____ / 5

Phonological Awareness

Name: _____ Date: _____

Record Sheet, Test 6

Produce Rhyming Words

Tell me a word that rhymes with . . .

	Word	Response
1.	day	_____
2.	jug	_____
3.	seed	_____
4.	tire	_____
5.	wood	_____

Score _____ / 5

Copyright © McGraw-Hill Education. Permission is granted to reproduce for classroom use.

Segment and Count Syllables

This phonological awareness test assesses a student's ability to count syllables in a word. Say a word. Have the student repeat the word and clap for each syllable, or word part, he or she hears. Then have the student tell the number of syllables in the word.

Instructions for Administering the Assessment

Make a copy of the record sheet for each child. Use the sheet to record the child's oral responses. Say these directions to the child:

I am going to say a word. I want you to repeat the word slowly and clap for each syllable, or word part, you hear. Let's do one together. Ready? The word is picnic. *Say and clap it with me:* pic-nic. *How many claps?* (2) *How many syllables?* (2)

Directions for Scoring

Give 1 point for each correct response. The highest score is 5.

Test 1, page A23
Answers: **1.** three syllables; **2.** four syllables; **3.** two syllables; **4.** one syllable; **5.** two syllables

Test 2, page A24
Answers: **1.** two syllables; **2.** one syllable; **3.** three syllables; **4.** four syllables; **5.** three syllables

Test 3, page A25
Answers: **1.** one syllable; **2.** four syllables; **3.** two syllables; **4.** two syllables; **5.** three syllables

Test 4, page A26
Answers: **1.** one syllable; **2.** three syllables; **3.** one syllable; **4.** two syllables; **5.** four syllables

Test 5, page A27
Answers: **1.** four syllables; **2.** one syllable; **3.** three syllables; **4.** two syllables; **5.** two syllables

Test 6, page A28
Answers: **1.** two syllables; **2.** three syllables; **3.** four syllables; **4.** one syllable; **5.** two syllables

Phonological Awareness

Name: _____ **Date:** _____

Record Sheet, Test 1

Segment and Count Syllables

The word is . . . . Say and clap the word. . . . How many syllables?

Word	Number of Syllables
1. umbrella	_____
2. caterpillar	_____
3. pumpkin	_____
4. kite	_____
5. turtle	_____

Score _____ / 5

Name: _____ Date: _____

Record Sheet, Test 2

Segment and Count Syllables

The word is . . . . Say and clap the word. . . . How many syllables?

Word	Number of Syllables
1. apple	_____
2. dress	_____
3. pajamas	_____
4. elevator	_____
5. holiday	_____

Score _____ / 5

Phonological Awareness

Name: _____ **Date:** _____

Record Sheet, Test 3

Segment and Count Syllables

The word is . . . . Say and clap the word. . . . How many syllables?

Word	Number of Syllables
1. farm	_____
2. harmonica	_____
3. baby	_____
4. finger	_____
5. animal	_____

Score _____ / 5

Phonological Awareness

Name: _____ Date: _____

Record Sheet, Test 4

Segment and Count Syllables

The word is . . . . Say and clap the word. . . . How many syllables?

Word	Number of Syllables
1. shop	_____
2. potato	_____
3. town	_____
4. lizard	_____
5. watermelon	_____

Score _____ / 5

Foundational Skills Assessment · Phonological Awareness

Name: _____ Date: _____

Record Sheet, Test 5

Segment and Count Syllables

The word is . . . . Say and clap the word. . . . How many syllables?

Word	Number of Syllables
1. alligator	_____
2. art	_____
3. kangaroo	_____
4. teacher	_____
5. river	_____

Score _____ / 5

Phonological Awareness

Name: _____ Date: _____

Record Sheet, Test 6

Segment and Count Syllables

The word is . . . . Say and clap the word. . . . How many syllables?

Word	Number of Syllables
1. water	_____
2. lemonade	_____
3. supermarket	_____
4. home	_____
5. napkin	_____

Score _____ / 5

Phonological Awareness

Blend Syllables

This phonological awareness test assesses a student's ability to combine syllables to form compound and multi-syllabic words. Say the parts of a word. Have the student say the complete word.

There are three sets of words. The sets progress in difficulty. If a student is unable to correctly say the first set of words, do not go on to the next set.

Instructions for Administering the Assessment

Make a copy of the record sheet for each child. Use the sheet to record the child's oral responses.

Say these directions to the child:

I am going to say the parts of a word. I want you to put the word parts together and say the whole word. Let's try one. Listen: can-dle. *Again:* can-dle. *What is the whole word?* (candle)

Directions for Scoring

Give 1 point for each correct response. The highest score for each set of items is 5.

Test 1, page A31

Answers for each set

Compound Words: **1.** pancake; **2.** baseball; **3.** popcorn; **4.** rainbow; **5.** airplane

Words with 2 Syllables: **1.** trumpet; **2.** costume; **3.** reptile; **4.** table; **5.** tiger

Words with 3 or More Syllables: **1.** cucumber; **2.** computer; **3.** alphabet; **4.** apartment; **5.** kindergarten

Test 2, page A32

Answers for each set

Compound Words: **1.** backyard; **2.** football; **3.** downtown; **4.** eyelid; **5.** horsefly

Words with 2 Syllables: **1.** number; **2.** sister; **3.** helmet; **4.** mistake; **5.** raisin

Words with 3 or More Syllables: **1.** banana; **2.** hospital; **3.** important; **4.** yesterday; **5.** information

Phonological Awareness

Test 3, page A33

Answers for each set

Compound Words: **1.** blackbird; **2.** feedback; **3.** bedtime; **4.** handball; **5.** flashlight

Words with 2 Syllables: **1.** bandage; **2.** shower; **3.** mountain; **4.** tower; **5.** picnic

Words with 3 or More Syllables: **1.** butterfly; **2.** customer; **3.** celery; **4.** library; **5.** decoration

Test 4, page A34

Answers for each set

Compound Words: **1.** snowball; **2.** seafood; **3.** bookcase; **4.** sandbox; **5.** backpack

Words with 2 Syllables: **1.** contest; **2.** music; **3.** nature; **4.** total; **5.** city

Words with 3 or More Syllables: **1.** volcano; **2.** however; **3.** tomorrow; **4.** hamburger; **5.** automatic

Test 5, page A35

Answers for each set

Compound Words: **1.** doorknob; **2.** bedroom; **3.** daytime; **4.** somewhere; **5.** cornmeal

Words with 2 Syllables: **1.** puppy; **2.** robin; **3.** wagon; **4.** metal; **5.** window

Words with 3 or More Syllables: **1.** cranberries; **2.** officer; **3.** afternoon; **4.** telephone; **5.** anybody

Test 6, page A36

Answers for each set

Compound Words: **1.** horseshoe; **2.** landmark; **3.** workout; **4.** railroad; **5.** handstand

Words with 2 Syllables: **1.** tractor; **2.** body; **3.** tuna; **4.** letter; **5.** spider

Words with 3 or More Syllables: **1.** gorilla; **2.** adventure; **3.** september; **4.** ladybug; **5.** caterpillar

Phonological Awareness

Name: _____ Date: _____

Record Sheet, Test 1

Blend Syllables

What is the whole word?

Compound Words

	Word Parts	Response
1.	pan-cake	_____
2.	base-ball	_____
3.	pop-corn	_____
4.	rain-bow	_____
5.	air-plane	_____

Score ___ / 5

Words with 3 or More Syllables

	Word Parts	Response
1.	cu-cum-ber	_____
2.	com-pu-ter	_____
3.	al-pha-bet	_____
4.	a-part-ment	_____
5.	kin-der-gar-ten	_____

Score ___ / 5

Words with 2 Syllables

	Word Parts	Response
1.	trum-pet	_____
2.	cos-tume	_____
3.	rep-tile	_____
4.	ta-ble	_____
5.	ti-ger	_____

Score ___ / 5

Phonological Awareness

Name: _____ Date: _____

Record Sheet, Test 2

Blend Syllables

What is the whole word?

Compound Words

	Word Parts	Response
1.	back-yard	_____
2.	foot-ball	_____
3.	down-town	_____
4.	eye-lid	_____
5.	horse-fly	_____

Score ___ / 5

Words with 3 or More Syllables

	Word Parts	Response
1.	ba-na-na	_____
2.	hos-pi-tal	_____
3.	im-por-tant	_____
4.	yes-ter-day	_____
5.	in-for-ma-tion	_____

Score ___ / 5

Words with 2 Syllables

	Word Parts	Response
1.	num-ber	_____
2.	sis-ter	_____
3.	hel-met	_____
4.	mis-take	_____
5.	rai-sin	_____

Score ___ / 5

Phonological Awareness

Name: _____ Date: _____

Record Sheet, Test 3

Blend Syllables

What is the whole word?

Compound Words

	Word Parts	Response
1.	black-bird	_____
2.	feed-back	_____
3.	bed-time	_____
4.	hand-ball	_____
5.	flash-light	_____

Score ___ / 5

Words with 3 or More Syllables

	Word Parts	Response
1.	but-ter-fly	_____
2.	cus-tom-er	_____
3.	cel-er-y	_____
4.	li-brar-y	_____
5.	dec-o-ra-tion	_____

Score ___ / 5

Words with 2 Syllables

	Word Parts	Response
1.	ban-dage	_____
2.	show-er	_____
3.	moun-tain	_____
4.	tow-er	_____
5.	pic-nic	_____

Score ___ / 5

Phonological Awareness

Name: _____ **Date:** _____

Record Sheet, Test 4

Blend Syllables

What is the whole word?

Compound Words

	Word Parts	Response
1.	snow-ball	_____
2.	sea-food	_____
3.	book-case	_____
4.	sand-box	_____
5.	back-pack	_____

Score ___ / 5

Words with 3 or More Syllables

	Word Parts	Response
1.	vol-ca-no	_____
2.	how-ev-er	_____
3.	to-mor-row	_____
4.	ham-bur-ger	_____
5.	au-to-mat-ic	_____

Score ___ / 5

Words with 2 Syllables

	Word Parts	Response
1.	con-test	_____
2.	mu-sic	_____
3.	na-ture	_____
4.	to-tal	_____
5.	cit-y	_____

Score ___ / 5

Phonological Awareness

Name: _____ Date: _____

Record Sheet, Test 5

Blend Syllables

What is the whole word?

Compound Words

	Word Parts	Response
1.	door-knob	_____
2.	bed-room	_____
3.	day-time	_____
4.	some-where	_____
5.	corn-meal	_____

Score ___ / 5

Words with 3 or More Syllables

	Word Parts	Response
1.	cran-ber-ries	_____
2.	of-fi-cer	_____
3.	af-ter-noon	_____
4.	tel-e-phone	_____
5.	an-y-bod-y	_____

Score ___ / 5

Words with 2 Syllables

	Word Parts	Response
1.	pup-py	_____
2.	rob-in	_____
3.	wag-on	_____
4.	met-al	_____
5.	win-dow	_____

Score ___ / 5

Phonological Awareness

Name: _____ Date: _____

Record Sheet, Test 6

Blend Syllables

What is the whole word?

Compound Words

	Word Parts	Response
1.	horse-shoe	_____
2.	land-mark	_____
3.	work-out	_____
4.	rail-road	_____
5.	hand-stand	_____

Score ___ / 5

Words with 3 or More Syllables

	Word Parts	Response
1.	go-ril-la	_____
2.	ad-ven-ture	_____
3.	sep-tem-ber	_____
4.	la-dy-bug	_____
5.	cat-er-pil-lar	_____

Score ___ / 5

Words with 2 Syllables

	Word Parts	Response
1.	trac-tor	_____
2.	bod-y	_____
3.	tu-na	_____
4.	let-ter	_____
5.	spi-der	_____

Score ___ / 5

Foundational Skills Assessment · Phonological Awareness

Phonological Awareness

Blend and Segment Onsets and Rimes

This phonological awareness test assesses a student's ability to combine onsets and rimes to form a word. Say the initial sound in a word (the onset) and then say the rest of the word (the rime). Have the student put the word together and repeat the whole word back to you.

Instructions for Administering the Assessment

Make a copy of the record sheet for each child. Use the sheet to record the child's oral responses. Say these directions to the child:

I am going to say a word in two parts. I want you to put the parts together and say the whole word. Let's try one. Listen: /g/-ame. Again: /g/-ame. What is the whole word? (game) That's right, the word is game.

Directions for Scoring

Give 1 point for each correct response. The highest score is 5.

Test 1, page A38

Answers: **1.** sit; **2.** bear; **3.** call; **4.** toe; **5.** pants

Test 2, page A39

Answers: **1.** cut; **2.** sell; **3.** hug; **4.** lip; **5.** bus

Test 3, page A40

Answers: **1.** pig; **2.** duck; **3.** men; **4.** job; **5.** tack

Test 4, page A41

Answers: **1.** tap; **2.** dug; **3.** dog; **4.** can; **5.** bend

Test 5, page A42

Answers: **1.** cup; **2.** pick; **3.** now; **4.** fan; **5.** beet

Test 6, page A43

Answers: **1.** cat; **2.** top; **3.** land; **4.** pen; **5.** bill

Name: _____ Date: _____

Blend and Segment Onsets and Rimes, Test 1

What is the whole word?

Onset and Rime	Response
1. /s/-it	_____
2. /b/-ear	_____
3. /k/-all	_____
4. /t/-oe	_____
5. /p/-ants	_____

Score ___ / 5

Name: _____ Date: _____

Blend and Segment Onsets and Rimes, Test 2

What is the whole word?

	Onset and Rime	Response
1.	/k/-ut	_____
2.	/s/-ell	_____
3.	/h/-ug	_____
4.	/l/-ip	_____
5.	/b/-us	_____

Score ____ / 5

Phonological Awareness

Name: _____ Date: _____

Blend and Segment Onsets and Rimes, Test 3

What is the whole word?

Onset and Rime	Response
1. /p/-ig	_____
2. /d/-uck	_____
3. /m/-en	_____
4. /j/-ob	_____
5. /t/-ack	_____

Score ___ / 5

Foundational Skills Assessment · Phonological Awareness

Name: _____ Date: _____

Blend and Segment Onsets and Rimes, Test 4

What is the whole word?

Onset and Rime	Response
1. /t/-ap	_____
2. /d/-ug	_____
3. /d/-og	_____
4. /k/-an	_____
5. /b/-end	_____

Score ____ / 5

Name: _____ Date: _____

Blend and Segment Onsets and Rimes, Test 5

What is the whole word?

	Onset and Rime	Response
1.	/k/-up	_____
2.	/p/-ick	_____
3.	/n/-ow	_____
4.	/f/-an	_____
5.	/b/-eet	_____

Score ___ / 5

Phonological Awareness

Name: _____ Date: _____

Blend and Segment Onsets and Rimes, Test 6

What is the whole word?

	Onset and Rime	**Response**
1.	/k/-at	_____
2.	/t/-op	_____
3.	/l/-and	_____
4.	/p/-en	_____
5.	/b/-ill	_____

Score _____ / 5

Phonemic Awareness

Count Phonemes

This phonemic awareness test assesses a student's ability to break a word into its separate sounds (phonemes) and count the sounds. Name each picture. Have the student repeat the word, segment it into sounds, and tell the number of sounds in the word.

Instructions for Administering the Assessment

Make a copy of the test page for each child. For Test 1, say the following directions to the child. Follow this same script for each test that follows, substituting the appropriate words from the test; words appear in **bold** before each answer.

I am going to say a word. I want you to say the word very slowly and tell me how many sounds you hear. Let's try one. Listen: fan. *Say it very slowly.* (/f/ /a/ /n/) *How many sounds do you hear?* (three)

1. *Look at Number 1* (point to the number). *This is a picture of a rock. Say the word* rock *very slowly. How many sounds do you hear?*

2. *Look at Number 2* (point to the number). *This is a picture of a bee. Say the word* bee *very slowly. How many sounds do you hear?*

3. *Look at Number 3* (point to the number). *This is a picture of a snake. Say the word* snake *very slowly. How many sounds do you hear?*

4. *Look at Number 4* (point to the number). *This is a picture of a plant. Say the word* plant *very slowly. How many sounds do you hear?*

5. *Look at Number 5* (point to the number). *This is a picture of feet. Say the word* feet *very slowly. How many sounds do you hear?*

Directions for Scoring

Give 1 point for each correct response. The highest score is 5.

Test 1, page A45
Answers: **1. rock:** three; **2. bee:** two; **3. snake:** four; **4. plant:** five; **5. feet:** three

Test 2, page A46
Answers: **1. dog:** three; **2. man:** three; **3. bell:** three; **4. flute:** four; **5. egg:** two

Test 3, page A47
Answers: **1. plate:** four; **2. cup:** three; **3. pants:** five; **4. well:** three; **5. pen:** three

Test 4, page A48
Answers: **1. bat:** three; **2. hand:** four; **3. book:** three; **4. skunk:** five; **5. geese:** three

Test 5, page A49
Answers: **1. boat:** three; **2. glove:** four; **3. spoon:** four; **4. fan:** three; **5. globe:** four

Test 6, page A50
Answers: **1. skate:** four; **2. frog:** four; **3. gate:** three; **4. pin:** three; **5. sheep:** three

Phonemic Awareness

Name: _____ Date: _____

Count Phonemes, Test 1

1

_____

2

_____

3

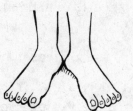

_____

4

_____

5

_____

Score: _____ / 5

Name: _____ Date: _____

Count Phonemes, Test 2

1

_____

2

_____

3

_____

4

_____

5

_____

Score: _____ / 5

Name: _____ **Date:** _____

Count Phonemes, Test 3

1

_____

2

_____

3

_____

4

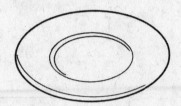

_____

5

_____

Score: _____ / 5

Name: _____ Date: _____

Count Phonemes, Test 4

1

_____

2

_____

3

_____

4

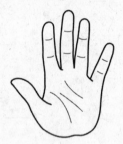

_____

5

_____

Score: _____ / 5

Name: _____ Date: _____

Count Phonemes, Test 5

1

_____

2

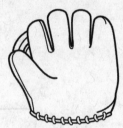

_____

3

_____

4

_____

5

_____

Score: _____ / 5

Name: _____ Date: _____

Count Phonemes, Test 6

1

_____

2

_____

3

_____

4

_____

5

_____

Score: _____ / 5

Phonemic Awareness

Isolate and Pronounce Phonemes

This phonemic awareness test assesses a student's ability to recognize individual sounds (phonemes) in a word. Say a word. Have the student say the first, last, or medial sound in the word.

Instructions for Administering the Assessment

Make a copy of the record sheet for each child. Use the sheet to record the child's oral responses.

Use the following directions depending on what is being assessed:

I am going to say a word. I want you to tell me the initial, or beginning, sound. Let's do an example. Listen: tag. *Say the initial, or beginning, sound in* tag. (/t/)

I am going to say a word. I want you to tell me the final, or ending, sound. Let's do an example. Listen: tag. *Say the final, or ending, sound in* tag. (/g/)

I am going to say a word. I want you to tell me the medial, or middle, sound. Let's do an example. Listen: tag. *Say the medial, or middle, sound in* tag. (/a/)

Directions for Scoring

Give 1 point for each correct response. The highest score for each set of items is 5.

Test 1, page A53

Answers for each set

Initial Sounds: **1.** /b/; **2.** /f/; **3.** /l/; **4.** /d/; **5.** /n/

Final Sounds: **1.** /d/; **2.** /g/; **3.** /m/; **4.** /n/; **5.** /p/

Medial Sounds: **1.** /a/; **2.** /ē/; **3.** /e/; **4.** /ā/; **5.** /i/

Test 2, page A54

Answers for each set

Initial Sounds: **1.** /l/; **2.** /t/; **3.** /r/; **4.** /p/; **5.** /k/

Final Sounds: **1.** /b/; **2.** /p/; **3.** /t/; **4.** /s/; **5.** /d/

Medial Sounds: **1.** /i/; **2.** /a/; **3.** /e/; **4.** /u/; **5.** /ō/

Phonemic Awareness

Test 3, page A55

Answers for each set

Initial Sounds: **1.** /l/; **2.** /d/; **3.** /v/; **4.** /n/; **5.** /f/

Final Sounds: **1.** /g/; **2.** /d/; **3.** /t/; **4.** /t/; **5.** /p/

Medial Sounds: **1.** /e/; **2.** /i/; **3.** /ē/; **4.** /ō/; **5.** /o/

Test 4, page A56

Answers for each set

Initial Sounds: **1.** /w/; **2.** /s/; **3.** /t/; **4.** /l/; **5.** /s/

Final Sounds: **1.** /s/; **2.** /f/; **3.** /k/; **4.** /b/; **5.** /t/

Medial Sounds: **1.** /a/; **2.** /ē/; **3.** /ü/; **4.** /i/; **5.** /e/

Test 5, page A57

Answers for each set

Initial Sounds: **1.** /n/; **2.** /h/; **3.** /g/; **4.** /n/; **5.** /z/

Final Sounds: **1.** /m/; **2.** /t/; **3.** /b/; **4.** /p/; **5.** /g/

Medial Sounds: **1.** /ō/; **2.** /i/; **3.** /ē/; **4.** /o/; **5.** /a/

Test 6, page A58

Answers for each set

Initial Sounds: **1.** /g/; **2.** /h/; **3.** /r/; **4.** /ch/; **5.** /b/

Final Sounds: **1.** /n/; **2.** /ē/; **3.** /d/; **4.** /p/; **5.** /k/

Medial Sounds: **1.** /e/; **2.** /a/; **3.** /i/; **4.** /ē/; **5.** /ā/

Phonemic Awareness

Name: _____ Date: _____

Record Sheet, Test 1

Isolate and Pronounce Phonemes

Initial Sounds

Say the initial, or beginning, sound in . . .

	Word	Response
1.	bag	_____
2.	fun	_____
3.	log	_____
4.	dip	_____
5.	net	_____

Score ___ / 5

Medial Sounds

Say the medial, or middle, sound in . . .

	Word	Response
1.	ran	_____
2.	team	_____
3.	set	_____
4.	wait	_____
5.	tip	_____

Score ___ / 5

Final Sounds

Say the final, or ending, sound in . . .

	Word	Response
1.	hid	_____
2.	wag	_____
3.	hum	_____
4.	pen	_____
5.	top	_____

Score ___ / 5

Phonemic Awareness

Name: _____ Date: _____

Record Sheet, Test 2

Isolate and Pronounce Phonemes

Initial Sounds

Say the initial, or beginning, sound in . . .

	Word	Response
1.	lob	_____
2.	tag	_____
3.	rip	_____
4.	put	_____
5.	kit	_____

Score ___ / 5

Medial Sounds

Say the medial, or middle, sound in . . .

	Word	Response
1.	lip	_____
2.	map	_____
3.	leg	_____
4.	hut	_____
5.	boat	_____

Score ___ / 5

Final Sounds

Say the final, or ending, sound in . . .

	Word	Response
1.	sub	_____
2.	sap	_____
3.	pit	_____
4.	gas	_____
5.	red	_____

Score ___ / 5

Foundational Skills Assessment · Phonemic Awareness

Phonemic Awareness

Name: _____ Date: _____

Record Sheet, Test 3

Isolate and Pronounce Phonemes

Initial Sounds

Say the initial, or beginning, sound in . . .

Word	Response
1. lad	_____
2. dot	_____
3. van	_____
4. not	_____
5. fit	_____

Score ___ / 5

Medial Sounds

Say the medial, or middle, sound in . . .

Word	Response
1. wet	_____
2. sip	_____
3. feet	_____
4. road	_____
5. job	_____

Score ___ / 5

Final Sounds

Say the final, or ending, sound in . . .

Word	Response
1. leg	_____
2. did	_____
3. wit	_____
4. bet	_____
5. ship	_____

Score ___ / 5

Phonemic Awareness

Name: _____ Date: _____

Record Sheet, Test 4

Isolate and Pronounce Phonemes

Initial Sounds

Say the initial, or beginning, sound in . . .

	Word	Response
1.	wig	_____
2.	sun	_____
3.	tan	_____
4.	lit	_____
5.	sit	_____

Score ___ / 5

Medial Sounds

Say the medial, or middle, sound in . . .

	Word	Response
1.	lap	_____
2.	week	_____
3.	tube	_____
4.	tin	_____
5.	head	_____

Score ___ / 5

Final Sounds

Say the final, or ending, sound in . . .

	Word	Response
1.	bus	_____
2.	leaf	_____
3.	cook	_____
4.	tub	_____
5.	rut	_____

Score ___ / 5

Foundational Skills Assessment · Phonemic Awareness

Phonemic Awareness

Name: _____ Date: _____

Record Sheet, Test 5

Isolate and Pronounce Phonemes

Initial Sounds

Say the initial, or beginning, sound in . . .

	Word	Response
1.	nut	_____
2.	hill	_____
3.	get	_____
4.	nod	_____
5.	zoo	_____

Score ___ / 5

Medial Sounds

Say the medial, or middle, sound in . . .

	Word	Response
1.	rode	_____
2.	dim	_____
3.	teen	_____
4.	hop	_____
5.	sag	_____

Score ___ / 5

Final Sounds

Say the final, or ending, sound in . . .

	Word	Response
1.	drum	_____
2.	rot	_____
3.	rub	_____
4.	soap	_____
5.	rag	_____

Score ___ / 5

Phonemic Awareness

Name: _____ Date: _____

Record Sheet, Test 6

Isolate and Pronounce Phonemes

Initial Sounds

Say the initial, or beginning, sound in . . .

	Word	Response
1.	got	_____
2.	hit	_____
3.	rob	_____
4.	chip	_____
5.	bat	_____

Score ___ / 5

Medial Sounds

Say the medial, or middle, sound in . . .

	Word	Response
1.	pet	_____
2.	fan	_____
3.	pin	_____
4.	meet	_____
5.	bait	_____

Score ___ / 5

Final Sounds

Say the final, or ending, sound in . . .

	Word	Response
1.	win	_____
2.	bee	_____
3.	rod	_____
4.	mop	_____
5.	kick	_____

Score ___ / 5

Phonemic Awareness

Match Phonemes

This phonemic awareness test assesses a student's ability to recognize the same sounds in different words. Say three words. Have the student say the words that have the same initial, final, or medial sound.

Instructions for Administering the Assessment

Make a copy of the record sheet for each child. Use the sheet to record the child's oral responses.

Use the following directions depending on what is being assessed:

I am going to say three words. I want you to tell me which two words begin with the same sound. Let's do an example. Listen: lap, pat, let. (Repeat.) *Which two words begin with the same sound?* (lap, let)

I am going to say three words. I want you to tell me which two words end with the same sound. Let's do an example. Listen: lap, pat, let. (Repeat.) *Which two words end with the same sound?* (pat, let)

I am going to say three words. I want you to tell me which two words have the same sound in the middle. Let's do an example. Listen: lap, pat, let. (Repeat.) *Which two words have the same sound in the middle?* (lap, pat)

Directions for Scoring

Give 1 point for each correct response. The highest score for each set of words is 5.

Test 1, page A61

Answers for each set

Initial Sounds: **1.** mob, mess; **2.** tack, toad; **3.** neck, nose; **4.** cut, cape; **5.** get, game

Final Sounds: **1.** seed, wood; **2.** hog, rag; **3.** take, pick; **4.** team, gum; **5.** foot, heat

Medial Sounds: **1.** red, net; **2.** mine, side; **3.** sail, fade; **4.** robe, loaf; **5.** cub, jug

Test 2, page A62

Answers for each set

Initial Sounds: **1.** man, mall; **2.** jam, join; **3.** same, sack; **4.** tar, take; **5.** hull, hut

Final Sounds: **1.** deep, drop; **2.** wide, read; **3.** cool, bell; **4.** sob, lab; **5.** grab, bib

Medial Sounds: **1.** big, lip; **2.** rake, paid; **3.** red, men; **4.** teeth, feet; **5.** note, coat

Phonemic Awareness

Test 3, page A63

Answers for each set

Initial Sounds: **1.** wet, wick; **2.** buck, belt; **3.** rot, rim; **4.** felt, few; **5.** loss, luck

Final Sounds: **1.** cliff, stuff; **2.** tug, wag; **3.** bake, peck; **4.** torn, gone; **5.** tax, fox

Medial Sounds: **1.** bug, rub; **2.** goal, bowl; **3.** pop, got; **4.** ride, time; **5.** week, meat

Test 4, page A64

Answers for each set

Initial Sounds: **1.** hose, home; **2.** will, went; **3.** dip, dull; **4.** pat, park; **5.** fall, fork

Final Sounds: **1.** rib, rob; **2.** just, neat; **3.** ten, been; **4.** cake, book; **5.** whip, pup

Medial Sounds: **1.** fine, mile; **2.** beat, leak; **3.** box, hot; **4.** toad, bone; **5.** flat, crab

Test 5, page A65

Answers for each set

Initial Sounds: **1.** pot, pill; **2.** give, gash; **3.** nest, nine; **4.** wind, won; **5.** zoo, zip

Final Sounds: **1.** hike, look; **2.** peep, rap; **3.** ball, smile; **4.** clay, say; **5.** fog, egg

Medial Sounds: **1.** bet, yes; **2.** goat, joke; **3.** seal, meet; **4.** rug, sun; **5.** sap, cat

Test 6, page A66

Answers for each set

Initial Sounds: **1.** ripe, rain; **2.** van, vat; **3.** pin, pain; **4.** den, dim; **5.** lime, lap

Final Sounds: **1.** chef, off; **2.** wake, cook; **3.** pool, tell; **4.** fish, bush; **5.** fuss, less

Medial Sounds: **1.** nod, pot; **2.** dime, vine; **3.** tote, loan; **4.** road, hope; **5.** head, beg

Phonemic Awareness

Name: _____ Date: _____

Record Sheet, Test 1

Match Phonemes

Initial Sounds

Which two words begin with the same sound?

Words	Response
1. mob, mess, pod	_____
2. lick, tack, toad	_____
3. neck, keep, nose	_____
4. cut, hut, cape	_____
5. get, game, sum	_____

Score ___ / 5

Final Sounds

Which two words end with the same sound?

Words	Response
1. seed, wood, sat	_____
2. hip, hog, rag	_____
3. take, tab, pick	_____
4. men, team, gum	_____
5. foot, heat, has	_____

Score ___ / 5

Medial Sounds

Which two words have the same sound in the middle?

Words	Response
1. red, net, nut	_____
2. mane, mine, side	_____
3. sail, tall, fade	_____
4. lot, robe, loaf	_____
5. cub, jug, web	_____

Score ___ / 5

Phonemic Awareness

Name: _____ **Date:** _____

Record Sheet, Test 2

Match Phonemes

Initial Sounds

Which two words begin with the same sound?

Words		Response
1.	man, mall, tan	_____
2.	jam, tick, join	_____
3.	tub, same, sack	_____
4.	tar, mean, take	_____
5.	hull, mat, hat	_____

Score ___ / 5

Medial Sounds

Which two words have the same sound in the middle?

Words		Response
1.	big, cap, lip	_____
2.	rake, bike, paid	_____
3.	red, mop, men	_____
4.	tape, teeth, feet	_____
5.	note, coat, sit	_____

Score ___ / 5

Final Sounds

Which two words end with the same sound?

Words		Response
1.	deep, dog, drop	_____
2.	wit, wide, read	_____
3.	boot, cool, bell	_____
4.	sob, lab, lag	_____
5.	grab, bib, bad	_____

Score ___ / 5

Phonemic Awareness

Name: _____ Date: _____

Record Sheet, Test 3

Match Phonemes

Initial Sounds

Which two words begin with the same sound?

	Words	Response
1.	wet, let, wick	_____
2.	buck, belt, tent	_____
3.	rot, rim, send	_____
4.	pen, felt, few	_____
5.	loss, top, luck	_____

Score ___ / 5

Medial Sounds

Which two words have the same sound in the middle?

	Words	Response
1.	bug, rub, beg	_____
2.	file, goal, bowl	_____
3.	pop, tag, got	_____
4.	rip, ride, time	_____
5.	week, meat, well	_____

Score ___ / 5

Final Sounds

Which two words end with the same sound?

	Words	Response
1.	cliff, stuff, stall	_____
2.	win, tug, wag	_____
3.	bake, need, peck	_____
4.	toe, torn, gone	_____
5.	tax, fox, tap	_____

Score ___ / 5

Phonemic Awareness

Name: _____ Date: _____

Record Sheet, Test 4

Match Phonemes

Initial Sounds

Which two words begin with the same sound?

	Words	Response
1.	hose, home, fill	_____
2.	will, bit, went	_____
3.	dip, fat, dull	_____
4.	pat, park, nod	_____
5.	fall, sat, fork	_____

Score ___ / 5

Medial Sounds

Which two words have the same sound in the middle?

	Words	Response
1.	fine, grin, mile	_____
2.	beat, leak, wall	_____
3.	fix, box, hot	_____
4.	toad, bone, cane	_____
5.	flat, toll, crab	_____

Score ___ / 5

Final Sounds

Which two words end with the same sound?

	Words	Response
1.	rib, jet, rob	_____
2.	just, jeep, neat	_____
3.	ten, been, them	_____
4.	coop, cake, book	_____
5.	fast, whip, pup	_____

Score ___ / 5

Foundational Skills Assessment • Phonemic Awareness

Phonemic Awareness

Name: _____ Date: _____

Record Sheet, Test 5

Match Phonemes

Initial Sounds

Which two words begin with the same sound?

Words	Response
1. rut, pot, pill	_____
2. give, fly, gash	_____
3. nest, fun, nine	_____
4. wind, won, tin	_____
5. zoo, jog, zip	_____

Score ___ / 5

Medial Sounds

Which two words have the same sound in the middle?

Words	Response
1. bet, yes, fan	_____
2. pail, goat, joke	_____
3. seal, sag, meet	_____
4. rug, sun, log	_____
5. sap, weed, cat	_____

Score ___ / 5

Final Sounds

Which two words end with the same sound?

Words	Response
1. hike, hole, look	_____
2. peep, rap, seem	_____
3. ball, smile, sip	_____
4. clay, say, see	_____
5. fog, fib, egg	_____

Score ___ / 5

Phonemic Awareness

Name: _____ Date: _____

Record Sheet, Test 6

Match Phonemes

Initial Sounds

Which two words begin with the same sound?

Words	Response
1. ripe, gate, rain	_____
2. van, vat, mad	_____
3. pin, pain, toss	_____
4. den, peg, dim	_____
5. lime, lap, ran	_____

Score ___ / 5

Medial Sounds

Which two words have the same sound in the middle?

Words	Response
1. nod, pot, pet	_____
2. dime, cone, vine	_____
3. tote, loan, fin	_____
4. mate, road, hope	_____
5. head, beg, sad	_____

Score ___ / 5

Final Sounds

Which two words end with the same sound?

Words	Response
1. chef, snip, off	_____
2. wake, cook, case	_____
3. pool, rope, tell	_____
4. fish, dust, bush	_____
5. fuss, less, pole	_____

Score ___ / 5

Phonemic Awareness

Blend Phonemes to Produce Words

This phonemic awareness test assesses a student's ability to combine phonemes to form words. Slowly say each sound in a word. Have the student say the word.

Instructions for Administering the Assessment

Make a copy of the record sheet for each child. Use the sheet to record the child's oral responses.

Say these directions to the child:

I am going to say a word, sound by sound. I want you to blend the sounds together and say the word. Let's try one. Listen: /s/ /a/ /d/. What word do you make when you blend the sounds /s/ /a/ /d/? (sad)

Directions for Scoring

Give 1 point for each correct response. The highest score for each set of items is 5.

Test 1, page A69

Answers for each set

Words with 3 Phonemes: **1.** fed; **2.** him; **3.** jug; **4.** fly; **5.** chin

Words with 4 Phonemes: **1.** brake (or break); **2.** sleep; **3.** nest; **4.** lamp; **5.** pinch

Test 2, page A70

Answers for each set

Words with 3 Phonemes: **1.** bad; **2.** rob; **3.** mud; **4.** fine; **5.** chop

Words with 4 Phonemes: **1.** smoke; **2.** treat; **3.** rust; **4.** glad; **5.** lunch

Test 3, page A71

Answers for each set

Words with 3 Phonemes: **1.** log; **2.** peg; **3.** hole; **4.** nail; **5.** shop

Words with 4 Phonemes: **1.** brave; **2.** train; **3.** spin; **4.** block; **5.** clash

Phonemic Awareness

Test 4, page A72

Answers for each set

Words with 3 Phonemes: **1.** lip; **2.** rug; **3.** jam; **4.** rain ; **5.** back

Words with 4 Phonemes: **1.** slide; **2.** sweet; **3.** plan; **4.** pump; **5.** flush

Test 5, page A73

Answers for each set

Words with 3 Phonemes: **1.** pet; **2.** tag; **3.** bib; **4.** snow; **5.** rock

Words with 4 Phonemes: **1.** green; **2.** brain; **3.** last; **4.** flip; **5.** bench

Test 6, page A74

Answers for each set

Words with 3 Phonemes: **1.** sip; **2.** rag; **3.** cone; **4.** race; **5.** ship

Words with 4 Phonemes: **1.** stone; **2.** flame; **3.** trap; **4.** flat; **5.** trash

Phonemic Awareness

Name: _____ Date: _____

Record Sheet, Test 1

Blend Phonemes to Produce Words

What word do you make when you blend the sounds…?

Words with 3 Phonemes

Phonemes	Response
1. /f/ /e/ /d/	_____
2. /h/ /i/ /m/	_____
3. /j/ /u/ /g/	_____
4. /f/ /l/ /ī/	_____
5. /ch/ /i/ /n/	_____

Score ___ / 5

Words with 4 Phonemes

Phonemes	Response
1. /b/ /r/ /ā/ /k/	_____
2. /s/ /l/ /ē/ /p/	_____
3. /n/ /e/ /s/ /t/	_____
4. /l/ /a/ /m/ /p/	_____
5. /p/ /i/ /n/ /ch/	_____

Score ___ / 5

Name: _____ Date: _____

Record Sheet, Test 2

Blend Phonemes to Produce Words

What word do you make when you blend the sounds…?

Words with 3 Phonemes

Phonemes	Response
1. /b/ /a/ /d/	_____
2. /r/ /o/ /b/	_____
3. /m/ /u/ /d/	_____
4. /f/ /ī/ /n/	_____
5. /ch/ /o/ /p/	_____

Score ___ / 5

Words with 4 Phonemes

Phonemes	Response
1. /s/ /m/ /ō/ /k/	_____
2. /t/ /r/ /ē/ /t/	_____
3. /r/ /u/ /s/ /t/	_____
4. /g/ /l/ /a/ /d/	_____
5. /l/ /u/ /n/ /ch/	_____

Score ___ / 5

Phonemic Awareness

Name: _____ Date: _____

Record Sheet, Test 3

Blend Phonemes to Produce Words

What word do you make when you blend the sounds…?

Words with 3 Phonemes

Phonemes	Response
1. /l/ /o/ /g/	_____
2. /p/ /e/ /g/	_____
3. /h/ /ō/ /l/	_____
4. /n/ /ā/ /l/	_____
5. /sh/ /o/ /p/	_____

Score ____ / 5

Words with 4 Phonemes

Phonemes	Response
1. /b/ /r/ /ā/ /v/	_____
2. /t/ /r/ /ā/ /n/	_____
3. /s/ /p/ /i/ /n/	_____
4. /b/ /l/ /o/ /k/	_____
5. /k/ /l/ /a/ /sh/	_____

Score ____ / 5

Name: _____ Date: _____

Record Sheet, Test 4

Blend Phonemes to Produce Words

What word do you make when you blend the sounds...?

Words with 3 Phonemes

Phonemes	Response

1. /l/ /i/ /p/   _____

2. /r/ /u/ /g/   _____

3. /j/ /a/ /m/   _____

4. /r/ /ā/ /n/   _____

5. /b/ /a/ /k/   _____

Score ___ / 5

Words with 4 Phonemes

Phonemes	Response

1. /s/ /l/ /ī/ /d/   _____

2. /s/ /w/ /ē/ /t/   _____

3. /p/ /l/ /a/ /n/   _____

4. /p/ /u/ /m/ /p/   _____

5. /f/ /l/ /u/ /sh/   _____

Score ___ / 5

Phonemic Awareness

Name: _____ Date: _____

Record Sheet, Test 5

Blend Phonemes to Produce Words

What word do you make when you blend the sounds…?

Words with 3 Phonemes

	Phonemes	Response
1.	/p/ /e/ /t/	_____
2.	/t/ /a/ /g/	_____
3.	/b/ /i/ /b/	_____
4.	/s/ /n/ /ō/	_____
5.	/r/ /o/ /k/	_____

Score ___ / 5

Words with 4 Phonemes

	Phonemes	Response
1.	/g/ /r/ /ē/ /n/	_____
2.	/b/ /r/ /ā/ /n/	_____
3.	/l/ /a/ /s/ /t/	_____
4.	/f/ /l/ /i/ /p/	_____
5.	/b/ /e/ /n/ /ch/	_____

Score ___ / 5

Name: _____ Date: _____

Record Sheet, Test 6

Blend Phonemes to Produce Words

What word do you make when you blend the sounds...?

Words with 3 Phonemes

	Phonemes	Response
1.	/s/ /i/ /p/	_____
2.	/r/ /a/ /g/	_____
3.	/k/ /ō/ /n/	_____
4.	/r/ /ā/ /s/	_____
5.	/sh/ /i/ /p/	_____

Score ___ / 5

Words with 4 Phonemes

	Phonemes	Response
1.	/s/ /t/ /ō/ /n/	_____
2.	/f/ /l/ /ā/ /m/	_____
3.	/t/ /r/ /a/ /p/	_____
4.	/f/ /l/ /a/ /t/	_____
5.	/t/ /r/ /a/ /sh/	_____

Score ___ / 5

Foundational Skills Assessment • Phonemic Awareness

Phonemic Awareness

Segment Words into Phonemes

This phonemic awareness test assesses a student's ability to break a word into its separate sounds. Say a word. Have the student segment the word into its sounds.

Instructions for Administering the Assessment

Make a copy of the record sheet for each child. Use the sheet to record the child's oral responses.

Say these directions to the child:

I am going to say a word. I want you to tell me all the sounds in the word. Let's try one. Tell me all the sounds you hear in the word pig. (/p/ /i/ /g/)

Directions for Scoring

Give 1 point for each correct response. The highest score for each set of items is 5.

Test 1, page A77

Answers for each set

Words with 3 Phonemes:
1. /r/ /u/ /b/; **2.** /g/ /o/ /t/; **3.** /f/ /ī/ /v/; **4.** /m/ /u/ /d/; **5.** /sh/ /ā/ /k/

Words with 4 Phonemes:
1. /t/ /r/ /ā/ /d/; **2.** /p/ /l/ /a/ /n/; **3.** /b/ /r/ /ā/ /v/; **4.** /d/ /e/ /s/ /k/; **5.** /k/ /a/ /m/ /p/

Test 2, page A78

Answers for each set

Words with 3 Phonemes:
1. /b/ /a/ /k/; **2.** /r/ /i/ /p/; **3.** /r/ /e/ /d/; **4.** /s/ /u/ /n/; **5.** /p/ /o/ /p/

Words with 4 Phonemes:
1. /s/ /l/ /a/ /p/; **2.** /s/ /t/ /ē/ /p/; **3.** /s/ /p/ /e/ /l/; **4.** /b/ /l/ /o/ /b/; **5.** /k/ /l/ /u/ /b/

Test 3, page A79

Answers for each set

Words with 3 Phonemes:
1. /j/ /a/ /m/; **2.** /t/ /e/ /n/; **3.** /k/ /i/ /t/; **4.** /j/ /o/ /b/; **5.** /b/ /u/ /s/

Words with 4 Phonemes:
1. /b/ /r/ /a/ /g/; **2.** /sh/ /e/ /l/ /f/; **3.** /sh/ /i/ /f/ /t/; **4.** /t/ /r/ /u/ /k/; **5.** /s/ /l/ /o/ /b/

Phonemic Awareness

Test 4, page A80

Answers for each set

Words with 3 Phonemes:
1. /f/ /a/ /n/; **2.** /s/ /i/ /p/; **3.** /s/ /u/ /m/; **4.** /sh/ /o/ /p/; **5.** /d/ /e/ /n/

Words with 4 Phonemes:
1. /s/ /p/ /i/ /l/; **2.** /k/ /l/ /a/ /m/; **3.** /p/ /o/ /n/ /d/; **4.** /s/ /l/ /u/ /g/; **5.** /d/ /r/ /e/ /s/

Test 5, page A81

Answers for each set

Words with 3 Phonemes:
1. /k/ /a/ /b/; **2.** /t/ /a/ /g/; **3.** /p/ /ē/ /l/; **4.** /k/ /i/ /k/; **5.** /r/ /u/ /g/

Words with 4 Phonemes:
1. /s/ /m/ /o/ /g/; **2.** /f/ /l/ /a/ /t/; **3.** /s/ /l/ /o/ /p/; **4.** /l/ /i/ /n/ /k/; **5.** /s/ /k/ /u/ /l/

Test 6, page A82

Answers for each set

Words with 3 Phonemes:
1. /p/ /a/ /d/; **2.** /v/ /e/ /t/; **3.** /m/ /u/ /g/; **4.** /z/ /i/ /p/; **5.** /d/ /o/ /l/

Words with 4 Phonemes:
1. /m/ /i/ /n/ /t/; **2.** /s/ /m/ /ô/ /l/; **3.** /s/ /p/ /i/ /n/; **4.** /d/ /r/ /u/ /m/; **5.** /b/ /e/ /s/ /t/

Phonemic Awareness

Name: _____ Date: _____

Record Sheet, Test 1

Segment Words into Phonemes

Tell me all the sounds you hear in the word . . . .

Words with 3 Phonemes

	Word	Response
1.	rub	_____
2.	got	_____
3.	five	_____
4.	mud	_____
5.	shake	_____

Score ___ / 5

Words with 4 Phonemes

	Word	Response
1.	trade	_____
2.	plan	_____
3.	brave	_____
4.	desk	_____
5.	camp	_____

Score ___ / 5

Phonemic Awareness

Name: _____ Date: _____

Record Sheet, Test 2

Segment Words into Phonemes

Tell me all the sounds you hear in the word . . . .

Words with 3 Phonemes

Word	Response
1. back	_____
2. rip	_____
3. red	_____
4. sun	_____
5. pop	_____

Score ___ / 5

Words with 4 Phonemes

Word	Response
1. slap	_____
2. steep	_____
3. spell	_____
4. blob	_____
5. club	_____

Score ___ / 5

Phonemic Awareness

Name: _____ Date: _____

Record Sheet, Test 3

Segment Words into Phonemes

Tell me all the sounds you hear in the word . . . .

Words with 3 Phonemes

Word	Response
1. jam	_____
2. ten	_____
3. kit	_____
4. job	_____
5. bus	_____

Score ___ / 5

Words with 4 Phonemes

Word	Response
1. brag	_____
2. shelf	_____
3. shift	_____
4. truck	_____
5. slob	_____

Score ___ / 5

Phonemic Awareness

Name: _____ Date: _____

Record Sheet, Test 4

Segment Words into Phonemes

Tell me all the sounds you hear in the word . . . .

Words with 3 Phonemes

Word	Response
1. fan	_____
2. sip	_____
3. sum	_____
4. shop	_____
5. den	_____

Score ___ / 5

Words with 4 Phonemes

Word	Response
1. spill	_____
2. clam	_____
3. pond	_____
4. slug	_____
5. dress	_____

Score ___ / 5

Phonemic Awareness

Name: _____ Date: _____

Record Sheet, Test 5

Segment Words into Phonemes

Tell me all the sounds you hear in the word . . . .

Words with 3 Phonemes

	Word	Response
1.	cab	_____
2.	tag	_____
3.	peel	_____
4.	kick	_____
5.	rug	_____

Score ___ / 5

Words with 4 Phonemes

	Word	Response
1.	smog	_____
2.	flat	_____
3.	slop	_____
4.	link	_____
5.	skull	_____

Score ___ / 5

Phonemic Awareness

Name: _____ Date: _____

Record Sheet, Test 6

Segment Words into Phonemes

Tell me all the sounds you hear in the word . . . .

Words with 3 Phonemes

Word	Response
1. pad	_____
2. vet	_____
3. mug	_____
4. zip	_____
5. doll	_____

Score ___ / 5

Words with 4 Phonemes

Word	Response
1. mint	_____
2. small	_____
3. spin	_____
4. drum	_____
5. best	_____

Score ___ / 5

Phonemic Awareness

Name: _____ Date: _____

Delete Phonemes to Make New Words, Test 1

This phonemic awareness test assesses a student's ability to manipulate sounds in words by deleting a phoneme from a word to make a new word. Say a word. Have the student delete a phoneme and say the new word. Make a copy of this page for each child, and record the child's oral responses. Give 1 point for each correct response. The highest score for each set of items is 5.

Delete Initial Sound

Listen to the word I say. Then delete the sound I say from the beginning of the word.

	Word		**Response**
1.	beat	*Delete /b/ from the beginning of beat.*	_____ (eat)
2.	cold	*Delete /k/ from the beginning of cold.*	_____ (old)
3.	cat	*Delete /k/ from the beginning of cat.*	_____ (at)
4.	table	*Delete /t/ from the beginning of table.*	_____ (able)
5.	cow	*Delete /k/ from the beginning of cow.*	_____ (ow)

Score ___ / 5

Delete Final Sound

Listen to the word I say. Then delete the sound I say from the end of the word.

	Word		**Response**
1.	seat	*Delete /t/ from the end of seat.*	_____ (sea)
2.	groan	*Delete /n/ from the end of groan.*	_____ (grow)
3.	stain	*Delete /n/ from the end of stain.*	_____ (stay)
4.	stoop	*Delete /p/ from the end of stoop.*	_____ (stew)
5.	sheep	*Delete /p/ from the end of sheep.*	_____ (she)

Score ___ / 5

Delete First Sound of Consonant Blend

Listen to the word I say. Then delete the sound I say from the beginning of the word.

	Word		**Response**
1.	slip	*Delete /s/ from the beginning of slip.*	_____ (lip)
2.	stun	*Delete /s/ from the beginning of stun.*	_____ (ton)
3.	block	*Delete /b/ from the beginning of block.*	_____ (lock)
4.	cram	*Delete /k/ from the beginning of cram.*	_____ (ram)
5.	crush	*Delete /k/ from the beginning of crush.*	_____ (rush)

Score ___ / 5

Name: _____ Date: _____

Delete Phonemes to Make New Words, Test 2

This phonemic awareness test assesses a student's ability to manipulate sounds in words by deleting a phoneme from a word to make a new word. Say a word. Have the student delete a phoneme and say the new word. Make a copy of this page for each child, and record the child's oral responses. Give 1 point for each correct response. The highest score for each set of items is 5.

Delete Initial Sound

Listen to the word I say. Then delete the sound I say from the beginning of the word.

	Word		**Response**
1.	bake	*Delete /b/ from the beginning of* bake.	_____ (ache)
2.	pink	*Delete /p/ from the beginning of* pink.	_____ (ink)
3.	tape	*Delete /t/ from the beginning of* tape.	_____ (ape)
4.	bin	*Delete /b/ from the beginning of* bin.	_____ (in)
5.	farm	*Delete /f/ from the beginning of* farm.	_____ (arm)

Score ___ / 5

Delete Final Sound

Listen to the word I say. Then delete the sound I say from the end of the word.

	Word		**Response**
1.	tone	*Delete /n/ from the end of* tone.	_____ (toe)
2.	soak	*Delete /k/ from the end of* soak.	_____ (so)
3.	wait	*Delete /t/ from the end of* wait.	_____ (way)
4.	pine	*Delete /n/ from the end of* pine.	_____ (pie)
5.	train	*Delete /n/ from the end of* train.	_____ (tray)

Score ___ / 5

Delete First Sound of Consonant Blend

Listen to the word I say. Then delete the sound I say from the beginning of the word.

	Word		**Response**
1.	played	*Delete /p/ from the beginning of* played.	_____ (laid)
2.	sweet	*Delete /s/ from the beginning of* sweet.	_____ (wheat)
3.	blend	*Delete /b/ from the beginning of* blend.	_____ (lend)
4.	stop	*Delete /s/ from the beginning of* stop.	_____ (top)
5.	grub	*Delete /g/ from the beginning of* grub.	_____ (rub)

Score ___ / 5

Phonemic Awareness

Name: _____ **Date:** _____

Delete Phonemes to Make New Words, Test 3

This phonemic awareness test assesses a student's ability to manipulate sounds in words by deleting a phoneme from a word to make a new word. Say a word. Have the student delete a phoneme and say the new word. Make a copy of this page for each child, and record the child's oral responses. Give 1 point for each correct response. The highest score for each set of items is 5.

Delete Initial Sound

Listen to the word I say. Then delete the sound I say from the beginning of the word.

	Word		**Response**
1.	towel	*Delete /t/ from the beginning of* towel.	_____ (owl)
2.	dear	*Delete /d/ from the beginning of* dear.	_____ (ear)
3.	tie	*Delete /t/ from the beginning of* tie.	_____ (I)
4.	pants	*Delete /p/ from the beginning of* pants.	_____ (ants)
5.	low	*Delete /l/ from the beginning of* low.	_____ (owe)

Score ____ / 5

Delete Final Sound

Listen to the word I say. Then delete the sound I say from the end of the word.

	Word		**Response**
1.	droop	*Delete /p/ from the end of* droop.	_____ (drew)
2.	soup	*Delete /p/ from the end of* soup.	_____ (sue)
3.	train	*Delete /n/ from the end of* train.	_____ (tray)
4.	inch	*Delete /ch/ from the end of* inch.	_____ (in)
5.	rose	*Delete /z/ from the end of* rose.	_____ (row)

Score ____ / 5

Delete First Sound of Consonant Blend

Listen to the word I say. Then delete the sound I say from the beginning of the word.

	Word		**Response**
1.	smile	*Delete /s/ from the beginning of* smile.	_____ (mile)
2.	strap	*Delete /s/ from the beginning of* strap.	_____ (trap)
3.	trust	*Delete /t/ from the beginning of* trust.	_____ (rust)
4.	sheet	*Delete /sh/ from the beginning of* sheet.	_____ (eat)
5.	slot	*Delete /s/ from the beginning of* slot.	_____ (lot)

Score ____ / 5

Name: _____ Date: _____

Delete Phonemes to Make New Words, Test 4

This phonemic awareness test assesses a student's ability to manipulate sounds in words by deleting a phoneme from a word to make a new word. Say a word. Have the student delete a phoneme and say the new word. Make a copy of this page for each child, and record the child's oral responses. Give 1 point for each correct response. The highest score for each set of items is 5.

Delete Initial Sound

Listen to the word I say. Then delete the sound I say from the beginning of the word.

	Word		**Response**
1.	leg	*Delete /l/ from the beginning of* leg.	_____ (egg)
2.	poke	*Delete /p/ from the beginning of* poke.	_____ (oak)
3.	fill	*Delete /f/ from the beginning of* fill.	_____ (ill)
4.	game	*Delete /g/ from the beginning of* game.	_____ (aim)
5.	paid	*Delete /p/ from the beginning of* paid.	_____ (aid)

Score ___ / 5

Delete Final Sound

Listen to the word I say. Then delete the sound I say from the end of the word.

	Word		**Response**
1.	road	*Delete /d/ from the end of* road.	_____ (row)
2.	meal	*Delete /l/ from the end of* meal.	_____ (me)
3.	pain	*Delete /n/ from the end of* pain.	_____ (pay)
4.	rain	*Delete /n/ from the end of* rain.	_____ (ray)
5.	belt	*Delete /t/ from the end of* belt.	_____ (bell)

Score ___ / 5

Delete First Sound of Consonant Blend

Listen to the word I say. Then delete the sound I say from the beginning of the word.

	Word		**Response**
1.	skin	*Delete /s/ from the beginning of* skin.	_____ (kin)
2.	crash	*Delete /k/ from the beginning of* crash.	_____ (rash)
3.	sled	*Delete /s/ from the beginning of* sled.	_____ (led)
4.	track	*Delete /t/ from the beginning of* track.	_____ (rack)
5.	snail	*Delete /s/ from the beginning of* snail.	_____ (nail)

Score ___ / 5

Phonemic Awareness

Name: _____ **Date:** _____

Delete Phonemes to Make New Words, Test 5

This phonemic awareness test assesses a student's ability to manipulate sounds in words by deleting a phoneme from a word to make a new word. Say a word. Have the student delete a phoneme and say the new word. Make a copy of this page for each child, and record the child's oral responses. Give 1 point for each correct response. The highest score for each set of items is 5.

Delete Initial Sound

Listen to the word I say. Then delete the sound I say from the beginning of the word.

	Word		**Response**
1.	sit	*Delete /s/ from the beginning of* sit.	_____ (it)
2.	nod	*Delete /n/ from the beginning of* nod.	_____ (odd)
3.	phone	*Delete /f/ from the beginning of* phone.	_____ (own)
4.	Sam	*Delete /s/ from the beginning of* Sam.	_____ (am)
5.	lash	*Delete /l/ from the beginning of* lash.	_____ (ash)
			Score ___ / 5

Delete Final Sound

Listen to the word I say. Then delete the sound I say from the end of the word.

	Word		**Response**
1.	place	*Delete /s/ from the end of* place.	_____ (play)
2.	feet	*Delete /t/ from the end of* feet.	_____ (fee)
3.	ramp	*Delete /p/ from the end of* ramp.	_____ (ram)
4.	felt	*Delete /t/ from the end of* felt.	_____ (fell)
5.	throat	*Delete /t/ from the end of* throat.	_____ (throw)
			Score ___ / 5

Delete First Sound of Consonant Blend

Listen to the word I say. Then delete the sound I say from the beginning of the word.

	Word		**Response**
1.	draft	*Delete /d/ from the beginning of* draft.	_____ (raft)
2.	stuck	*Delete /s/ from the beginning of* stuck.	_____ (tuck)
3.	sleep	*Delete /s/ from the beginning of* sleep.	_____ (leap)
4.	prank	*Delete /p/ from the beginning of* prank.	_____ (rank)
5.	click	*Delete /k/ from the beginning of* click.	_____ (lick)
			Score ___ / 5

Phonemic Awareness

Name: _____ **Date:** _____

Delete Phonemes to Make New Words, Test 6

This phonemic awareness test assesses a student's ability to manipulate sounds in words by deleting a phoneme from a word to make a new word. Say a word. Have the student delete a phoneme and say the new word. Make a copy of this page for each child, and record the child's oral responses. Give 1 point for each correct response. The highest score for each set of items is 5.

Delete Initial Sound

Listen to the word I say. Then delete the sound I say from the beginning of the word.

	Word		**Response**
1.	same	*Delete /s/ from the beginning of same.*	_____ (aim)
2.	fat	*Delete /f/ from the beginning of fat.*	_____ (at)
3.	hair	*Delete /h/ from the beginning of hair.*	_____ (air)
4.	chin	*Delete /ch/ from the beginning of chin.*	_____ (in)
5.	jar	*Delete /j/ from the beginning of jar.*	_____ (are)

Score ___ / 5

Delete Final Sound

Listen to the word I say. Then delete the sound I say from the end of the word.

	Word		**Response**
1.	weed	*Delete /d/ from the end of weed.*	_____ (we)
2.	cart	*Delete /t/ from the end of cart.*	_____ (car)
3.	plant	*Delete /t/ from the end of plant.*	_____ (plan)
4.	side	*Delete /d/ from the end of side.*	_____ (sigh)
5.	wage	*Delete /j/ from the end of wage.*	_____ (way)

Score ___ / 5

Delete First Sound of Consonant Blend

Listen to the word I say. Then delete the sound I say from the beginning of the word.

	Word		**Response**
1.	bridge	*Delete /b/ from the beginning of bridge.*	_____ (ridge)
2.	drench	*Delete /d/ from the beginning of drench.*	_____ (wrench)
3.	clean	*Delete /k/ from the beginning of clean.*	_____ (lean)
4.	blame	*Delete /b/ from the beginning of blame.*	_____ (lame)
5.	flight	*Delete /f/ from the beginning of flight.*	_____ (light)

Score ___ / 5

Phonemic Awareness

Name: _____ **Date:** _____

Add Phonemes to Make New Words, Test 1

This phonemic awareness test assesses a student's ability to manipulate sounds in words by adding a phoneme to a word to make a new word. Say a word. Have the student add a phoneme and say the new word. Make a copy of this page for each child, and record the child's oral responses. Give 1 point for each correct response. The highest score for each set of items is 5.

Add Initial Sound

Listen to the word I say. Then add the sound I say to the beginning of the word.

	Word		**Response**	
1.	an	*Add /k/ to the beginning of* an.	_____	(can)
2.	ice	*Add /m/ to the beginning of* ice.	_____	(mice)
3.	eel	*Add /s/ to the beginning of* eel.	_____	(seal)
4.	out	*Add /p/ to the beginning of* out.	_____	(pout)
5.	ox	*Add /f/ to the beginning of* ox.	_____	(fox)

Score ___ / 5

Add Final Sound

Listen to the word I say. Then add the sound I say to the end of the word.

	Word		**Response**	
1.	bee	*Add /d/ to the end of* bee.	_____	(bead)
2.	way	*Add /v/ to the end of* way.	_____	(wave)
3.	he	*Add /t/ to the end of* he.	_____	(heat)
4.	no	*Add /z/ to the end of* no.	_____	(nose)
5.	boo	*Add /m/ to the end of* boo.	_____	(boom)

Score ___ / 5

Add First Sound of Consonant Blend

Listen to the word I say. Then add the sound I say to the beginning of the word.

	Word		**Response**	
1.	ranch	*Add /b/ to the beginning of* ranch.	_____	(branch)
2.	loud	*Add /k/ to the beginning of* loud.	_____	(cloud)
3.	win	*Add /t/ to the beginning of* win.	_____	(twin)
4.	tar	*Add /s/ to the beginning of* tar.	_____	(star)
5.	ray	*Add /g/ to the beginning of* ray.	_____	(gray)

Score ___ / 5

Name: _____ Date: _____

Add Phonemes to Make New Words, Test 2

This phonemic awareness test assesses a student's ability to manipulate sounds in words by adding a phoneme to a word to make a new word. Say a word. Have the student add a phoneme and say the new word. Make a copy of this page for each child, and record the child's oral responses. Give 1 point for each correct response. The highest score for each set of items is 5.

Add Initial Sound

Listen to the word I say. Then add the sound I say to the beginning of the word.

	Word		Response
1.	odd	*Add /r/ to the beginning of odd.*	_____ (rod)
2.	egg	*Add /p/ to the beginning of egg.*	_____ (peg)
3.	am	*Add /h/ to the beginning of am.*	_____ (ham)
4.	old	*Add /k/ to the beginning of old.*	_____ (cold)
5.	own	*Add /m/ to the beginning of own.*	_____ (moan)

Score ___ / 5

Add Final Sound

Listen to the word I say. Then add the sound I say to the end of the word.

	Word		Response
1.	knee	*Add /t/ to the end of knee.*	_____ (neat)
2.	bow	*Add /n/ to the end of bow.*	_____ (bone)
3.	do	*Add /n/ to the end of do.*	_____ (dune)
4.	key	*Add /p/ to the end of key.*	_____ (keep)
5.	go	*Add /t/ to the end of go.*	_____ (goat)

Score ___ / 5

Add First Sound of Consonant Blend

Listen to the word I say. Then add the sound I say to the beginning of the word.

	Word		Response
1.	lame	*Add /f/ to the beginning of lame.*	_____ (flame)
2.	ride	*Add /t/ to the beginning of ride.*	_____ (tried)
3.	rank	*Add /d/ to the beginning of rank.*	_____ (drank)
4.	lend	*Add /b/ to the beginning of lend.*	_____ (blend)
5.	rip	*Add /g/ to the beginning of rip.*	_____ (grip)

Score ___ / 5

Phonemic Awareness

Name: _____ Date: _____

Add Phonemes to Make New Words, Test 3

This phonemic awareness test assesses a student's ability to manipulate sounds in words by adding a phoneme to a word to make a new word. Say a word. Have the student add a phoneme and say the new word. Make a copy of this page for each child, and record the child's oral responses. Give 1 point for each correct response. The highest score for each set of items is 5.

Add Initial Sound

Listen to the word I say. Then add the sound I say to the beginning of the word.

	Word		Response
1.	an	*Add /v/ to the beginning of an.*	_____ (van)
2.	oak	*Add /s/ to the beginning of oak.*	_____ (soak)
3.	at	*Add /k/ to the beginning of at.*	_____ (cat)
4.	in	*Add /t/ to the beginning of in.*	_____ (tin)
5.	are	*Add /t/ to the beginning of are.*	_____ (tar)

Score ___ / 5

Add Final Sound

Listen to the word I say. Then add the sound I say to the end of the word.

	Word		Response
1.	tea	*Add /m/ to the end of tea.*	_____ (team)
2.	day	*Add /t/ to the end of day.*	_____ (date)
3.	lie	*Add /f/ to the end of lie.*	_____ (life)
4.	pay	*Add /s/ to the end of pay.*	_____ (pace)
5.	two	*Add /n/ to the end of two.*	_____ (tune)

Score ___ / 5

Add First Sound of Consonant Blend

Listen to the word I say. Then add the sound I say to the beginning of the word.

	Word		Response
1.	link	*Add /k/ to the beginning of link.*	_____ (clink)
2.	rag	*Add /d/ to the beginning of rag.*	_____ (drag)
3.	lot	*Add /p/ to the beginning of lot.*	_____ (plot)
4.	rust	*Add /k/ to the beginning of rust.*	_____ (crust)
5.	lump	*Add /s/ to the beginning of lump.*	_____ (slump)

Score ___ / 5

Name: _____ Date: _____

Add Phonemes to Make New Words, Test 4

This phonemic awareness test assesses a student's ability to manipulate sounds in words by adding a phoneme to a word to make a new word. Say a word. Have the student add a phoneme and say the new word. Make a copy of this page for each child, and record the child's oral responses. Give 1 point for each correct response. The highest score for each set of items is 5.

Add Initial Sound

Listen to the word I say. Then add the sound I say to the beginning of the word.

	Word		**Response**
1.	oat	*Add /v/ to the beginning of oat.*	_____ (vote)
2.	ice	*Add /r/ to the beginning of ice.*	_____ (rice)
3.	up	*Add /k/ to the beginning of up.*	_____ (cup)
4.	add	*Add /l/ to the beginning of add.*	_____ (lad)
5.	ear	*Add /t/ to the beginning of ear.*	_____ (tear)

Score ___ / 5

Add Final Sound

Listen to the word I say. Then add the sound I say to the end of the word.

	Word		**Response**
1.	fee	*Add /d/ to the end of fee.*	_____ (feed)
2.	how	*Add /s/ to the end of how.*	_____ (house)
3.	may	*Add /n/ to the end of may.*	_____ (main)
4.	buy	*Add /t/ to the end of buy.*	_____ (bite)
5.	know	*Add /t/ to the end of know.*	_____ (note)

Score ___ / 5

Add First Sound of Consonant Blend

Listen to the word I say. Then add the sound I say to the beginning of the word.

	Word		**Response**
1.	lid	*Add /s/ to the beginning of lid.*	_____ (slid)
2.	lane	*Add /p/ to the beginning of lane.*	_____ (plane)
3.	paid	*Add /s/ to the beginning of paid.*	_____ (spade)
4.	lock	*Add /f/ to the beginning of lock.*	_____ (flock)
5.	rim	*Add /t/ to the beginning of rim.*	_____ (trim)

Score ___ / 5

Phonemic Awareness

Name: _____ Date: _____

Add Phonemes to Make New Words, Test 5

This phonemic awareness test assesses a student's ability to manipulate sounds in words by adding a phoneme to a word to make a new word. Say a word. Have the student add a phoneme and say the new word. Make a copy of this page for each child, and record the child's oral responses. Give 1 point for each correct response. The highest score for each set of items is 5.

Add Initial Sound

Listen to the word I say. Then add the sound I say to the beginning of the word.

	Word		**Response**
1.	add	*Add /p/ to the beginning of* add.	_____ (pad)
2.	us	*Add /b/ to the beginning of* us.	_____ (bus)
3.	air	*Add /t/ to the beginning of* air.	_____ (tear)
4.	oar	*Add /m/ to the beginning of* oar.	_____ (more)
5.	own	*Add /t/ to the beginning of* own.	_____ (tone)

Score ___ / 5

Add Final Sound

Listen to the word I say. Then add the sound I say to the end of the word.

	Word		**Response**
1.	tie	*Add /m/ to the end of* tie.	_____ (time)
2.	day	*Add /z/ to the end of* day.	_____ (daze)
3.	see	*Add /t/ to the end of* see.	_____ (seat)
4.	Sue	*Add /p/ to the end of* Sue.	_____ (soup)
5.	low	*Add /n/ to the end of* low.	_____ (loan)

Score ___ / 5

Add First Sound of Consonant Blend

Listen to the word I say. Then add the sound I say to the beginning of the word.

	Word		**Response**
1.	rise	*Add /p/ to the beginning of* rise.	_____ (prize)
2.	lab	*Add /s/ to the beginning of* lab.	_____ (slab)
3.	lush	*Add /p/ to the beginning of* lush.	_____ (plush)
4.	rake	*Add /b/ to the beginning of* rake.	_____ (break)
5.	tone	*Add /s/ to the beginning of* tone.	_____ (stone)

Score ___ / 5

Phonemic Awareness

Name: _____ Date: _____

Add Phonemes to Make New Words, Test 6

This phonemic awareness test assesses a student's ability to manipulate sounds in words by adding a phoneme to a word to make a new word. Say a word. Have the student add a phoneme and say the new word. Make a copy of this page for each child, and record the child's oral responses. Give 1 point for each correct response. The highest score for each set of items is 5.

Add Initial Sound

Listen to the word I say. Then add the sound I say to the beginning of the word.

	Word		**Response**
1.	all	*Add /f/ to the beginning of* all.	_____ (fall)
2.	own	*Add /l/ to the beginning of* own.	_____ (lone)
3.	is	*Add /h/ to the beginning of* is.	_____ (his)
4.	oat	*Add /b/ to the beginning of* oat.	_____ (boat)
5.	an	*Add /m/ to the beginning of* an.	_____ (man)

Score ___ / 5

Add Final Sound

Listen to the word I say. Then add the sound I say to the end of the word.

	Word		**Response**
1.	lay	*Add /t/ to the end of* lay.	_____ (late)
2.	tie	*Add /m/ to the end of* tie.	_____ (time)
3.	toe	*Add /d/ to the end of* toe.	_____ (toad)
4.	ray	*Add /n/ to the end of* ray.	_____ (rain)
5.	high	*Add /v/ to the end of* high.	_____ (hive)

Score ___ / 5

Add First Sound of Consonant Blend

Listen to the word I say. Then add the sound I say to the beginning of the word.

	Word		**Response**
1.	pill	*Add /s/ to the beginning of* pill.	_____ (spill)
2.	poke	*Add /s/ to the beginning of* poke.	_____ (spoke)
3.	lace	*Add /p/ to the beginning of* lace.	_____ (place)
4.	lap	*Add /k/ to the beginning of* lap.	_____ (clap)
5.	lap	*Add /f/ to the beginning of* lap.	_____ (flap)

Score ___ / 5

Phonemic Awareness

Name: _____ **Date:** _____

Substitute Phonemes to Make New Words, Test 1

This phonemic awareness test assesses a student's ability to manipulate sounds in words by substituting one phoneme for another to make a new word. Say a word. Have the student replace one phoneme and say the new word. Make a copy of this page for each child, and record the child's oral responses. Give 1 point for each correct response. The highest score for each set of items is 5.

Initial Sound Substitution

Listen to the word I say. Then change the sound I say at the beginning of the word.

	Word		**Response**	
1.	ham	*Change the /h/ to /r/.*	_____	(ram)
2.	face	*Change the /f/ to /p/.*	_____	(pace)
3.	jet	*Change the /j/ to /s/.*	_____	(set)
4.	line	*Change the /l/ to /n/.*	_____	(nine)
5.	house	*Change the /h/ to /m/.*	_____	(mouse)

Score ___ / 5

Final Sound Substitution

Listen to the word I say. Then change the sound I say at the end of the word.

	Word		**Response**	
1.	has	*Change the /z/ to /t/.*	_____	(hat)
2.	fig	*Change the /g/ to /n/.*	_____	(fin)
3.	safe	*Change the /f/ to /m/.*	_____	(same)
4.	hot	*Change the /t/ to /p/.*	_____	(hop)
5.	rode	*Change the /d/ to /z/.*	_____	(rose)

Score ___ / 5

Medial Sound Substitution

Listen to the word I say. Then change the sound I say in the middle of the word.

1.	lip	*Change the /i/ to /a/.*	_____	(lap)
2.	sad	*Change the /a/ to /ī/.*	_____	(side)
3.	rake	*Change the /ā/ to /o/.*	_____	(rock)
4.	rode	*Change the /ō/ to /e/.*	_____	(red)
5.	pile	*Change the /ī/ to /i/.*	_____	(pill)

Score ___ / 5

Name: _____ Date: _____

Substitute Phonemes to Make New Words, Test 2

This phonemic awareness test assesses a student's ability to manipulate sounds in words by substituting one phoneme for another to make a new word. Say a word. Have the student replace one phoneme and say the new word. Make a copy of this page for each child, and record the child's oral responses. Give 1 point for each correct response. The highest score for each set of items is 5.

Initial Sound Substitution

Listen to the word I say. Then change the sound I say at the beginning of the word.

	Word		**Response**
1.	lice	*Change the /l/ to /m/.*	_____ (mice)
2.	cut	*Change the /k/ to /n/.*	_____ (nut)
3.	ditch	*Change the /d/ to /p/.*	_____ (pitch)
4.	bat	*Change the /b/ to /f/.*	_____ (fat)
5.	case	*Change the /k/ to /f/.*	_____ (face)

Score ___ / 5

Final Sound Substitution

Listen to the word I say. Then change the sound I say at the end of the word.

	Word		**Response**
1.	win	*Change the /n/ to /g/.*	_____ (wig)
2.	tape	*Change the /p/ to /m/.*	_____ (tame)
3.	food	*Change the /d/ to /l/.*	_____ (fool)
4.	tack	*Change the /k/ to /p/.*	_____ (tap)
5.	dig	*Change the /g/ to /m/.*	_____ (dim)

Score ___ / 5

Medial Sound Substitution

Listen to the word I say. Then change the sound I say in the middle of the word.

	Word		**Response**
1.	cup	*Change the /u/ to /a/.*	_____ (cap)
2.	math	*Change the /a/ to /ô/.*	_____ (moth)
3.	kick	*Change the /i/ to /ù/.*	_____ (cook)
4.	tap	*Change the /a/ to /ī/.*	_____ (type)
5.	tin	*Change the /i/ to /a/.*	_____ (tan)

Score ___ / 5

Phonemic Awareness

Name: _____ Date: _____

Substitute Phonemes to Make New Words, Test 3

This phonemic awareness test assesses a student's ability to manipulate sounds in words by substituting one phoneme for another to make a new word. Say a word. Have the student replace one phoneme and say the new word. Make a copy of this page for each child, and record the child's oral responses. Give 1 point for each correct response. The highest score for each set of items is 5.

Initial Sound Substitution

Listen to the word I say. Then change the sound I say at the beginning of the word.

	Word		**Response**
1.	said	*Change the /s/ to /r/.*	_____ (red)
2.	rice	*Change the /r/ to /n/.*	_____ (nice)
3.	took	*Change the /t/ to /b/.*	_____ (book)
4.	root	*Change the /r/ to /b/.*	_____ (boot)
5.	gem	*Change the /j/ to /h/.*	_____ (hem)

Score ___ / 5

Final Sound Substitution

Listen to the word I say. Then change the sound I say at the end of the word.

	Word		**Response**
1.	leave	*Change the /v/ to /n/.*	_____ (lean)
2.	came	*Change the /m/ to /n/.*	_____ (cane)
3.	gain	*Change the /n/ to /m/.*	_____ (game)
4.	sip	*Change the /p/ to /t/.*	_____ (sit)
5.	kit	*Change the /t/ to /d/.*	_____ (kid)

Score ___ / 5

Medial Sound Substitution

Listen to the word I say. Then change the sound I say in the middle of the word.

	Word		**Response**
1.	rack	*Change the /a/ to /ā/.*	_____ (rake)
2.	rap	*Change the /a/ to /i/.*	_____ (rip)
3.	bit	*Change the /i/ to /a/.*	_____ (bat)
4.	team	*Change the /ē/ to /ā/.*	_____ (tame)
5.	cub	*Change the /u/ to /a/.*	_____ (cab)

Score ___ / 5

Phonemic Awareness

Name: _____ Date: _____

Substitute Phonemes to Make New Words, Test 4

This phonemic awareness test assesses a student's ability to manipulate sounds in words by substituting one phoneme for another to make a new word. Say a word. Have the student replace one phoneme and say the new word. Make a copy of this page for each child, and record the child's oral responses. Give 1 point for each correct response. The highest score for each set of items is 5.

Initial Sound Substitution

Listen to the word I say. Then change the sound I say at the beginning of the word.

	Word		Response
1.	tip	*Change the /t/ to /r/.*	_____ (rip)
2.	pace	*Change the /p/ to /k/.*	_____ (case)
3.	less	*Change the /l/ to /m/.*	_____ (mess)
4.	fine	*Change the /f/ to /l/.*	_____ (line)
5.	when	*Change the /hw/ to /h/.*	_____ (hen)

Score ___ / 5

Final Sound Substitution

Listen to the word I say. Then change the sound I say at the end of the word.

	Word		Response
1.	pen	*Change the /n/ to /t/.*	_____ (pet)
2.	load	*Change the /d/ to /f/.*	_____ (loaf)
3.	boat	*Change the /t/ to /n/.*	_____ (bone)
4.	tail	*Change the /l/ to /p/.*	_____ (tape)
5.	mat	*Change the /t/ to /p/.*	_____ (map)

Score ___ / 5

Medial Sound Substitution

Listen to the word I say. Then change the sound I say in the middle of the word.

	Word		Response
1.	late	*Change the /ā/ to /ī/.*	_____ (light)
2.	lick	*Change the /i/ to /ü/.*	_____ (look)
3.	bat	*Change the /a/ to /ō/.*	_____ (boat)
4.	den	*Change the /e/ to /u/.*	_____ (done)
5.	pool	*Change the /ü/ to /u̇/.*	_____ (pull)

Score ___ / 5

Foundational Skills Assessment • Phonemic Awareness

Phonemic Awareness

Name: _____ **Date:** _____

Substitute Phonemes to Make New Words, Test 5

This phonemic awareness test assesses a student's ability to manipulate sounds in words by substituting one phoneme for another to make a new word. Say a word. Have the student replace one phoneme and say the new word. Make a copy of this page for each child, and record the child's oral responses. Give 1 point for each correct response. The highest score for each set of items is 5.

Initial Sound Substitution

Listen to the word I say. Then change the sound I say at the beginning of the word.

	Word		**Response**	
1.	rode	*Change the /r/ to /l/.*	_____	(load)
2.	jog	*Change the /j/ to /h/.*	_____	(hog)
3.	yes	*Change the /y/ to /m/.*	_____	(mess)
4.	moat	*Change the /m/ to /b/.*	_____	(boat)
5.	vet	*Change the /v/ to /n/.*	_____	(net)

Score ___ / 5

Final Sound Substitution

Listen to the word I say. Then change the sound I say at the end of the word.

	Word		**Response**	
1.	cage	*Change the /j/ to /n/.*	_____	(cane)
2.	laugh	*Change the /f/ to /k/.*	_____	(lack)
3.	hug	*Change the /g/ to /m/.*	_____	(hum)
4.	toad	*Change the /d/ to /n/.*	_____	(tone)
5.	sick	*Change the /k/ to /p/.*	_____	(sip)

Score ___ / 5

Medial Sound Substitution

Listen to the word I say. Then change the sound I say in the middle of the word.

	Word		**Response**	
1.	cape	*Change the /ā/ to /u/.*	_____	(cup)
2.	ram	*Change the /a/ to /ü/.*	_____	(room)
3.	gem	*Change the /e/ to /a/.*	_____	(jam)
4.	time	*Change the /ī/ to /ā/.*	_____	(tame)
5.	rip	*Change the /i/ to /ī/.*	_____	(ripe)

Score ___ / 5

Phonemic Awareness

Name: _____ Date: _____

Substitute Phonemes to Make New Words, Test 6

This phonemic awareness test assesses a student's ability to manipulate sounds in words by substituting one phoneme for another to make a new word. Say a word. Have the student replace one phoneme and say the new word. Make a copy of this page for each child, and record the child's oral responses. Give 1 point for each correct response. The highest score for each set of items is 5.

Initial Sound Substitution

Listen to the word I say. Then change the sound I say at the beginning of the word.

	Word		Response
1.	tote	*Change the /t/ to /v/.*	_____ (vote)
2.	lick	*Change the /l/ to /w/.*	_____ (wick)
3.	hood	*Change the /h/ to /g/.*	_____ (good)
4.	mill	*Change the /m/ to /h/.*	_____ (hill)
5.	fed	*Change the /f/ to /r/.*	_____ (red)

Score ___ / 5

Final Sound Substitution

Listen to the word I say. Then change the sound I say at the end of the word.

	Word		Response
1.	rag	*Change the /g/ to /t/.*	_____ (rat)
2.	comb	*Change the /m/ to /n/.*	_____ (cone)
3.	bun	*Change the /n/ to /k/.*	_____ (buck)
4.	moat	*Change the /t/ to /l/.*	_____ (mole)
5.	cave	*Change the /v/ to /k/.*	_____ (cake)

Score ___ / 5

Medial Sound Substitution

Listen to the word I say. Then change the sound I say in the middle of the word.

	Word		Response
1.	bud	*Change the /u/ to /i/.*	_____ (bid)
2.	cat	*Change the /a/ to /u/.*	_____ (cut)
3.	made	*Change the /ā/ to /u/.*	_____ (mud)
4.	fig	*Change the /i/ to /o/.*	_____ (fog)
5.	bill	*Change the /i/ to /ō/.*	_____ (bowl)

Score ___ / 5

Foundational Skills Assessment • **Phonemic Awareness**

Phonemic Awareness

Represent Phonemes with Letters, Test 1

This phonemic awareness test assesses a student's ability to connect sound to letter. Name a picture. Have the student circle the letter for the first, last, or middle sound in the picture name.

Instructions for Administering the Assessment

Make a copy of pages A113, A114, and A115 for each child.

Say these directions to the child.

Page A113: Initial Consonants

1. *Look at Number 1* (point to the number). *This is a picture of a cat. Circle the letter that stands for the sound at the beginning of* cat.

2. *Look at Number 2* (point to the number). *This is a picture of a table. Circle the letter that stands for the sound at the beginning of* table.

3. *Look at Number 3* (point to the number). *This is a picture of a bee. Circle the letter that stands for the sound at the beginning of* bee.

4. *Look at Number 4* (point to the number). *This is a picture of a rake. Circle the letter that stands for the sound at the beginning of* rake.

5. *Look at Number 5* (point to the number). *This is a picture of a vest. Circle the letter that stands for the sound at the beginning of* vest.

Page A114: Final Consonants

1. *Look at Number 1* (point to the number). *This is a picture of a bat. Circle the letter that stands for the sound at the end of* bat.

2. *Look at Number 2* (point to the number). *This is a picture of a pig. Circle the letter that stands for the sound at the end of* pig.

3. *Look at Number 3* (point to the number). *This is a picture of a bell. Circle the letter that stands for the sound at the end of* bell.

4. *Look at Number 4* (point to the number). *This is a picture of a web. Circle the letter that stands for the sound at the end of* web.

5. *Look at Number 5* (point to the number). *This is a picture of a book. Circle the letter that stands for the sound at the end of* book.

Phonemic Awareness

Page A115: Vowels

1. *Look at Number 1* (point to the number). *This is a picture of a rug. Circle the letter that stands for the sound you hear in the middle of* rug.

2. *Look at Number 2* (point to the number). *This is a picture of a cap. Circle the letter that stands for the sound you hear in the middle of* cap.

3. *Look at Number 3* (point to the number). *This is a picture of a mop. Circle the letter that stands for the sound you hear in the middle of* mop.

4. *Look at Number 4* (point to the number). *This is a picture of a bed. Circle the letter that stands for the sound you hear in the middle of* bed.

5. *Look at Number 5* (point to the number). *This is a picture of a wig. Circle the letter that stands for the sound you hear in the middle of* wig.

Directions for Scoring

Give 1 point for each correct response. The highest score for each set of items is 5.

Answers for each set

Page A113: **1.** c; **2.** t; **3.** b; **4.** r; **5.** v

Page A114: **1.** t; **2.** g; **3.** l; **4.** b; **5.** k

Page A115: **1.** u; **2.** a; **3.** o; **4.** e; **5.** i

Phonemic Awareness

Represent Phonemes with Letters, Test 2

This phonemic awareness test assesses a student's ability to connect sound to letter. Name a picture. Have the student circle the letter for the first, last, or middle sound in the picture name.

Instructions for Administering the Assessment

Make a copy of pages A116, A117, and A118 for each child.

Say these directions to the child.

Page A116: Initial Consonants

1. *Look at Number 1* (point to the number). *This is a picture of a basket. Circle the letter that stands for the sound at the beginning of* basket.

2. *Look at Number 2* (point to the number). *This is a picture of a fox. Circle the letter that stands for the sound at the beginning of* fox.

3. *Look at Number 3* (point to the number). *This is a picture of a log. Circle the letter that stands for the sound at the beginning of* log.

4. *Look at Number 4* (point to the number). *This is a picture of pants. Circle the letter that stands for the sound at the beginning of* pants.

5. *Look at Number 5* (point to the number). *This is a picture of a dog. Circle the letter that stands for the sound at the beginning of* dog.

Page A117: Final Consonants

1. *Look at Number 1* (point to the number). *This is a picture of a flag. Circle the letter that stands for the sound at the end of* flag.

2. *Look at Number 2* (point to the number). *This is a picture of a bus. Circle the letter that stands for the sound at the end of* bus.

3. *Look at Number 3* (point to the number). *This is a picture of a box. Circle the letter that stands for the sound at the end of* box.

4. *Look at Number 4* (point to the number). *This is a picture of a star. Circle the letter that stands for the sound at the end of* star.

5. *Look at Number 5* (point to the number). *This is a picture of a kite. Circle the letter that stands for the sound at the end of* kite.

Phonemic Awareness

Page A118: Vowels

1. *Look at Number 1* (point to the number). *This is a picture of a leg. Circle the letter that stands for the sound you hear in the middle of* leg.

2. *Look at Number 2* (point to the number). *This is a picture of fish. Circle the letter that stands for the sound you hear in the middle of* fish.

3. *Look at Number 3* (point to the number). *This is a picture of the sun. Circle the letter that stands for the sound you hear in the middle of* sun.

4. *Look at Number 4* (point to the number). *This is a picture of a clock. Circle the letter that stands for the sound you hear in the middle of* clock.

5. *Look at Number 5* (point to the number). *This is a picture of a tack. Circle the letter that stands for the sound you hear in the middle of* tack.

Directions for Scoring

Give 1 point for each correct response. The highest score for each set of items is 5.

Answers for each set

Initial Consonants, page A116: **1.** b; **2.** f; **3.** l; **4.** p; **5.** d

Final Consonants, page A117: **1.** g; **2.** s; **3.** x; **4.** r; **5.** t

Vowels, page A118: **1.** e; **2.** i; **3.** u; **4.** o; **5.** a

Represent Phonemes with Letters, Test 3

This phonemic awareness test assesses a student's ability to connect sound to letter. Name a picture. Have the student circle the letter for the first, last, or middle sound in the picture name.

Instructions for Administering the Assessment

Make a copy of pages A119, A120, and A121 for each child.

Say these directions to the child.

Page A119: Initial Consonants

1. *Look at Number 1* (point to the number). *This is a picture of a neck. Circle the letter that stands for the sound at the beginning of* neck.

2. *Look at Number 2* (point to the number). *This is a picture of a goat. Circle the letter that stands for the sound at the beginning of* goat.

3. *Look at Number 3* (point to the number). *This is a picture of a wall. Circle the letter that stands for the sound at the beginning of* wall.

4. *Look at Number 4* (point to the number). *This is a picture of a lizard. Circle the letter that stands for the sound at the beginning of* lizard.

5. *Look at Number 5* (point to the number). *This is a picture of pancakes. Circle the letter that stands for the sound at the beginning of* pancakes.

Page A120: Final Consonants

1. *Look at Number 1* (point to the number). *This is a picture of the number five. Circle the letter that stands for the sound at the end of* five.

2. *Look at Number 2* (point to the number). *This is a picture of a seal. Circle the letter that stands for the sound at the end of* seal.

3. *Look at Number 3* (point to the number). *This is a picture of a lion. Circle the letter that stands for the sound at the end of* lion.

4. *Look at Number 4* (point to the number). *This is a picture of tape. Circle the letter that stands for the sound at the end of* tape.

5. *Look at Number 5* (point to the number). *This is a picture of an ear. Circle the letter that stands for the sound at the end of* ear.

Phonemic Awareness

Page A121: Vowels

1. *Look at Number 1* (point to the number). *This is a picture of a duck. Circle the letter that stands for the sound you hear in the middle of* duck.

2. *Look at Number 2* (point to the number). *This is a picture of a pot. Circle the letter that stands for the sound you hear in the middle of* pot.

3. *Look at Number 3* (point to the number). *This is a picture of a pen. Circle the letter that stands for the sound you hear in the middle of* pen.

4. *Look at Number 4* (point to the number). *This is a picture of a rat. Circle the letter that stands for the sound you hear in the middle of* rat.

5. *Look at Number 5* (point to the number). *This is a picture of a fin. Circle the letter that stands for the sound you hear in the middle of* fin.

Directions for Scoring

Give 1 point for each correct response. The highest score for each set of items is 5.

Answers for each set

Initial Consonants, page A119: **1.** n; **2.** g; **3.** w; **4.** l; **5.** p

Final Consonants, page A120: **1.** v; **2.** l; **3.** n; **4.** p; **5.** r

Vowels, page A121: **1.** u; **2.** o; **3.** e; **4.** a; **5.** i

Phonemic Awareness

Represent Phonemes with Letters, Test 4

This phonemic awareness test assesses a student's ability to connect sound to letter. Name a picture. Have the student circle the letter for the first, last, or middle sound in the picture name.

Instructions for Administering the Assessment

Make a copy of pages A122, A123, and A124 for each child.

Say these directions to the child.

Page A122: Initial Consonants

1. *Look at Number 1* (point to the number). *This is a picture of a zebra. Circle the letter that stands for the sound at the beginning of* zebra.

2. *Look at Number 2* (point to the number). *This is a picture of a bear. Circle the letter that stands for the sound at the beginning of* bear.

3. *Look at Number 3* (point to the number). *This is a picture of yarn. Circle the letter that stands for the sound at the beginning of* yarn.

4. *Look at Number 4* (point to the number). *This is a picture of a pineapple. Circle the letter that stands for the sound at the beginning of* pineapple.

5. *Look at Number 5* (point to the number). *This is a picture of rain. Circle the letter that stands for the sound at the beginning of* rain.

Page A123: Final Consonants

1. *Look at Number 1* (point to the number). *This is a picture of a lock. Circle the letter that stands for the sound at the end of* lock.

2. *Look at Number 2* (point to the number). *This is a picture of a car. Circle the letter that stands for the sound at the end of* car.

3. *Look at Number 3* (point to the number). *This is a picture of a sheep. Circle the letter that stands for the sound at the end of* sheep.

4. *Look at Number 4* (point to the number). *This is a picture of a leaf. Circle the letter that stands for the sound at the end of* leaf.

5. *Look at Number 5* (point to the number). *This is a picture of a whale. Circle the letter that stands for the sound at the end of* whale.

Phonemic Awareness

Page A124: Vowels

1. *Look at Number 1* (point to the number). *This is a picture of a tent. Circle the letter that stands for the sound you hear in the middle of* tent.

2. *Look at Number 2* (point to the number). *This is a picture of a crab. Circle the letter that stands for the sound you hear in the middle of* crab.

3. *Look at Number 3* (point to the number). *This is a picture of socks. Circle the letter that stands for the sound you hear in the middle of* socks.

4. *Look at Number 4* (point to the number). *This is a picture of lips. Circle the letter that stands for the sound you hear in the middle of* lips.

5. *Look at Number 5* (point to the number). *This is a picture of a truck. Circle the letter that stands for the sound you hear in the middle of* truck.

Directions for Scoring

Give 1 point for each correct response. The highest score for each set of items is 5.

Answers for each set

Initial Consonants, page A122: **1.** z; **2.** b; **3.** y; **4.** p; **5.** r

Final Consonants, page A123: **1.** k; **2.** r; **3.** p; **4.** f; **5.** l

Vowels, page A124: **1.** e; **2.** a; **3.** o; **4.** i; **5.** u

Phonemic Awareness

Represent Phonemes with Letters, Test 5

This phonemic awareness test assesses a student's ability to connect sound to letter. Name a picture. Have the student circle the letter for the first, last, or middle sound in the picture name.

Instructions for Administering the Assessment

Make a copy of pages A125, A126, and A127 for each child.

Say these directions to the child.

Page A125: Initial Consonants

1. *Look at Number 1* (point to the number). *This is a picture of a deer. Circle the letter that stands for the sound at the beginning of* deer.

2. *Look at Number 2* (point to the number). *This is a picture of feet. Circle the letter that stands for the sound at the beginning of* feet.

3. *Look at Number 3* (point to the number). *This is a picture of a hippo. Circle the letter that stands for the sound at the beginning of* hippo.

4. *Look at Number 4* (point to the number). *This is a picture of a worm. Circle the letter that stands for the sound at the beginning of* worm.

5. *Look at Number 5* (point to the number). *This is a picture of a rabbit. Circle the letter that stands for the sound at the beginning of* rabbit.

Page A126: Final Consonants

1. *Look at Number 1* (point to the number). *This is a picture of an egg. Circle the letter that stands for the sound at the end of* egg.

2. *Look at Number 2* (point to the number). *This is a picture of a crib. Circle the letter that stands for the sound at the end of* crib.

3. *Look at Number 3* (point to the number). *This is a picture of bread. Circle the letter that stands for the sound at the end of* bread.

4. *Look at Number 4* (point to the number). *This is a picture of a drum. Circle the letter that stands for the sound at the end of* drum.

5. *Look at Number 5* (point to the number). *This is a picture of an owl. Circle the letter that stands for the sound at the end of* owl.

Phonemic Awareness

Page A127: Vowels

1. *Look at Number 1* (point to the number). *This is a picture of a mask. Circle the letter that stands for the sound you hear in the middle of* mask.

2. *Look at Number 2* (point to the number). *This is a picture of a doll. Circle the letter that stands for the sound you hear in the middle of* doll.

3. *Look at Number 3* (point to the number). *This is a picture of a cup. Circle the letter that stands for the sound you hear in the middle of* cup.

4. *Look at Number 4* (point to the number). *This is a picture of a shell. Circle the letter that stands for the sound you hear in the middle of* shell.

5. *Look at Number 5* (point to the number). *This is a picture of the number six. Circle the letter that stands for the sound you hear in the middle of* six.

Directions for Scoring

Give 1 point for each correct response. The highest score for each set of items is 5.

Answers for each set

Initial Consonants, page A125: **1.** d; **2.** f; **3.** h; **4.** w; **5.** r

Final Consonants, page A126: **1.** g; **2.** b; **3.** d; **4.** m; **5.** l

Vowels, page A127: **1.** a; **2.** o; **3.** u; **4.** e; **5.** i

Phonemic Awareness

Represent Phonemes with Letters, Test 6

This phonemic awareness test assesses a student's ability to connect sound to letter. Name a picture. Have the student circle the letter for the first, last, or middle sound in the picture name.

Instructions for Administering the Assessment

Make a copy of pages A128, A129, and A130 for each child.

Say these directions to the child.

Page A128: Initial Consonants

1. *Look at Number 1* (point to the number). *This is a picture of a jar. Circle the letter that stands for the sound at the beginning of* jar.

2. *Look at Number 2* (point to the number). *This is a picture of a monkey. Circle the letter that stands for the sound at the beginning of* monkey.

3. *Look at Number 3* (point to the number). *This is a picture of a butterfly. Circle the letter that stands for the sound at the beginning of* butterfly.

4. *Look at Number 4* (point to the number). *This is a picture of a ladybug. Circle the letter that stands for the sound at the beginning of* ladybug.

5. *Look at Number 5* (point to the number). *This is a picture of a camel. Circle the letter that stands for the sound at the beginning of* camel.

Page A129: Final Consonants

1. *Look at Number 1* (point to the number). *This is a picture of a cloud. Circle the letter that stands for the sound at the end of* cloud.

2. *Look at Number 2* (point to the number). *This is a picture of an ox. Circle the letter that stands for the sound at the end of* ox.

3. *Look at Number 3* (point to the number). *This is a picture of a door. Circle the letter that stands for the sound at the end of* door.

4. *Look at Number 4* (point to the number). *This is a picture of a balloon. Circle the letter that stands for the sound at the end of* balloon.

5. *Look at Number 5* (point to the number). *This is a picture of a dress. Circle the letter that stands for the sound at the end of* dress.

Phonemic Awareness

Page A130: Vowels

1. *Look at Number 1* (point to the number). *This is a picture of a map. Circle the letter that stands for the sound you hear in the middle of* map.

2. *Look at Number 2* (point to the number). *This is a picture of a fence. Circle the letter that stands for the sound you hear in the middle of* fence.

3. *Look at Number 3* (point to the number). *This is a picture of blocks Circle the letter that stands for the sound you hear in the middle of* blocks.

4. *Look at Number 4* (point to the number). *This is a picture of a stump. Circle the letter that stands for the sound you hear in the middle of* stump.

5. *Look at Number 5* (point to the number). *This is a picture of a hill. Circle the letter that stands for the sound you hear in the middle of* hill.

Directions for Scoring

Give 1 point for each correct response. The highest score for each set of items is 5.

Answers for each set

Initial Consonants, page A128: **1.** j; **2.** m; **3.** b; **4.** l; **5.** c

Final Consonants, page A129: **1.** d; **2.** x; **3.** r; **4.** n; **5.** s

Vowels, page A130: **1.** a; **2.** e; **3.** o; **4.** u; **5.** i

Name: _____ Date: _____

Represent Phonemes with Letters, Test 1
Initial Consonants

1      **t**   **f**   **c**

2      **m**   **t**   **w**

3      **b**   **l**   **n**

4      **k**   **g**   **r**

5      **s**   **p**   **v**

Score ___ / 5

Name: _____ Date: _____

Represent Phonemes with Letters, Test 1
Final Consonants

1      **d**   **t**   **g**

2      **g**   **c**   **v**

3      **d**   **l**   **m**

4      **b**   **p**   **d**

5      **l**   **n**   **k**

Score ____ / 5

Name: _____ Date: _____

Represent Phonemes with Letters, Test 1
Vowels

1 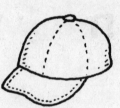   **i**   **e**   **u**

2 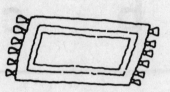   **e**   **u**   **a**

3    **e**   **o**   **u**

4    **a**   **i**   **e**

5    **i**   **o**   **u**

Score ___ / 5

Name: _____ Date: _____

Represent Phonemes with Letters, Test 2
Initial Consonants

1  **m**   **b**   **c**

2  **f**   **n**   **w**

3 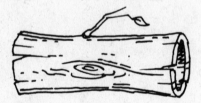 **d**   **t**   **l**

4  **g**   **c**   **p**

5  **d**   **l**   **s**

Score ___ / 5

Phonemic Awareness

Name: _____ Date: _____

Represent Phonemes with Letters, Test 2
Final Consonants

1      d   t   g

2   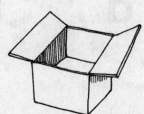   m   s   v

3      l   t   x

4      s   r   g

5      t   c   k

Score ___ / 5

Name: _____ Date: _____

Represent Phonemes with Letters, Test 2
Vowels

1  a   e   o

2  e   u   i

3  i   a   u

4  o   i   e

5  i   u   a

Score ___ / 5

Name: _____ **Date:** _____

Represent Phonemes with Letters, Test 3
Initial Consonants

1  **n** **b** **f**

2 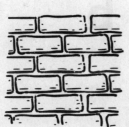 **g** **p** **n**

3  **d** **w** **k**

4  **l** **c** **p**

5  **n** **p** **b**

Score ___ / 5

Name: _____ Date: _____

Represent Phonemes with Letters, Test 3
Final Consonants

1      k   v   p

2   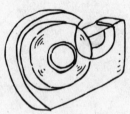   k   p   l

3      t   b   n

4      m   z   p

5      k   r   c

Score ___ / 5

Name: _____ Date: _____

Represent Phonemes with Letters, Test 3
Vowels

1    i   u   o

2    o   a   e

3    e   i   u

4    a   o   e

5    i   a   u

Score ___ / 5

Name: _____ Date: _____

Represent Phonemes with Letters, Test 4
Initial Consonants

1    **z**   **b**   **f**

2    **b**   **t**   **s**

3    **d**   **y**   **m**

4    **l**   **k**   **p**

5    **r**   **t**   **n**

Score ___ / 5

Name: _____ Date: _____

Represent Phonemes with Letters, Test 4
Final Consonants

1    **k**   **v**   **l**

2    **p**   **r**   **s**

3    **p**   **b**   **t**

4    **d**   **n**   **f**

5    **c**   **n**   **l**

Score ___ / 5

Name: _____ Date: _____

Represent Phonemes with Letters, Test 4
Vowels

1 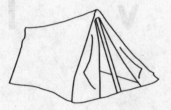   **e**   **o**   **u**

2    **i**   **a**   **o**

3    **o**   **a**   **u**

4 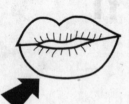   **i**   **o**   **e**

5    **i**   **u**   **e**

Score ___ / 5

Name: _____ Date: _____

Represent Phonemes with Letters, Test 5
Initial Consonants

1      **d**   **h**   **p**

2   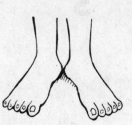   **n**   **f**   **w**

3      **l**   **h**   **p**

4      **s**   **w**   **c**

5      **b**   **s**   **v**

Score ___ / 5

Name: _____ Date: _____

Represent Phonemes with Letters, Test 5
Final Consonants

1 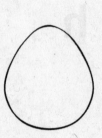   **p**   **t**   **g**

2    **b**   **s**   **w**

3 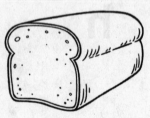   **l**   **d**   **c**

4    **m**   **k**   **b**

5    **c**   **l**   **z**

Score ____ / 5

Name: _____ Date: _____

Represent Phonemes with Letters, Test 5
Vowels

1  a   i   e

2  o   u   a

3  o   u   i

4  a   u   e

5  o   i   e

Score ___ / 5

Name: _____ Date: _____

Represent Phonemes with Letters, Test 6
Initial Consonants

1  **j   k   n**

2  **n   m   w**

3  **t   b   l**

4  **l   g   p**

5  **v   s   c**

Score ___ / 5

Name: _____ Date: _____

Represent Phonemes with Letters, Test 6
Final Consonants

1      **t**   **d**   **c**

2      **x**   **b**   **c**

3      **r**   **m**   **d**

4   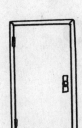   **k**   **n**   **p**

5      **n**   **s**   **b**

Score ___ / 5

Phonemic Awareness

Name: _____ Date: _____

Represent Phonemes with Letters, Test 6
Vowels

1 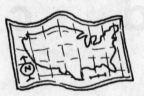   **a**   **e**   **o**

2    **e**   **o**   **a**

3    **e**   **o**   **u**

4    **u**   **i**   **e**

5 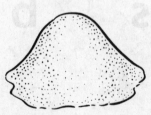   **i**   **o**   **e**

Score ___ / 5

Distinguish Long from Short Vowels

This phonemic awareness test assesses a student's ability to distinguish between long and short vowels. Say a pair of words. Ask the student to identify the word with a long or short vowel sound.

Instructions for Administering the Assessment

Make a copy of the record sheet for each child. Record the child's oral responses.

Say these directions to the child based on the assessment focus:

I am going to say two words. I want you to tell me which word has a short vowel sound. Let's try an example. Listen: cot, coat. *Which word has a short vowel sound:* cot *or* coat? (cot)

I am going to say two words. I want you to tell me which word has a long vowel sound. Let's try an example. Listen: cot, coat. *Which word has a long vowel sound:* cot *or* coat? (coat)

Directions for Scoring

Give 1 point for each correct response. The highest score for each set of items is 5.

Test 1, page A133

Answers for each set

Short Vowels: **1.** man; **2.** rip; **3.** met; **4.** hop; **5.** slid

Long Vowels: **1.** pine; **2.** robe; **3.** tape; **4.** cube; **5.** bead

Test 2, page A134

Answers for each set

Short Vowels: **1.** fin; **2.** tub; **3.** set; **4.** bit; **5.** clam

Long Vowels: **1.** spine; **2.** cope; **3.** pail; **4.** neat; **5.** vane

Test 3, page A135

Answers for each set

Short Vowels: **1.** fad; **2.** dim; **3.** ran; **4.** bet; **5.** rod

Long Vowels: **1.** mean; **2.** hide; **3.** feed; **4.** bait; **5.** mile

Phonemic Awareness

Test 4, page A136

Answers for each set

Short Vowels: **1.** sell; **2.** pan; **3.** got; **4.** cut; **5.** ten

Long Vowels: **1.** weed; **2.** cane; **3.** ride; **4.** steep; **5.** kite

Test 5, page A137

Answers for each set

Short Vowels: **1.** cap; **2.** wet; **3.** shin; **4.** plan; **5.** mop

Long Vowels: **1.** note; **2.** grime; **3.** gape; **4.** lease; **5.** wage

Test 6, page A138

Answers for each set

Short Vowels: **1.** wit; **2.** mad; **3.** will; **4.** sop; **5.** met

Long Vowels: **1.** slime; **2.** mate; **3.** feel; **4.** light; **5.** plain

Name: _____ Date: _____

Record Sheet, Test 1

Distinguish Long from Short Vowels

Short Vowels

Which word has a short vowel sound?

Words	Response
1. man *or* mane?	_____
2. ripe *or* rip?	_____
3. meet *or* met?	_____
4. hop *or* hope?	_____
5. slide *or* slid?	_____

Score ___ / 5

Long Vowels

Which word has a long vowel sound?

Words	Response
1. pine *or* pin?	_____
2. rob *or* robe?	_____
3. tap *or* tape?	_____
4. cub *or* cube?	_____
5. bead *or* bed?	_____

Score ___ / 5

Phonemic Awareness

Name: _____ **Date:** _____

Record Sheet, Test 2

Distinguish Long from Short Vowels

Short Vowels

Which word has a short vowel sound?

	Words	Response
1.	fin *or* fine?	_____
2.	tube *or* tub?	_____
3.	seat *or* set?	_____
4.	bit *or* bite?	_____
5.	claim *or* clam?	_____

Score ___ / **5**

Long Vowels

Which word has a long vowel sound?

	Words	Response
1.	spine *or* spin?	_____
2.	cop *or* cope?	_____
3.	pal *or* pail?	_____
4.	net *or* neat?	_____
5.	vane *or* van?	_____

Score ___ / **5**

Phonemic Awareness

Name: _____ Date: _____

Record Sheet, Test 3

Distinguish Long from Short Vowels

Short Vowels

Which word has a short vowel sound?

	Words	Response
1.	fad *or* fade?	_____
2.	dime *or* dim?	_____
3.	rain *or* ran?	_____
4.	bet *or* beat?	_____
5.	road *or* rod?	_____

Score ___ / 5

Long Vowels

Which word has a long vowel sound?

	Words	Response
1.	mean *or* men?	_____
2.	hid *or* hide?	_____
3.	fed *or* feed?	_____
4.	bat *or* bait?	_____
5.	mile *or* mill?	_____

Score ___ / 5

Phonemic Awareness

Name: _____ **Date:** _____

Record Sheet, Test 4

Distinguish Long from Short Vowels

Short Vowels

Which word has a short vowel sound?

	Words	Response
1.	sell *or* seal?	_____
2.	pain *or* pan?	_____
3.	goat *or* got?	_____
4.	cut *or* cute?	_____
5.	teen *or* ten?	_____

Score _____ **/ 5**

Long Vowels

Which word has a long vowel sound?

	Words	Response
1.	weed *or* wed?	_____
2.	can *or* cane?	_____
3.	rid *or* ride?	_____
4.	step *or* steep?	_____
5.	kite *or* kit?	_____

Score _____ **/ 5**

Phonemic Awareness

Name: _____ **Date:** _____

Record Sheet, Test 5

Distinguish Long from Short Vowels

Short Vowels

Which word has a short vowel sound?

Words	Response
1. cap *or* cape?	_____
2. wheat *or* wet?	_____
3. shine *or* shin?	_____
4. plan *or* plane?	_____
5. mope *or* mop?	_____

Score _____ / 5

Long Vowels

Which word has a long vowel sound?

Words	Response
1. note *or* not?	_____
2. grim *or* grime?	_____
3. gap *or* gape?	_____
4. less *or* lease?	_____
5. wage *or* wag?	_____

Score _____ / 5

Phonemic Awareness

Name: _____ Date: _____

Record Sheet, Test 6

Distinguish Long from Short Vowels

Short Vowels

Which word has a short vowel sound?

Words	Response
1. wit *or* white?	_____
2. maid *or* mad?	_____
3. will *or* while?	_____
4. sop *or* soap?	_____
5. meat *or* met?	_____

Score ___ / 5

Long Vowels

Which word has a long vowel sound?

Words	Response
1. slime *or* slim?	_____
2. mat *or* mate?	_____
3. fell *or* feel?	_____
4. lit *or* light?	_____
5. plain *or* plan?	_____

Score ___ / 5

Letter Naming and Sight Words

Letter Naming Fluency Assessment
Instructions for Administering Letter Naming Fluency

1. Make a copy of the Letter Naming Fluency record sheet. Use this sheet to record the student's oral responses.

2. Say these directions to the student:

Here are some letters. Tell me the names of as many letters as you can. When I say, "Begin" start here (point to the first letter) *and go across the page. Point to each letter and tell me the name of that letter. If you come to a letter that you don't know, I'll tell it to you. Put your finger on the first letter. Ready, begin.*

3. Start your stopwatch. Follow along with your copy of the Letter Naming Fluency record sheet. Put a slash (/) through letters named incorrectly. Place a check above letters named correctly.

4. At the end of 1 minute, place a bracket (]) after the last letter named and say, *Stop.*

Directions for Scoring

1. If the student does not get any correct letter names within the first 10 letters (1 row), discontinue the task and record a score of zero.

2. If the student hesitates for 3 seconds on a letter, score the letter incorrect, and provide the correct letter to the student.

3. If the student provides the letter sound rather than the letter name, say: *Remember to tell me the letter name, not the sound it makes.* If the student continues providing letter sounds, mark each letter as incorrect, and make a note of this behavior at the bottom of the page.

4. Score a point for each correct letter the student names and record the total number of correct letters at the bottom of the sheet.

5. If students fail to meet the following benchmarks, then more intensive instruction in the alphabetic principle is required.

> Beginning of Year: 40 correct letters
>
> Middle of Year: 50 correct letters
>
> End of Year: 60 correct letters

Letter Naming and Sight Words

Name: _____ Date: _____

Record Sheet, Test 1

Letter Naming Fluency	# correct
g H t X r F C j T z	__ /10
K l q z b n y s I O	__ /10
A e V u Q Y z M j a	__ /10
f i W R g U d z S c	__ /10
k M g D o J n p m h	__ /10
C N E b u a g w V f	__ /10
G Y i d e n S T t c	__ /10
R F a m Z I w v C n	__ /10
f s P o Y W E j k Q	__ /10
D U g e A b i y B d	__ /10
N f p R F q l K p M	__ /10
L a W f U c O b x Z	__ /10

Total ___ /120

Letter Naming and Sight Words

Name: _____ Date: _____

Record Sheet, Test 2

Letter Naming Fluency	# correct
p a B o c F T o d X	__ /10
D p M i G j b h b z	__ /10
q b n d h H J t n K	__ /10
R y b c e U e X a r	__ /10
I E g f b h D m F c	__ /10
y F m s a Z T A g k	__ /10
i W J Y f e E k M x	__ /10
A g S c h R I j V f	__ /10
i K g r d c L Y i D v	__ /10
J t e C k N h G I Z	__ /10
V g H F j f C l e u	__ /10
b k S u Y B I d L Q	__ /10

Total ____ /120

Foundational Skills Assessment · Letter Naming and Sight Words

Letter Naming and Sight Words

Name: _____ **Date:** _____

Record Sheet, Test 3

Letter Naming Fluency	# correct
a O q T v Q i e F n	__ /10
u K g C b U o M F e	__ /10
Z i u o J t h A p H	__ /10
j B O c u b P q K e	__ /10
w M a H A i r I d F	__ /10
E t S i m f T C w a	__ /10
r V D U I o s E Q e	__ /10
o N r c q G M b Y r	__ /10
t q L i B s d c H u	__ /10
P i G f w g U k I Z	__ /10
i I R y V g c I D v	__ /10
S x a K s e L d R z	__ /10

Total ___ /120

Letter Naming and Sight Words

Name: _____ **Date:** _____

Record Sheet, Test 4

Letter Naming Fluency	# correct
A o m h q g i T c l	__ /10
f c n F R e j s R t	__ /10
b E c d w D e B L o	__ /10
d K e S a Q g i D e	__ /10
f C j c V a G b I g	__ /10
j q f H L k S A u F	__ /10
Y M R a e g H c h D	__ /10
w u B z J l g c K h	__ /10
j Q d b o U x N m B	__ /10
X f b V m d Z x C h	__ /10
y M w C m N i b G T	__ /10
f b O g A f P i q W	__ /10

Total ___ /120

Letter Naming and Sight Words

Name: _____ **Date:** _____

Record Sheet, Test 5

Letter Naming Fluency										# correct
S	E	a	T	m	D	h	I	d	U	__ /10
m	D	K	X	L	f	s	a	t	r	__ /10
f	j	F	E	h	n	D	L	r	K	__ /10
l	A	q	S	y	i	W	U	g	e	__ /10
o	n	L	d	a	j	D	F	o	P	__ /10
P	b	e	V	g	O	j	I	M	T	__ /10
r	T	A	S	G	n	B	d	H	o	__ /10
U	d	r	M	x	e	H	z	y	e	__ /10
K	U	y	j	o	T	i	c	Y	x	__ /10
F	g	i	M	b	o	L	t	H	l	__ /10
z	d	S	J	y	N	k	D	m	A	__ /10
R	C	o	k	f	m	b	x	y	c	__ /10

Total ___ /120

Letter Naming and Sight Words

Name: _____ **Date:** _____

Record Sheet, Test 6

Letter Naming Fluency	# correct
A G X i r e s D P u	__ /10
e b j O A g W s k f	__ /10
Q a c p J e r s E N	__ /10
i F H d p m T h j P	__ /10
M Z t n S Y a B c I	__ /10
o X u K T i U o b J	__ /10
S i C f H i B N S m	__ /10
g m g e K f l w d M	__ /10
E h l I u F g a t o	__ /10
W q O k f L R q M r	__ /10
K p I V T r m u D s	__ /10
r V d C G s L y v p	__ /10

Total ____ /120

Foundational Skills Assessment • Letter Naming and Sight Words

Sight Word Fluency Assessment

Instructions for Administering the Assessment

Make two copies of the record sheet. Use one to record the student's responses. Give the student the other sheet, and have the student put his or her finger on the first word in the first row. Explain that you would like the student to read as many words as he or she can in one minute. Tell the student to point to each word and say the word. Then say: *When you are ready, you may begin.* Start your stopwatch, timing the student for one minute as he or she reads the words.

1. Follow along as the student reads. Place a check above each word that is said correctly.

2. Place a line through each word that is read incorrectly or omitted.

3. If the student substitutes or mispronounces a word, put a line through the word and write the word the student said above it.

4. If the student does not correctly say a word within 3 seconds, say the word for the student and mark the word as incorrect.

5. Say *Stop* at the end of one minute and place a bracket (]) after the last word read by the student.

Directions for Scoring

1. Count the total number of words read. This includes the words that are read correctly and incorrectly. Record that number on the table at the bottom of the sheet.

2. Count the number of errors for each line of words in the # of errors column. Record the total number of errors in the bottom table.

3. Use this formula to score Oral Reading Accuracy:

$$\frac{\text{Total No. of Words Read} - \text{No. of Errors}}{\text{Total Number of Words Read}} \times 100$$

Letter Naming and Sight Words

Name: _____ Date: _____

Record Sheet, Test 1

Sight Word Fluency					# of errors
and	are	do	for	go	__ /5
has	is	she	here	of	__ /5
see	who	look	said	my	__ /5
play	like	see	he	want	__ /5
the	what	help	good	this	__ /5
out	run	new	live	her	__ /5
some	grow	none	fall	carry	__ /5
food	build	give	ago	eat	__ /5
oh	sure	four	near	woman	__ /5
gone	learn	know	write	push	__ /5
through	guess	surprise	above	children	__ /5
thought	laugh	round	climb	heard	__ /5

Total number of words read in one minute	
Number of errors	
Accuracy rate (use Oral Reading Accuracy formula)	

Letter Naming and Sight Words

Name: _____ **Date:** _____

Record Sheet, Test 2

Sight Word Fluency					# of errors
go	and	for	come	do	__ /5
does	me	can	here	are	__ /5
we	to	you	is	of	__ /5
help	look	have	with	the	__ /5
he	they	what	too	play	__ /5
be	not	up	fun	move	__ /5
no	call	so	or	were	__ /5
soon	done	upon	our	full	__ /5
door	warm	after	early	old	__ /5
water	nothing	knew	animal	blue	__ /5
again	many	school	could	three	__ /5
caught	favorite	front	people	work	__ /5

Total number of words read in one minute	
Number of errors	
Accuracy rate (use Oral Reading Accuracy formula)	

Letter Naming and Sight Words

Name: _____ **Date:** _____

Record Sheet, Test 3

Sight Word Fluency					# of errors
is	has	see	here	me	__ /5
to	was	she	of	does	__ /5
this	they	want	my	with	__ /5
good	said	who	where	have	__ /5
little	play	go	like	can	__ /5
one	day	more	ate	few	__ /5
two	by	they	over	use	__ /5
very	began	another	then	jump	__ /5
love	been	eyes	only	great	__ /5
enough	brother	over	more	father	__ /5
toward	push	brought	wonder	grow	__ /5
walk	poor	because	picture	large	__ /5

Total number of words read in one minute	
Number of errors	
Accuracy rate (use Oral Reading Accuracy formula)	

Foundational Skills Assessment • Letter Naming and Sight Words

Name: _____ Date: _____

Record Sheet, Test 4

Sight Word Fluency					# of errors
to	and	the	he	was	___ /5
have	me	we	she	come	___ /5
see	look	said	with	of	___ /5
like	who	too	where	are	___ /5
they	for	what	you	does	___ /5
am	any	boy	from	into	___ /5
happy	flew	well	fun	new	___ /5
put	pretty	why	other	green	___ /5
brown	poor	color	right	found	___ /5
friend	should	would	about	small	___ /5
year	month	money	young	away	___ /5
picture	question	instead	brother	busy	___ /5

Total number of words read in one minute	
Number of errors	
Accuracy rate (use Oral Reading Accuracy formula)	

Letter Naming and Sight Words

Name: _____ Date: _____

Record Sheet, Test 5

Sight Word Fluency					# of errors
is	he	can	we	are	__ /5
my	for	do	come	me	__ /5
see	too	said	look	want	__ /5
where	you	play	little	help	__ /5
does	have	good	this	has	__ /5
but	yes	say	way	find	__ /5
make	start	small	yellow	eight	__ /5
around	funny	under	black	again	__ /5
year	their	once	young	better	__ /5
your	mother	their	because	love	__ /5
month	surprise	another	friend	eyes	__ /5
enough	tomorrow	listen	children	busy	__ /5

Total number of words read in one minute	
Number of errors	
Accuracy rate (use Oral Reading Accuracy formula)	

Letter Naming and Sight Words

Name: _____ **Date:** _____

Record Sheet, Test 6

Sight Word Fluency					# of errors
to	has	do	go	and	__ /5
for	can	you	have	my	__ /5
we	they	with	want	she	__ /5
good	too	who	what	was	__ /5
help	where	this	little	like	__ /5
red	girl	get	went	well	__ /5
will	how	there	now	away	__ /5
about	every	today	down	walk	__ /5
buy	white	place	hard	large	__ /5
brought	find	surprise	girl	gone	__ /5
toward	eight	great	tomorrow	few	__ /5
together	once	instead	answer	night	__ /5

Total number of words read in one minute	
Number of errors	
Accuracy rate (use Oral Reading Accuracy formula)	

Phonics and Structural Analysis

Phonics and Structural Analysis Survey

based on **The Quick Phonics Screener**
Jan Hasbrouck, Ph.D.
© 2006-2010 JH Consulting

The purpose of the Phonics and Structural Analysis Survey (PSAS) is to provide informal diagnostic information that can be used to help (a) PLAN a student's instructional program in basic word reading skills, and (b) MONITOR THE PROGRESS or IMPROVEMENT in phonics and structural analysis skill development. The PSAS has not been normed or standardized. It is meant to be used as an informal classroom assessment tool.

Phonics and Structural Analysis

Directions for Administration and Scoring

1. Say to the student:

"I'm going to ask you to read some letters, words, and sentences to me so I can find out what kinds of words are easy for you to read and what kinds of words you still need to learn. I want you to try to do your best. We probably won't do this whole page; we'll stop if it gets too hard. Do you have any questions?"

Start the PSAS assessment where you believe the student's skills are fairly strong. For beginning readers, start with sounds or letter names.

For Skill 1, first (a) have the student tell the name of each letter. Then (b) have the student tell the sound each letter makes.

For the *NAMES* skill, have the student name the letter Q, not the *qu* digraph. For the *SOUNDS* task, have the student give you the short sound for each of the vowels. If the student says the long sound (letter name), say: *"That is one sound that letter makes. Do you know the short sound for that letter?"* For the letter *c*, ask for the "hard sound" /k/, as in *cat*. For the letter *g* ask for the "hard sound" /g/, as in *gas*. For the letter *y* ask for the /y/ sound, as in *yes*. If the student offers a correct alternative sound for these letters, you should say, *"Yes, that is one sound for that letter. Do you know another sound that letter makes?"*

If a student reads 6/10 or more in Skill 2a, you may skip Skill 1 Letter Sounds.

2. If the student has difficulty (half or fewer correct on any task) move up the page to an easier skill. If the student does well (more than half correct on a task), move down to a harder skill.

3. On Skills 2–6: If the student reads all or almost all words correctly on part (a) of the skill (reading words), you may want to skip part (b) of the skill (reading sentences). If the next skill is difficult for the student, you can go back and complete the part of a previous skill that was skipped.

4. When the student is reading the words in text, only count errors on the target words (those underlined and in italics).

5. Stop the assessment when the student appears frustrated or tired. It is OK to stop in the middle of a skill. Not all skills must be administered, but try to assess as many as possible so you will have sufficient information to plan instruction or monitor progress.

Phonics and Structural Analysis

6. Mark errors and make notes or comments to help you remember how the student responded. Note that in Skill 9, students read the entire word, not syllable-by-syllable. The teacher's copy is written in syllables to facilitate marking/recording of errors within a word. For Skills 11-15, students read the entire word, and syllabication is not featured in the teacher's copy.

7. The PSAS is scored by each individual skill *only*. Record the ratio of correct responses over the total number possible, (e.g., 13/21 or 8/10 for each skill). Use the scoring chart that corresponds to each test to record PSAS results.

Phonics and Structural Analysis Survey Scoring Sheet, Test 1

1. Letters					Score						Score
(a) Names	m	t	a	s		**(b) Sounds**	/m/	/t/	/a/	/s/	Consonants:
	i	r	d	f			/i/	/r/	/d/	/f/	/21
	o	g	l	h			/o/	/g/	/l/	/h/	
	u	c	n	b			/u/	/k/	/n/	/b/	
	j	k	y	e			/j/	/k/	/y/	/e/	Vowels:
	w	p	v	z			/w/	/p/	/v/	/z/	
	x	qu			/26		/ks/	/kw/			/5

2. VC and CVC					Comments	Score
(a) In List	lat	hod	teb	vun		
	pog	bis	yug	rak		
	miz	fev				/10
(b) In Text	*Put* the *hat in* the *big bag.* *Dad sat on* the *red rug.*		The *bed had* a *tag on it.* *Sid had* a *pal in* the *dog.*			/20

3. Consonant Digraphs					Comments	Score
(a) In List	shep	kang	geck	whut		
	lath	chid	thun	rosh		
	nich	whit				/10
(b) In Text	*Shut* it *when* you get *back.* *That dish* is red.		I had a *long chat with* him. *Kick* or *push* it to me.			/10

8. **NOTE:** *Results from the PSAS **CAN ONLY** be used to determine a student's strengths/needs in key phonics and structural analysis skills, **NOT** his or her grade-level performance in reading.*

Phonics and Structural Analysis

	Phonics and Structural Analysis Survey, Test 1				
Skill 1(a)	m t a s i r d f o				
	g l h u c n b j k				
Skill 1(b)	y e w p v z x qu				
Skill 2(a)	lat	hod	teb	vun	pog
	bis	yug	rak	miz	fev
Skill 2(b)	Put the hat in the big bag. The bed had a tag on it. Dad sat on the red rug. Sid had a pal in the dog.				
Skill 3(a)	shep	kang	geck	whut	lath
	chid	thun	rosh	nich	whit
Skill 3(b)	Shut it when you get back. I had a long chat with him. That dish is red. Kick or push it to me.				
Skill 4(a)	lont	dist	preb	blut	himt
	selb	flin	crit	grun	tumk
Skill 4(b)	You must grab the left hand so it will not slip. Plan to buy a sled as a gift just for Fred.				
Skill 5(a)	hipe	fude	bame	mize	vene
	rane	lide	sule	nele	roke
Skill 5(b)	Eve and Steve use a bike to ride to the game. The note at home came from Dave.				

Phonics and Structural Analysis

	Phonics and Structural Analysis Survey, Test 1
Skill 6(a)	dort kirk tarb ferl purd parn torp surk nirn ferm
Skill 6(b)	A girl burst out singing at the birthday party on the porch. The third short story in the book is called "Perfect Art."
Skill 7(a)	fitch sudge blux quab celb gerd knaf gnab wrib dalk
Skill 7(b)	The queen and the knight often talk. The nice gent made a pledge to help. I put the sign on the box. Don't watch the wrong one.
Skill 8	oab toat meap peal koom doot ait faim holp solb aym cray poud louk foid hoit oyd royn pau kaut lawk sawp roe doel gew fewd hald dalt figh drigh
Skill 9(a)	tuna market random pencil lighthouse border button palace signal basket
Skill 9(b)	element calendar ambulance banana forgetful September department carpenter propeller telephone
Skill 9(c)	America television impossible elevator watermelon convertible calculator operation discovery indentation
Skill 10	disagree disgrace nonsense nonfat inexact inability premade presold resell remake unfair unlock context conform suggestion ration nervous wondrous darkness fairness capable teachable mislaid mistake hopeful sorrowful secondary primary experiment ornament

Phonics and Structural Analysis

	Phonics and Structural Analysis Survey, Test 1			
Skill 11(a)	hats dishes axes	sticks brushes boxes	kisses arches breezes	glasses benches sizes
Skill 11(b)	flies ponies selves	cries stories wives	babies elves knives	cookies wolves shelves
Skill 12(a)	hums bikes played	snoops teaches acting	tracks fished swaying	fixes funded throwing
Skill 12(b)	fries bragged fanning	glories hopped startling	quizzes tried cycling	multiplies magnified populating
Skill 13(a)	boy's teacher's men's	dog's mouse's students'	child's birds' doctors'	queen's girls' children's
Skill 13(b)	I'm we've couldn't	he'd they'll haven't	it's can't mustn't	she's didn't shouldn't
Skill 14(a)	colder smoother warmest	faster narrower freshest	louder slowest longest	smaller roundest newest
Skill 14(b)	bigger madder slimmest	fatter wetter hottest	gladder fittest reddest	thinner saddest hippest

Phonics and Structural Analysis

Phonics and Structural Analysis Survey Scoring Sheet, Test 1

I. Letters

(a) Names				Score	(b) Sounds					Score
m	t	a	s			/m/	/t/	/a/	/s/	Consonants:
i	r	d	f			/i/	/r/	/d/	/f/	/21
o	g	l	h			/o/	/g/	/l/	/h/	
u	c	n	b			/u/	/k/	/n/	/b/	
j	k	y	e			/j/	/k/	/y/	/e/	Vowels:
w	p	v	z			/w/	/p/	/v/	/z/	
x	qu			/26		/ks/	/kw/			/5

2. VC and CVC

					Comments	Score
(a) In List	lat	hod	teb	vun		
	pog	bis	yug	rak		
	miz	fev				/10
(b) In Text	*Put* the *hat* *in* the *big bag.*		The *bed had* a *tag* *on it.*			
	Dad sat on the *red rug.*		*Sid had* a *pal in* the *dog.*			/20

3. Consonant Digraphs

					Comments	Score
(a) In List	shep	kang	geck	whut		
	lath	chid	thun	rosh		
	nich	whit				/10
(b) In Text	*Shut* it *when* you get *back.*		I had a *long chat with* him.			
	That dish is red.		*Kick* or *push* it to me.			/10

4. CVCC and CCVC

					Comments	Score
(a) In List	lont	dist	preb	blut		
	himt	selb	flin	crit		
	grun	tumk				/10
(b) In Text	You *must grab* the *left hand* so it will not *slip.*		*Plan* to buy a *sled* as a *gift just* for *Fred.*			/10

5. Silent *e*

					Comments	Score
(a) In List	hipe	fude	bame	mize		
	vene	rane	lide	sule		
	nele	roke				/10
(b) In Text	*Eve* and *Steve use* a *bike* to *ride* to the *game.*		The *note* at *home came* from *Dave.*			/10

Phonics and Structural Analysis

Copyright © McGraw-Hill Education

Phonics and Structural Analysis Survey Scoring Sheet, Test 1

6. r-Controlled Vowels		Comments	Score
(a) In List	dort kirk tarb ferl purd parn torp surk nirn ferm		/10
(b) In Text	A *girl* *burst* out singing at the *birthday* *party* on the *porch*.	The *third* *short* *story* in the book is called *"Perfect* *Art."*	/10

7. Advanced Consonants (-*tch*, -*dge*, -*x*, *qu*, soft *c* & *g*, *kn*, *gn*, *wr*, -*lk*)		Comments	Score
(a) In List	fitch sudge blux quab celb gerd knaf gnab wrib dalk		/10
(b) In Text	The *queen* and the *knight* often *talk*. The *nice* *gent* made a *pledge* to help.	I put the *sign* on the *box*. Don't *watch* the *wrong* one.	/10

8. Vowel Teams		Comments	Score
oa, ea, oo, ai, ol, ay, ou, oi, oy, au, aw, oe, ew, al, igh	oab toat meap peal koom doot ait faim holp salb aym cray poud louk foid hoit oyd royn pau kaut lawk sawp roe doel gew fewd hald dalt figh drigh		/30

9. Multi-Syllable		Comments	Score
(a) 2-Syllable	tu-na mar-ket ran-dom pen-cil light-house bor-der but-ton pal-ace sig-nal bas-ket		/10
(b) 3-Syllable	el-e-ment cal-en-dar am-bu-lance ba-nan-a for-get-ful Sep-tem-ber de-part-ment car-pen-ter pro-pel-ler tel-e-phone		/10
(c) 4-Syllable	A-mer-i-ca tel-e-vi-sion im-pos-si-ble el-e-va-tor wa-ter-mel-on con-ver-ti-ble cal-cu-la-tor op-er-a-tion dis-cov-er-y in-den-ta-tion		/10

10. Prefixes and Suffixes				Comments	Score
dis-, non-, in-, pre-, re-, un-, con-, mis-, -tion, -ous, -ness, -able, -ful, -ary, -ment	disagree disgrace inexact inability resell remake context conform nervous wondrous capable teachable hopeful sorrowful experiment ornament	nonsense nonfat premade presold unfair unlock suggestion ration darkness fairness mislaid mistake secondary primary			/30

Phonics and Structural Analysis

Phonics and Structural Analysis Survey Scoring Sheet, Test 1

11. Plurals (-s, -es)					Comments	Score
(a) No spelling changes	hats dishes axes	sticks brushes boxes	kisses arches breezes	glasses benches sizes		/12
(b) With spelling changes (*y to i, f, fe to v*)	flies ponies selves	cries stories wives	babies elves knives	cookies wolves shelves		/12

12. Inflectional Verb Endings (-s, -es, -ed, -ing)				Comments	Score
(a) No spelling changes	hums fixes fished acting	snoops bikes funded swaying	tracks teaches played throwing		/12
(b) With spelling changes	fries multiplies tried startling	glories bragged magnified cycling	quizzes hopped fanning populating		/12

13. Possessives and Contractions				Comments	Score
(a) Possessives (singular, plural, and irregular)	boy's queen's birds' students'	dog's teacher's girls' doctors'	child's mouse's men's children's		/12
(b) Contractions (pronoun-verb and with *not*)	I'm she's can't haven't	he'd we've didn't mustn't	it's they'll couldn't shouldn't		/12

14. Comparative Endings (-er, -est)				Comments	Score
(a) No spelling changes	colder smaller slowest freshest	faster smoother roundest longest	louder narrower warmest newest		/12
(b) With spelling changes	bigger thinner fittest hottest	fatter madder saddest reddest	gladder wetter slimmest hippest		/12

Phonics and Structural Analysis

	Phonics and Structural Analysis Survey, Test 2				
Skill 1(a)	qu j u h d s m r t v x e i w l o z y				
Skill 1(b)	k f b n p a g c				
Skill 2(a)	dok	lib	gup	hak	teg
	sib	cug	raf	mip	hev
Skill 2(b)	Did the rat rip his cot? Let us in! Dad set his top hat on the bed. The pan has a bit on it.				
Skill 3(a)	heng	whem	nesh	guth	vech
	juck	veng	pung	lish	neth
Skill 3(b)	Hit that gong, Buck! A fish will rush to get bugs. Sam hung it in his shop. Beth sang on a path.				
Skill 4(a)	snil	vint	glod	bolp	swev
	runk	hend	flaf	krik	bemt
Skill 4(b)	He went fast on the snow on his sled trip. Clem must swim in the rest on the pond.				
Skill 5(a)	dobe	jepe	huve	rame	fice
	hule	hake	pife	pebe	tose
Skill 5(b)	The mole will use a hole to poke his nose in it. His home in the cave was made of fine stone.				

Phonics and Structural Analysis

Phonics and Structural Analysis Survey, Test 2

Skill 6(a)	bort tirk sarb werl murd sarn zorp burk mirn serm
Skill 6(b)	Cars swerve around the sharp curve on the dirt road. The store clerk confirms that we returned the shorts.
Skill 7(a)	titch dudge dux quaf celd ged knak gnan wrif falk
Skill 7(b)	She wrote a story for six pages. There is a gnarled tree by the bridge. He knit the stitch quickly. You walk with a smile on your face.
Skill 8	coan goam seak keat poot bool cail wain folb boln fay dray cout foud croil doip moy stoy vaut faul awt traw droe loe tew prew kal stal brigh pigh
Skill 9(a)	follow mustard mascot carrot homework jelly kingdom riches princess mistake
Skill 9(b)	December Saturday vanishing camera ladybug overboard gravity victory gardener multiply
Skill 9(c)	invitation information fertilizer helicopter emergency January delivery invisible electrician binoculars
Skill 10	disarm dislike nonfiction nonprofit unbroken undone inactive incomplete precook premade reappear retell concur concede misbehave misread action invention infectious courageous cleverness goodness agreeable approachable stressful harmful monetary military enjoyment replacement

Phonics and Structural Analysis

	Phonics and Structural Analysis Survey, Test 2			
Skill 11(a)	wigs lashes hoaxes	socks crashes foxes	passes porches mazes	misses ranches prizes
Skill 11(b)	fries bunnies selves	cities fifties lives	bodies knives calves	daddies halves scarves
Skill 12(a)	sips reaches roasted	tells blushes packing	lacks drilled lending	hisses handed smashing
Skill 12(b)	dries stopped batting	relies patted digging	varies pried baking	carries muddied judging
Skill 13(a)	dad's woman's hogs'	mule's snake's spouses'	clerk's buds' geese's	hen's writers' fish's
Skill 13(b)	I've they've doesn't	we'd we'll hasn't	he's isn't won't	you've aren't wouldn't
Skill 14(a)	neater harder sweetest	longer plainer strongest	tighter cleanest dampest	richer blackest brightest
Skill 14(b)	trimmer primmer tannest	hotter drabber biggest	smugger dimmest snuggest	redder glummest flattest

Phonics and Structural Analysis

Phonics and Structural Analysis Survey Scoring Sheet, Test 2

1. Letters		Score						Score
(a) Names	qu j u h d s m r t v x e i w l o z y k f b n p a g c	/26	**(b) Sounds**	/kw/ /j/ /u/ /h/ /d/ /s/ /m/ /r/ /t/ /v/ /ks/ /e/ /i/ /w/ /l/ /o/ /z/ /y/ /k/ /f/ /b/ /n/ /p/ /a/ /g/ /k/			Consonants: /21 Vowels: /5

2. VC and CVC		Comments	Score
(a) In List	dok lib gup hak teg sib cug raf mip hev		/10
(b) In Text	_Did_ the _rat_ _rip_ _his_ _cot_? _Let_ _us_ _in_! _Dad_ _set_ _his_ _top_ _hat_ _on_ the The _pan_ _has_ a _bit_ _on_ _it_. _bed_.		/20

3. Consonant Digraphs		Comments	Score
(a) In List	heng whem nesh guth vech juck veng pung lish neth		/10
(b) In Text	Hit _that_ _gong_, _Buck_! A _fish_ will _rush_ to get bugs. Sam _hung_ it in his _shop_. _Beth_ _sang_ on a _path_.		/10

4. CVCC and CCVC		Comments	Score
(a) In List	snil vint glod bolp swev runk hend flaf krik bemt		/10
(b) In Text	He _went_ _fast_ on the _Clem_ _must_ _swim_ in the _snow_ on his _sled_ _trip_. _rest_ of the _pond_.		/10

5. Silent e		Comments	Score
(a) In List	dobe jepe huve rame fice hule hake pife pebe tose		/10
(b) In Text	The _mole_ will _use_ a _hole_ to _poke_ his _nose_ in it. His _home_ in the _cave_ was _made_ of _fine_ _stone_.		/10

Phonics and Structural Analysis

Phonics and Structural Analysis Survey Scoring Sheet, Test 2

6. *r*-Controlled Vowels		Comments	Score
(a) In List	bort tirk sarb werl murd sarn zorp burk mirn serm		/10
(b) In Text	Cars *swerve* around the *sharp* *curve* on the *dirt* road. The *store* *clerk* *confirms* that we *returned* the *shorts*.		/10

7. Advanced Consonants (*-tch, -dge, -x, qu,* soft *c* & *g, kn, gn, wr, -lk*)		Comments	Score
(a) In List	titch dudge dux quaf celd ged knak gnan wriff falk		/10
(b) In Text	She *wrote* a story for *six* *pages*. There is a *gnarled* tree by the *bridge*. He *knit* the *stitch* *quickly*. You *walk* with a smile on your *face*.		/10

8. Vowel Teams							Comments	Score
oa, ea, oo, ai, oi, ay, ou, oi, oy, au, aw, oe, ew, al, igh	coan cail cout vaut tew	goam wain foud faul prew	seak folb croil awt kal	keat boln doip traw stal	poot fay moy droe brigh	bool dray stoy loe pigh		/30

9. Multi-Syllable		Comments	Score
(a) 2-Syllable	fol-low mus-tard mas-cot car-rot home-work jel-ly king-dom rich-es prin-cess mis-take		/10
(b) 3-Syllable	De-cem-ber Sat-ur-day van-ish-ing cam-er-a la-dy-bug o-ver-board grav-i-ty vic-tor-y gar-den-er mul-ti-ply		/10
(c) 4-Syllable	in-vi-ta-tion in-for-ma-tion fer-ti-li-zer he-li-cop-ter e-mer-gen-cy Jan-u-ar-y de-liv-er-y in-vis-i-ble e-lec-tri-cian bi-noc-u-lars		/10

10. Prefixes and Suffixes				Comments	Score
dis-, non-, in-, pre-, re-, un-, con-, mis-, -tion, -ous, -ness, -able, -ful, -ary, -ment	disarm nonprofit inactive premade concur misread infectious goodness stressful military	dislike unbroken incomplete reappear concede action courageous agreeable harmful enjoyment	nonfiction undone precook retell misbehave invention cleverness approachable monetary replacement		/30

Phonics and Structural Analysis

11. Plurals (-*s*, -*es*)					Comments	Score
(a) No spelling changes	wigs lashes hoaxes	socks crashes foxes	passes porches mazes	misses ranches prizes		/12
(b) With spelling changes (*y to i, f, fe to v*)	fries bunnies selves	cities fifties lives	bodies knives calves	daddies halves scarves		/12

12. Inflectional Verb Endings (-*s*, -*es*, -*ed*, -*ing*)				Comments	Score
(a) No spelling changes	sips hisses drilled packing	tells reaches handed lending	lacks blushes roasted smashing		/12
(b) With spelling changes	dries carries pried digging	relies stopped muddied baking	varies patted batting judging		/12

13. Possessives and Contractions				Comments	Score
(a) Possessives (singular, plural, and irregular)	dad's hen's buds' spouses'	mule's woman's writers' geese's	clerk's snake's hogs' fish's		/12
(b) Contractions (pronoun-verb and with *not*)	I've you've isn't hasn't	we'd they've aren't won't	he's we'll doesn't wouldn't		/12

14. Comparative Endings (-*er*, -*est*)				Comments	Score
(a) No spelling changes	neater richer cleanest strongest	longer harder blackest dampest	tighter plainer sweetest brightest		/12
(b) With spelling changes	trimmer redder dimmest biggest	hotter primmer glummest snuggest	smugger drabber tannest flattest		/12

Phonics and Structural Analysis

	Phonics and Structural Analysis Survey, Test 3
Skill 1(a)	l p e t r c s u y h o d x qu k a n z
Skill 1(b)	f i w v b g m j
Skill 2(a)	kas wum fut lod meb bim lat mef vot dil
Skill 2(b)	Mom is not as sad as Pat. The cat ran to the top. A man sat on a cup. Did Tim nap in the big bed?
Skill 3(a)	whad wack thep dush chev ting lith whin reck shum
Skill 3(b)	Mash the egg in this dish. When did Meg sing? Ted had chips with his duck. Did Gus get much cash?
Skill 4(a)	bilt smop resk swin timp griv gelp spaf drev bosk
Skill 4(b)	A gust of wind bent the rest of the mast. My plan is to drag a clam on land and grab it.
Skill 5(a)	dife bupe mobe leme pite vake gace debe sofe tule
Skill 5(b)	Steve had to use the rope to rise out of the huge hole. He came to the wide lake and dove in.

Phonics and Structural Analysis

	Phonics and Structural Analysis Survey, Test 3
Skill 6(a)	lort hirk narb terl burd zarn borp vurk sirn bern
Skill 6(b)	We saw a dark storm turn and whirl over the river. She urged me with firm words to fix the yard.
Skill 7(a)	sitch gudge gux quag celf gerf knal gnam wrik halk
Skill 7(b)	We buy quality rice in bulk. She untied the knot to fix it. The gnat flew on my wrist and made it itch. That is a giant bandage!
Skill 8	doat roak deat creal dool scoob pait raim polt olb aym nayt roum spouv oik fois coyn boyl gaut faul awk nawd moev oen tew lew palt kalb twigh kighp
Skill 9(a)	enter workout level staircase dollar penpal backpack boiler teacher apple
Skill 9(b)	holiday afternoon fantastic computer terrific understand happening recommend lemonade balcony
Skill 9(c)	predicament experiment community astronomer declaration horizontal prehistoric anybody renewable constitution
Skill 10	disconnect dishonest nonfact nonnews incorrect indefinite prepaid preschool rewrite renew uncover undecided concert confident misspell misplace attention location famous enormous kindness smoothness curable washable careful thankful ordinary honorary movement improvement

Phonics and Structural Analysis

Phonics and Structural Analysis Survey, Test 3			
Skill 11(a)	cats wishes sixes	bells clashes taxes	losses trenches gazes	classes torches blazes
Skill 11(b)	tries pennies wolves	puppies studies halves	buddies leaves wharves	hobbies thieves loaves
Skill 12(a)	rots pitches camped	slips flinches drinking	quits planted tossing	wishes cracked raining
Skill 12(b)	plies ripped jogging	denies grinned cutting	empties fried smiling	marries applied trading
Skill 13(a)	seal's girl's tribes'	actor's raven's pests'	band's ducks' people's	hare's kids' deer's
Skill 13(b)	we're he'll hadn't	she'd I'll weren't	you're wasn't didn't	you'll don't can't
Skill 14(a)	higher smarter thickest	quicker blonder firmest	cheaper hollowest widest	older darkest lightest
Skill 14(b)	sadder grimmer thinnest	dimmer bigger drabbest	fitter gladdest fattest	squatter wettest hippest

Phonics and Structural Analysis

Phonics and Structural Analysis Survey Scoring Sheet, Test 3

1. Letters

(a) Names					Score	(b) Sounds					Score
l	p	e	t				/l/	/p/	/e/	/t/	Consonants:
r	c	s	u				/r/	/k/	/s/	/u/	
y	h	o	d				/y/	/h/	/o/	/d/	/21
x	qu	k	a				/ks/	/kw/	/k/	/a/	
n	z	f	i				/n/	/z/	/f/	/i/	Vowels:
w	v	b	g				/w/	/v/	/b/	/g/	
m	j				/26		/m/	/j/			/5

2. VC and CVC

						Comments	Score
(a) In List	kas	wum	fut	lod	meb		
	bim	lat	mef	vot	dil		/10
(b) In Text	_Mom is not as sad as Pat_.		The _cat ran_ to the _top_.				
	A _man sat on_ a _cup_.		_Did Tim nap in_ the _big bed_?				/20

3. Consonant Digraphs

						Comments	Score
(a) In List	whad	wack	thep	dush	chev		
	ting	lith	whin	reck	shum		/10
(b) In Text	_Mash_ the egg in _this dish_.		_When_ did Meg _sing_?				
	Ted had _chips with_ his _duck_.		Did Gus get _much cash_?				/10

4. CVCC and CCVC

						Comments	Score
(a) In List	bilt	smop	resk	swin	timp		
	griv	gelp	spaf	drev	bosk		/10
(b) In Text	A _gust_ of _wind bent_ the _rest_ of the _mast_.		My _plan_ is to _drag_ a _clam_ on _land_ and _grab_ it.				/10

5. Silent e

						Comments	Score
(a) In List	dife	bupe	mobe	leme	pite		
	vake	gace	debe	sofe	tule		/10
(b) In Text	_Steve_ had to _use_ the _rope_ to _rise_ out of the _huge hole_.		He _came_ to the _wide lake_ and _dove_ in.				/10

Phonics and Structural Analysis

Phonics and Structural Analysis Survey Scoring Sheet, Test 3

6. *r*-Controlled Vowels		Comments	Score
(a) In List	lort hirk narb terl burd zarn borp vurk sirn bern		/10
(b) In Text	We saw a *dark storm turn* and *whirl over* the *river*. She *urged* me with *firm words* to fix the *yard*.		/10

7. Advanced Consonants (*-tch, -dge, -x, qu*, soft *c* & *g, kn, gn, wr, -lk*)		Comments	Score
(a) In List	sitch gudge gux quag celf gerf knal gnam wrik halk		/10
(b) In Text	We buy *quality rice* in *bulk*. The *gnat* flew on my *wrist* and made it *itch*. She untied the *knot* to *fix* it. That is a *giant bandage*!		/10

8. Vowel Teams		Comments	Score
oa, ea, oo, ai, oi, ay, ou, oi, oy, au, aw, oe, ew, al, igh	doat roak deat creal dool scoob pait raim polt olb aym nayt roum spouv oik fois coyn boyl gaut faul awk nawd moev oen tew lew palt kalb tigh kighp		/30

9. Multi-Syllable		Comments	Score
(a) 2-Syllable	en-ter work-out lev-el stair-case dol-lar pen-pal back-pack boil-er teach-er ap-ple		/10
(b) 3-Syllable	hol-i-day af-ter-noon fan-tas-tic com-put-er ter-rif-ic un-der-stand hap-pen-ing rec-om-mend lem-o-nade bal-con-y		/10
(c) 4-Syllable	pre-dic-a-ment ex-per-i-ment com-mun-i-ty as-tron-o-mer dec-lar-a-tion hor-i-zon-tal pre-his-tor-ic an-y-bod-y re-new-a-ble con-sti-tu-tion		/10

10. Prefixes and Suffixes		Comments	Score
dis-, non-, in-, pre-, re-, un-, con-, mis-, -tion, -ous, -ness, -able, -ful, -ary, -ment	disconnect dishonest nonfact nonnews incorrect indefinite prepaid preschool rewrite renew uncover undecided concert confident misspell misplace attention location famous enormous kindness smoothness curable washable careful thankful ordinary honorary movement improvement		/30

Phonics and Structural Analysis

Phonics and Structural Analysis Survey Scoring Sheet, Test 3					
11. Plurals (-s, -es)				**Comments**	**Score**
(a) No spelling changes	cats wishes sixes	bells clashes taxes	losses trenches gazes	classes torches blazes		/12
(b) With spelling changes (*y to i, f, fe to v*)	tries pennies wolves	puppies studies halves	buddies leaves wharves	hobbies thieves loaves		/12
12. Inflectional Verb Endings (-s, -es, -ed, -ing)				**Comments**	**Score**
(a) No spelling changes	rots wishes planted drinking	slips pitches cracked tossing	quits flinches camped raining			/12
(b) With spelling changes	plies marries fried cutting	denies ripped applied smiling	empties grinned jogging trading			/12
13. Possessives and Contractions				**Comments**	**Score**
(a) Possessives (singular, plural, and irregular)	seal's hare's ducks' pests'	actor's girl's kids' people's	band's raven's tribes' deer's			/12
(b) Contractions (pronoun-verb and with *not*)	we're you'll wasn't weren't	she'd he'll don't didn't	you're I'll hadn't can't			/12
14. Comparative Endings (-er, -est)				**Comments**	**Score**
(a) No spelling changes	higher older hollowest firmest	quicker smarter darkest widest	cheaper blonder thickest lightest			/12
(b) With spelling changes	sadder squatter gladdest drabbest	dimmer grimmer wettest fattest	fitter bigger thinnest hippest			/12

Phonics and Structural Analysis

Phonics and Structural Analysis Survey, Test 4

Skill 1(a)	h e r l o d p n f j u c w t s qu g k
Skill 1(b)	i b a z v y m x
Skill 2(a)	tov bis ret pev dit huf lom wak kuv daf
Skill 2(b)	A bug hid in the jug. Ted let Kim hit the can. The mop can sop it up a bit. Did Lin win at tag?
Skill 3(a)	losh kuck whap theg veck chep kang shen whev tich
Skill 3(b)	When can Phil get his wish? Ned did his math with Jan. This map has a gash in it. I had chat with Ben in his shed.
Skill 4(a)	vust vemp glub plid trep brin skub wesp nist demp
Skill 4(b)	The bat fled his damp nest and went on a trip to grab a bug. Yank the flap up and get in the tent, Brad!
Skill 5(a)	kace kide pame fite vone lote gude lide wike pute
Skill 5(b)	Dale rode his bike to the pine grove. Eve and Jake will ride the same mule.

Phonics and Structural Analysis

	Phonics and Structural Analysis Survey, Test 4
Skill 6(a)	jort girk zarb berl rurd varn dorp durk pirn zerm
Skill 6(b)	He blurted out important orders that his poor dog ignored. An artist drew the bird perched with a worm in the yard.
Skill 7(a)	nitch hudge mux quak celg geb knan gnas wrim jalk
Skill 7(b)	Mom will mix and knead dough for a batch of muffins. He quit the game and began to sulk. She gnashed her teeth when she plunged into cold water. The officer has a badge and writes parking tickets.
Skill 8	roan koad leal teap zoot toop vaim jaik kol tolt skay blay mout boun zoi joi loy woy vaul taup spaw yaw noe boe kewl bew kal balt bigh pight
Skill 9(a)	order diner suitcase outside burger running lady football sunshine notebook
Skill 9(b)	reporter vitamin computer elephant envelope acrobat customer feverish foundation tomato
Skill 9(c)	February alligator celebration cemetery memorial spectacular dictionary caterpillar millimeter ordinary
Skill 10	disloyal dismount nonverbal nonhuman insincere infrequent pretest prearrange restart repaint unlucky unheated consent conduct mispronounce mistreat decoration injection nervous various thickness swiftness respectable breakable restful wasteful solitary literary judgement refinement

Phonics and Structural Analysis

Phonics and Structural Analysis Survey, Test 4

Skill 11(a)	beds flashes waxes	hills sashes boxes	grasses inches pinches	bosses perches buzzes
Skill 11(b)	skies kitties cherries	mommies pansies thirties	buggies sheaves leaves	rallies groceries hooves
Skill 12(a)	grabs fizzes blended	spends munches yelling	licks picked swinging	reaches fluffed stretching
Skill 12(b)	tries gripped winning	tidies nodded popping	unifies plied skating	planned shied inhaling
Skill 13(a)	king's painter's skunks'	chimp's moth's frogs'	niece's coaches' nurses'	stork's classmates' mice's
Skill 13(b)	I'd she'll mustn't	they're I'm aren't	they'd haven't shouldn't	you'd wouldn't isn't
Skill 14(a)	higher taller newest	shallower leaner sickest	tighter lowest proudest	shorter fairest bleakest
Skill 14(b)	flatter tanner maddest	snugger hipper grimmest	slimmer trimmest squattest	glummer smuggest primmest

Phonics and Structural Analysis

Phonics and Structural Analysis Survey Scoring Sheet, Test 4

1. Letters		Score			Score
(a) Names	h e r l o d p n f j u c w t s qu g k i b a z v y m x	/26	**(b) Sounds**	/h/ /e/ /r/ /l/ /o/ /d/ /p/ /n/ /f/ /j/ /u/ /k/ /w/ /t/ /s/ /kw/ /g/ /k/ /i/ /b/ /a/ /z/ /v/ /y/ /m/ /ks/	Consonants: /21 Vowels: /5

2. VC and CVC		Comments	Score
(a) In List	tov bis ret pev dit huf lom wak kuv daf		/10
(b) In Text	A *bug* *hid* *in* the *jug*. The *mop* *can* *sop* *it* up a *bit*. *Ted* *let* *Kim* *hit* the *can*. *Did* *Lin* *win* *at* *tag*?		/20

3. Consonant Digraphs		Comments	Score
(a) In List	losh kuck whap theg veck chep kang shen whev tich		/10
(b) In Text	*When* can *Phil* get his *wish*? Ned did his *math* *with* Jan. *This* map has a *gash* in it. I had a *chat* *with* Ben in his *shed*.		/10

4. CVCC and CCVC		Comments	Score
(a) In List	vust vemp glub plid trep brin skub wesp nist demp		/10
(b) In Text	The bat *fled* his *damp* *nest* and *went* on a *trip* to *grab* a bug. *Yank* the *flap* up and get in the *tent*, *Brad*!		/10

5. Silent *e*		Comments	Score
(a) In List	kace kide pame fite vone lote gude lide wike pute		/10
(b) In Text	*Dale* *rode* his *bike* to the *pine* *grove*. *Eve* and *Jake* will *ride* the *same* *mule*.		/10

Phonics and Structural Analysis

Phonics and Structural Analysis Survey Scoring Sheet, Test 4

6. *r*-Controlled Vowels		Comments	Score
(a) In List	jort girk zarb berl rurd varn dorp durk pirn zerm		/10
(b) In Text	He *blurted* out *important* *orders* his *poor* dog *ignored*. An *artist* drew the *bird* *perched* with a *worm* in the *yard*.		/10

7. Advanced Consonants (-*tch*, -*dge*, -*x*, *qu*, soft *c* & *g*, *kn*, *gn*, *wr*, -*lk*)		Comments	Score
(a) In List	nitch hudge mux quak celg geb knan gnas wrim jalk		/10
(b) In Text	Mom will *mix* and *knead* dough for a *batch* of muffins. He *quit* the game and began to *sulk*. She *gnashed* her teeth when she *plunged* into cold water. The *officer* has a *badge* and *writes* parking tickets.		/10

8. Vowel Teams		Comments	Score
oa, ea, oo, ai, ol, ay, ou, oi, oy, au, aw, oe, ew, al, igh	roan koad leal teap zoot toop vaim jaik kol tolt skay blay mout boun zoi joi loy woy vaul taup spaw yaw noe boe kewl bew kal balt bigh pight		/30

9. Multi-Syllable		Comments	Score
(a) 2-Syllable	or-der di-ner suit-case out-side bur-ger run-ning la-dy foot-ball sun-shine note-book		/10
(b) 3-Syllable	re-por-ter vi-ta-min com-pu-ter el-e-phant en-vel-ope ac-ro-bat cus-tom-er fe-ver-ish foun-da-tion to-ma-to		/10
(c) 4-Syllable	Feb-ru-ar-y al-li-ga-tor cel-e-bra-tion cem-e-ter-y mem-or-i-al spec-tac-u-lar dic-tion-ar-y cat-ter-pil-lar mil-li-me-ter or-din-ar-y		/10

10. Prefixes and Suffixes		Comments	Score
dis-, non-, in-, pre-, re-, un-, con-, mis-, -tion, -ous, -ness, -able, -ful, -ary, -ment	disloyal dismount nonverbal nonhuman insincere infrequent pretest prearrange restart repaint unlucky unheated consent conduct mispronounce mistreat decoration injection nervous various thickness swiftness respectable breakable restful wasteful solitary literary judgement refinement		/30

Phonics and Structural Analysis

Phonics and Structural Analysis Survey Scoring Sheet, Test 4			
II. Plurals (-s, -es)		**Comments**	**Score**
(a) No spelling changes	beds hills grasses bosses flashes sashes inches perches waxes boxes pinches buzzes		/12
(b) With spelling changes (*y to i, f, fe to v*)	skies mommies buggies rallies kitties pansies sheaves groceries cherries thirties leaves hooves		/12
I2. Inflectional Verb Endings (-s, -es, -ed, -ing)		**Comments**	**Score**
(a) No spelling changes	grabs spends licks reaches fizzes munches picked fluffed blended yelling swinging stretching		/12
(b) With spelling changes	tries tidies unifies planned gripped nodded plied shied winning popping skating inhaling		/12
I3. Possessives and Contractions		**Comments**	**Score**
(a) Possessives (singular, plural, and irregular)	king's chimp's niece's stork's painter's moth's coaches' classmates' skunks' frogs' nurses' mice's		/12
(b) Contractions (pronoun-verb and with *not*)	I'd they're they'd you'd she'll I'm haven't wouldn't mustn't aren't shouldn't isn't		/12
I4. Comparative Endings (-er, -est)		**Comments**	**Score**
(a) No spelling changes	higher shallower tighter shorter taller leaner lowest fairest newest sickest proudest bleakest		/12
(b) With spelling changes	flatter snugger slimmer glummer tanner hipper trimmest smuggest maddest grimmest squattest primmest		/12

Phonics and Structural Analysis

	Phonics and Structural Analysis Survey, Test 5
Skill 1(a)	w n j o v s e f c z k p r a h u x g
Skill 1(b)	b y i m d l t qu
Skill 2(a)	dib ruk jav nef bak jun hof luf lis wiv
Skill 2(b)	The big man let Jim sit. Is it wet? The cod fit in the pot. Kim got in bed but Ben sat up.
Skill 3(a)	whag jing teck lath chet pesh shup gith reng thun
Skill 3(b)	What did Bill get on his chin? This song is such fun! Is a rat back in his shop? That fish is not rich.
Skill 4(a)	grep clup stob yenk bluv dift tesp gost drep galt
Skill 4(b)	Glen got a lump of gunk to prop up his desk. The cost of the best sink will bust his bank.
Skill 5(a)	bole rume voke vace sipe kize gupe kele dape tede
Skill 5(b)	Steve wove a nice rope and gave it to me. Clive came home to gaze at the waves.

Phonics and Structural Analysis

Phonics and Structural Analysis Survey, Test 5

Skill 6(a)	hort sirk warb derl durd harn gorp nurk girn merm
Skill 6(b)	The first sport I played was hard to learn, but I did score. Thursday she felt sore, having hurt herself on the floor.
Skill 7(a)	zitch kudge plux qual celk gern knam gnaf wrin kalk
Skill 7(b)	She will wrap her knee after the race. Rotten milk makes us cringe. Let's catch the bugs that gnaw on our flowers. The player will quietly flex on the edge of the field.
Skill 8	hoat soan keal beap rool poog waint faing prold trolk blay cray pount noud poil poid noy moy baul staud maw chaw stoe coe pewn frew kal pralt digh twight
Skill 9(a)	edit bucket sandbox swingset ribbon catfish puppy juggle circus kitchen
Skill 9(b)	jellyfish energy totally entertain appetite liberty continent property hurricane medicine
Skill 9(c)	education naturally population excusable electricity situation original territory kilometer graduation
Skill 10	disobey disorder nonguest nonviral inaccurate invest predate preheat relaunch remind unfamiliar unequal conspire convene misuse misquote pollution migration numerous furious politeness softness trainable moveable helpful forgetful cautionary voluntary impairment government

Phonics and Structural Analysis

Phonics and Structural Analysis Survey, Test 5			
Skill 11(a)	cots rashes tuxes	rugs splashes mixes	messes riches glazes	dresses bunches sneezes
Skill 11(b)	berries tabbies sixties	bellies trophies jetties	copies eighties shelves	duties families thieves
Skill 12(a)	trips meshes pushed	mails buzzes stacking	brags spilled waiting	fetches mended fussing
Skill 12(b)	carries mopped clapping	simplifies clipped chopping	replies dried escaping	dragged spied sliding
Skill 13(a)	mom's judge's boys'	fawn's eel's apes'	singer's pets' wives'	bull's knights' oxen's
Skill 13(b)	you're I'll won't	she's they'll weren't	they've couldn't hasn't	he'd doesn't don't
Skill 14(a)	louder meaner richest	briefer milder nearest	older nearest slickest	plumper greenest wildest
Skill 14(b)	sadder grimmer snuggest	fatter gladder biggest	drabber dimmest reddest	thinner hottest wettest

Phonics and Structural Analysis

Phonics and Structural Analysis Survey Scoring Sheet, Test 5

1. Letters		Score						Score
(a) Names	w n j o v s e f c z k p r a h u x g b y i m d l t qu	/26	**(b) Sounds**	/w/ /n/ /v/ /s/ /k/ /z/ /r/ /a/ /ks/ /g/ /i/ /m/ /t/ /kw/	/j/ /o/ /e/ /f/ /k/ /p/ /h/ /u/ /b/ /y/ /d/ /l/			Consonants: /21 Vowels: /5

2. VC and CVC			Comments	Score
(a) In List	dib ruk jav nef bak jun hof luf lis wiv			/10
(b) In Text	The _big_ _man_ _let_ _Jim_ _sit_. The _cod_ _fit_ _in_ the _pot_.	_Is_ _it_ _wet_? _Kim_ _got_ _in_ _bed_ but _Ben_ _sat_ _up_.		/20

3. Consonant Digraphs			Comments	Score
(a) In List	whag jing teck lath chet pesh shup gith reng thun			/10
(b) In Text	_What_ did Bill get on his _chin_? Is a rat _back_ is his _shop_?	_This_ _song_ is _such_ fun! _That_ _fish_ is not _rich_.		/10

4. CVCC and CCVC			Comments	Score
(a) In List	grep clup stob yenk bluv dift tesp gost drep galt			/10
(b) In Text	_Glen_ got a _lump_ of _gunk_ to _prop_ up his _desk_.	The _cost_ of the _best_ _sink_ will _bust_ his _bank_.		/10

5. Silent _e_			Comments	Score
(a) In List	bole rume voke vace sipe kize gupe kele dape tede			/10
(b) In Text	_Steve_ _wove_ a _nice_ _rope_ and _gave_ it to me.	_Clive_ _came_ _home_ to _gaze_ at the _waves_.		/10

Phonics and Structural Analysis

Phonics and Structural Analysis Survey Scoring Sheet, Test 5

6. *r*-Controlled Vowels

		Comments	Score
(a) In List	hort sirk warb derl durd harn gorp nurk girn merm		/10
(b) In Text	The *first* *sport* I played was *hard* to *learn*, but I did *score*. *Thursday* she felt *sore*, having *hurt* *herself* on the *floor*.		/10

7. Advanced Consonants (*-tch, -dge, -x, qu,* soft *c* & *g, kn, gn, wr, -lk*)

		Comments	Score
(a) In List	zitch kudge plux qual celk gern knam gnaf wrin kalk		/10
(b) In Text	She will *wrap* her *knee* after the *race*. Rotten *milk* makes us *cringe*. Let's *catch* the bugs that *gnaw* on our flowers. The player will *quietly* *flex* on the *edge* of the field.		/10

8. Vowel Teams

oa, ea, oo, ai, ol, ay, ou, oi, oy, au, aw, oe, ew, al, igh						Comments	Score
hoat	soan	keal	beap	rool	poog		
waint	faing	prold	trolk	blay	cray		
pount	noud	poil	poid	noy	moy		
baul	staud	maw	chaw	stoe	coe		
pewn	frew	kal	pralt	digh	twight		/30

9. Multi-Syllable

		Comments	Score
(a) 2-Syllable	ed-it buck-et sand-box swing-set rib-bon cat-fish pup-py jug-gle cir-cus kit-chen		/10
(b) 3-Syllable	jel-ly-fish en-er-gy to-tal-ly en-ter-tain a-ppe-tite li-ber-ty con-ti-nent pro-per-ty hur-ri-cane me-di-cine		/10
(c) 4-Syllable	ed-u-ca-tion na-tu-ral-ly pop-u-la-tion ex-cus-a-ble e-lec-tric-i-ty sit-u-a-tion or-i-gin-al ter-ri-tor-y kil-o-me-ter grad-u-a-tion		/10

10. Prefixes and Suffixes

dis-, non-, in-, pre-, re-, un-, con-, mis-, -tion, -ous, -ness, -able, -ful, -ary, -ment				Comments	Score
disobey	disorder	nonguest	nonviral		
inaccurate	invest	predate	preheat		
relaunch	remind	unfamiliar	unequal		
conspire	convene	misuse	misquote		
pollution	migration	numerous	furious		
politeness	softness	trainable	moveable		
helpful	forgetful	cautionary	voluntary		
impairment	government				/30

Phonics and Structural Analysis

Phonics and Structural Analysis Survey Scoring Sheet, Test 5						
11. Plurals (-s, -es)					**Comments**	**Score**
(a) No spelling changes	cots rashes tuxes	rugs splashes mixes	messes riches glazes	dresses bunches sneezes		/12
(b) With spelling changes (y to i, f, fe to v)	berries tabbies sixties	bellies trophies jetties	copies eighties shelves	duties families thieves		/12
12. Inflectional Verb Endings (-s, -es, -ed, -ing)					**Comments**	**Score**
(a) No spelling changes	trips fetches spilled stacking	mails meshes mended waiting	brags buzzes pushed fussing			/12
(b) With spelling changes	carries dragged dried chopping	simplifies mopped spied escaping	replies clipped clapping sliding			/12
13. Possessives and Contractions					**Comments**	**Score**
(a) Possessives (singular, plural, and irregular)	mom's bull's pets' apes'	fawn's judge's knights' wives'	singer's eel's boys' oxen's			/12
(b) Contractions (pronoun-verb and with *not*)	you're he'd couldn't weren't	she's I'll doesn't hasn't	they've they'll won't don't			/12
14. Comparative Endings (-er, -est)					**Comments**	**Score**
(a) No spelling changes	louder plumper nearest nearest	briefer meaner greenest slickest	older milder richest wildest			/12
(b) With spelling changes	sadder thinner dimmest biggest	fatter grimmer hottest reddest	drabber gladder snuggest wettest			/12

Phonics and Structural Analysis

	Phonics and Structural Analysis Survey, Test 6
Skill 1(a)	d g h t qu i l y w b a j s r e v c f
Skill 1(b)	z n k p m u o x
Skill 2(a)	lud til fot nep kem das het pif bel vot
Skill 2(b)	The cat fit in his lap. Ron got the wet log. Ken can let the dog dig. Did Jen set the pen on the rug?
Skill 3(a)	shem hing sech thev huck wheg leck shab dack whep
Skill 3(b)	Did Nick get his ship back? Ben did not get his bath. When did that chap get rich? Wish me luck!
Skill 4(a)	drev gled bolk stot memp rupt plup vunk smet fesk
Skill 4(b)	Did he risk the rest of his plan to set the trap? His hand slid past the grim grin on the mask.
Skill 5(a)	fane hite pofe jeve sume wote beme nafe mide hube
Skill 5(b)	The huge rope by the gate was a live snake! The time came for June to hide her phone.

Phonics and Structural Analysis

	Phonics and Structural Analysis Survey, Test 6
Skill 6(a)	kort wirk darb zerl furd marn jorp furk dirn lerm
Skill 6(b)	The horse nurses its thirsty young in the barn at birth. Part of a day of chores on the farm is to serve corn.
Skill 7(a)	gitch ludge slux quan celm gerv knat gnaz wriz palk
Skill 7(b)	We saw a nest of wrens and a fox. I know a good place to stretch at the gym. Ducks are quacking under the ridge. The garden gnome is next to the plant's stalk.
Skill 8	joam coan fean sweak sloon stoot slait baisk spol rolt scray vays zout moust poil zoi goyn floy naut faus spraw graw joes stoed stewk prewn malg balnd wight tright
Skill 9(a)	bedroom costume rescue petting poster kitten mayor shower fountain benches
Skill 9(b)	disaster tornado medium radio recording gasoline hibernate kangaroo umbrella vanilla
Skill 9(c)	literature congratulations determination biology temperature dictionary triangular operator coordinate rectangular
Skill 10	disown dissappear nonrigid nonlocal informal inoffensive prejudge precaution recount rerun uneven uncommon construct contain misdial miscast graduation protection mysterious spacious greatness softness laughable avoidable cheerful colorful honorary momentary treatment employment

Phonics and Structural Analysis

Phonics and Structural Analysis Survey, Test 6			
Skill 11(a)	huts slashes faxes	blocks bushes suffixes	tresses lunches bronzes	glasses wrenches waltzes
Skill 11(b)	spies tummies bullies	guppies armies elves	follies lilies dwarves	twenties canaries midwives
Skill 12(a)	costs mashes grilled	throws twitches clicking	spells picked staying	hushes barked singing
Skill 12(b)	tallies hummed studied	marries begged dripping	implies cried placing	flipped replied inflating
Skill 13(a)	duke's sister's dancers'	mare's turtle's bears'	pilot's pupils' women's	man's chiefs' sheep's
Skill 13(b)	he's you'd isn't	it's we've didn't	I've wasn't haven't	they're can't wouldn't
Skill 14(a)	brisker slighter dullest	poorer fewer tallest	yellower kindest oddest	deeper weakest boldest
Skill 14(b)	hotter squatter saddest	smugger wetter gladdest	madder fittest trimmest	flatter primmest slimmest

Phonics and Structural Analysis

Phonics and Structural Analysis Survey Scoring Sheet, Test 6

1. Letters

(a) Names					Score	(b) Sounds					Score
d	g	h	t			/d/	/g/	/h/	/t/		Consonants:
qu	i	l	y			/kw/	/i/	/l/	/y/		
w	b	a	j			/w/	/b/	/a/	/j/		/21
s	r	e	v			/s/	/r/	/e/	/v/		
c	f	z	n			/k/	/f/	/z/	/n/		Vowels:
k	p	m	u			/k/	/p/	/m/	/u/		
o	x				/26	/o/	/ks/				/5

2. VC and CVC

						Comments	Score
(a) In List	lud	til	fot	nep	kem		
	das	het	pif	bel	vot		/10
(b) In Text	The _cat fit in his lap_. _Ken can let_ the _dog dig_.		Ron _got_ the _wet log_. _Did_ Jen _set_ the _pen on_ the _rug_?				/20

3. Consonant Digraphs

						Comments	Score
(a) In List	shem	hing	sech	thev	huck		
	wheg	leck	shab	dack	whep		/10
(b) In Text	Did _Nick_ get his _ship back_? _When_ did _that chap_ get _rich_?		Ben did not get his _bath_. _Wish_ me _luck_!				/10

4. CVCC and CCVC

						Comments	Score
(a) In List	drev	gled	bolk	stot	memp		
	rupt	plup	vunk	smet	fesk		/10
(b) In Text	Did he _risk_ the _rest_ of his _plan_ to set the _trap_?		His _hand slid past_ the _grim grin_ on the _mask_.				/10

5. Silent e

						Comments	Score
(a) In List	fane	hite	pofe	jeve	sume		
	wote	beme	nafe	mide	hube		/10
(b) In Text	The _huge rope_ by the _gate_ was a _live snake_!		The _time came_ for _June_ to _hide_ her _phone_.				/10

Phonics and Structural Analysis

Phonics and Structural Analysis Survey Scoring Sheet, Test 6

6. *r*-Controlled Vowels					Comments	Score
(a) In List	kort wirk darb zerl furd marn jorp furk dirn lerm					/10
(b) In Text	The *horse* *nurses* its *thirsty* young in the *barn* at *birth*.		*Part* of a day of *chores* on the *farm* is to *serve* *corn*.			/10

7. Advanced Consonants (*-tch, -dge, -x, qu,* soft *c* & *g, kn, gn, wr, -lk*)					Comments	Score
(a) In List	gitch ludge slux quan celm gerv knat gnaz wriz palk					/10
(b) In Text	We saw a nest of *wrens* and a *fox*. Ducks are *quacking* under the *ridge*.		I *know* a good *place* to *stretch* at the *gym*. The garden *gnome* is next to the plant's *stalk*.			/10

8. Vowel Teams						Comments	Score
oa, ea, oo, ai, oi, ay, ou, oi, oy, au, aw, oe, ew, al, igh	joam stoot scray zoi spraw prewn	coan slait vays goyn graw malg	fean baisk zout floy joes balnd	sweak spol moust naut stoed wight	sloon rolt poil faus stewk tright		/30

9. Multi-Syllable					Comments	Score
(a) 2-Syllable	bed-room cos-tume res-cue pet-ting pos-ter kit-ten ma-yor show-er foun-tain ben-ches					/10
(b) 3-Syllable	dis-as-ter tor-na-do me-di-um ra-di-o re-cor-ding gas-o-line hi-ber-nate kan-ga-roo um-brel-la va-nil-la					/10
(c) 4-Syllable	lit-er-a-ture con-grat-u-la-tions de-ter-min-a-tion bi-o-lo-gy tem-per-a-ture dic-tion-ar-y tri-an-gu-lar op-er-a-tor co-or-di-nate rec-tan-gu-lar					/10

10. Prefixes and Suffixes					Comments	Score
dis-, non-, in-, pre-, re-, un-, con-, -mis, -tion, -ous, -ness, -able, -ful, -ary, -ment	disown informal recount construct graduation greatness cheerful treatment	disappear inoffensive rerun contain protection softness colorful employment	nonrigid prejude uneven misdial mysterious laughable honorary	nonlocal precaution uncommon miscast spacious avoidable momentary		/30

Phonics and Structural Analysis

Phonics and Structural Analysis Survey Scoring Sheet, Test 6						
11. Plurals (-s, -es)					**Comments**	**Score**
(a) No spelling changes	huts slashes faxes	blocks bushes suffixes	tresses lunches bronzes	glasses wrenches waltzes		/12
(b) With spelling changes (y to i, f, fe to v)	spies tummies bullies	guppies armies elves	follies lilies dwarves	twenties canaries wives		/12
12. Inflectional Verb Endings (-s, -es, -ed, -ing)					**Comments**	**Score**
(a) No spelling changes	costs hushes picked clicking	throws mashes barked staying	spells twitches grilled singing			/12
(b) With spelling changes	tallies flipped cried dripping	marries hummed replied placing	implies begged studied inflating			/12
13. Possessives and Contractions					**Comments**	**Score**
(a) Possessives (singular, plural, and irregular)	duke's man's pupils' bears'	mare's sister's chiefs' women's	pilot's turtle's dancers' sheep's			/12
(b) Contractions (pronoun-verb and with not)	he's they're wasn't didn't	it's you'd can't haven't	I've we've isn't wouldn't			/12
14. Comparative Endings (-er, -est)					**Comments**	**Score**
(a) No spelling changes	brisker deeper kindest tallest	poorer slighter weakest oddest	yellower fewer dullest boldest			/12
(b) With spelling changes	hotter flatter fittest gladdest	smugger squatter primmest trimmest	madder wetter saddest slimmest			/12

Fluency
Assessment

Jazz

My name is Phillip. This is my pet hamster Jazz.

He is brown with spots of white.

He has a little pink nose.

He is small and very cute.

This is his cage. It is where he plays and sleeps.

He sleeps most of the day. He plays at night.

There is a wheel in his cage. Jazz likes to run.

He goes up on the wheel.

He goes down on the wheel.

Then Jazz drinks some water and eats.

I change his water and food every day.

Jazz is the best.

✔ Who is Jazz?

✔ What does the narrator think of Jazz?

Name: _____ Date: _____

Jazz

10	My name is Phillip. This is my pet hamster Jazz.
17	He is brown with spots of white.
23	He has a little pink nose.
29	He is small and very cute.
40	This is his cage. It is where he plays and sleeps.
50	He sleeps most of the day. He plays at night.
61	There is a wheel in his cage. Jazz likes to run.
67	He goes up on the wheel.
73	He goes down on the wheel.
80	Then Jazz drinks some water and eats.
88	I change his water and food every day.
92	Jazz is the best.

 Who is Jazz?

 What does the narrator think of Jazz?

Words Read	-	Errors	=	WCPM

☐ **Fall (51 WCPM)**
☐ **Winter (72 WCPM)**
☐ **Spring (89 WCPM)**

WCPM	÷	Words Read	=	Accuracy %

PROSODY				
	L1	L2	L3	L4
Reading in Phrases	O	O	O	O
Pace	O	O	O	O
Syntax	O	O	O	O
Self-correction	O	O	O	O
Intonation	O	O	O	O

So Many Ants

There are many kinds of ants.

Most ants are small.

But some are big. Ants can be one inch long.

Most ants are black.

There are yellow and green ants too.

There are even purple ants.

Some ants live in trees.

Others make nests in sand.

Ants are strong. They can lift big things.

They can lift things that are bigger than them!

Ants help each other. Some ants make nests.

Other ants protect the nests.

A different group looks for food.

There is another important job.

It is to care for baby ants.

Look for ants in a park. They are fun to watch!

✔ What is the MAIN idea of the article?

✔ How do ants help each other?

Name: _____ Date: _____

So Many Ants

6	There are many kinds of ants.
10	Most ants are small.
20	But some are big. Ants can be one inch long.
24	Most ants are black.
31	There are yellow and green ants too.
36	There are even purple ants.
41	Some ants live in trees.
46	Others make nests in sand.
54	Ants are strong. They can lift big things.
63	They can lift things that are bigger than them!
71	Ants help each other. Some ants make nests.
76	Other ants protect the nests.
82	A different group looks for food.
87	There is another important job.
94	It is to care for baby ants.
105	Look for ants in a park. They are fun to watch!

 What is the MAIN idea of the article?

✓ How do ants help each other?

Words Read	-	Errors	=	WCPM

☐ **Fall (51 WCPM)**
☐ **Winter (72 WCPM)**
☐ **Spring (89 WCPM)**

WCPM	÷	Words Read	=	Accuracy %

PROSODY	L1	L2	L3	L4
Reading in Phrases	O	O	O	O
Pace	O	O	O	O
Syntax	O	O	O	O
Self-correction	O	O	O	O
Intonation	O	O	O	O

Elephant and Turtle

Elephant sat up and looked at the clock.

He would be late for school!

Elephant got dressed. He ate a banana.

He grabbed his books.

He put them in a backpack.

Elephant ran down the street.

He had to get to school!

On the way, he saw Turtle.

Turtle was also late for school.

Turtle walked very slowly.

Elephant knew that Turtle would be very late.

He knew that Turtle would get in trouble.

So Elephant had an idea.

He put Turtle in his backpack.

Elephant ran all the way to school.

They got to class before the bell rang.

They were not late.

👆 How does Elephant help Turtle?

👆 What is the message of this story?

Name: _____   Date: _____

Elephant and Turtle

8	Elephant sat up and looked at the clock.
14	He would be late for school!
21	Elephant got dressed. He ate a banana.
25	He grabbed his books.
31	He put them in a backpack.
36	Elephant ran down the street.
42	He had to get to school!
48	On the way, he saw Turtle.
54	Turtle was also late for school.
58	Turtle walked very slowly.
66	Elephant knew that Turtle would be very late.
74	He knew that Turtle would get in trouble.
79	So Elephant had an idea.
85	He put Turtle in his backpack.
92	Elephant ran all the way to school.
100	They got to class before the bell rang.
104	They were not late.

 How does Elephant help Turtle?

 What is the message of this story?

Words Read	-	Errors	=	WCPM

☐ **Fall (51 WCPM)**
☐ **Winter (72 WCPM)**
☐ **Spring (89 WCPM)**

WCPM	÷	Words Read	=	Accuracy %

PROSODY				
	L1	L2	L3	L4
Reading in Phrases	O	O	O	O
Pace	O	O	O	O
Syntax	O	O	O	O
Self-correction	O	O	O	O
Intonation	O	O	O	O

Bird Homes

Where do birds live? Birds live in many places.

This bird lives in a park. It hops in the grass.

It picks up twigs with its beak.

The bird uses twigs to make a nest.

Look into the nest. What do you see?

You may see eggs. You may see baby birds.

This bird lives in the woods.

Do you hear that sound?

The bird is pecking a hole in a tree. It is loud.

His beak is strong to peck a hole.

It cuts a hole in the tree for a home.

✔ What do birds use to make a nest?

✔ Why does a bird make a hole in a tree?

Name: _____ Date: _____

Bird Homes

9	Where do birds live? Birds live in many places.
20	This bird lives in a park. It hops in the grass.
27	It picks up twigs with its beak.
35	The bird uses twigs to make a nest.
43	Look into the nest. What do you see?
52	You may see eggs. You may see baby birds.
58	This bird lives in the woods.
63	Do you hear that sound?
75	The bird is pecking a hole in a tree. It is loud.
83	His beak is strong to peck a hole.
93	It cuts a hole in the tree for a home.

 What do birds use to make a nest?

 Why does a bird make a hole in a tree?

Words Read	-	Errors	=	WCPM

☐ **Fall (51 WCPM)**
☐ **Winter (72 WCPM)**
☐ **Spring (89 WCPM)**

WCPM	÷	Words Read	=	Accuracy %

PROSODY

	L1	L2	L3	L4
Reading in Phrases	O	O	O	O
Pace	O	O	O	O
Syntax	O	O	O	O
Self-correction	O	O	O	O
Intonation	O	O	O	O

Crab and Clam

One day, Crab saw Clam on the beach.

He said, "You are like me."

Crab had a shell. Clam had one, too.

Clam said, "Yes, and we both live near the sea."

Crab had many strong legs.

He could run very fast.

He said, "Can you run, Clam?"

"No," said Clam. He was slow.

Clam had one foot.

He used it to get around. It could scoop sand.

Clam ate plants.

He asked, "What do you eat, Crab?"

"I eat clams!" said Crab.

Crab didn't look so friendly anymore.

Clam moved as fast as he could.

"Bye!" yelled Clam.

✓ How are Clam and Crab alike?

✓ Why does Clam leave at the end of the story?

Name: _____ Date: _____

Crab and Clam

8	One day, Crab saw Clam on the beach.
14	He said, "You are like me."
22	Crab had a shell. Clam had one, too.
32	Clam said, "Yes, and we both live near the sea."
37	Crab had many strong legs.
42	He could run very fast.
48	He said, "Can you run, Clam?"
54	"No," said Clam. He was slow.
58	Clam had one foot.
68	He used it to get around. It could scoop sand.
71	Clam ate plants.
78	He asked, "What do you eat, Crab?"
83	"I eat clams!" said Crab.
89	Crab didn't look so friendly anymore.
96	Clam moved as fast as he could.
99	"Bye!" yelled Clam.

 How are Clam and Crab alike?

 Why does Clam leave at the end of the story?

Words Read	-	Errors	=	WCPM

☐ **Fall (51 WCPM)**
☐ **Winter (72 WCPM)**
☐ **Spring (89 WCPM)**

WCPM	÷	Words Read	=	Accuracy %

PROSODY				
	L1	L2	L3	L4
Reading in Phrases	O	O	O	O
Pace	O	O	O	O
Syntax	O	O	O	O
Self-correction	O	O	O	O
Intonation	O	O	O	O

Let's Ski!

Many children ski. It is fun to ski in the snow.

Children dress to stay warm.

They dress to stay dry.

Snow is very cold. It is wet.

They wear goggles.

These keep snow out of their eyes.

Children use small skis. They are easy to use.

First they go down small hills. They don't go fast.

They practice a lot on small hills.

Later they jump over small bumps.

It is fun to ski over bumps of snow.

Adults must be near when children ski.

Adults make sure no one gets hurt. Let's ski!

✓ What do goggles do?

✓ Who needs to be close when children ski?

Name: _____ Date: _____

Let's Ski!

11	Many children ski. It is fun to ski in the snow.
16	Children dress to stay warm.
21	They dress to stay dry.
28	Snow is very cold. It is wet.
31	They wear goggles.
38	These keep snow out of their eyes.
47	Children use small skis. They are easy to use.
57	First they go down small hills. They don't go fast.
64	They practice a lot on small hills.
70	Later they jump over small bumps.
79	It is fun to ski over bumps of snow.
86	Adults must be near when children ski.
95	Adults make sure no one gets hurt. Let's ski!

 What do goggles do?

Who needs to be close when children ski?

Words Read	-	Errors	=	WCPM

☐ **Fall (51 WCPM)**
☐ **Winter (72 WCPM)**
☐ **Spring (89 WCPM)**

WCPM	÷	Words Read	=	Accuracy %

PROSODY				
	L1	L2	L3	L4
Reading in Phrases	O	O	O	O
Pace	O	O	O	O
Syntax	O	O	O	O
Self-correction	O	O	O	O
Intonation	O	O	O	O

Mandy and Paul

Mandy always plays ball with Paul.

They like to play on the lawn.

Mandy is six and Paul is four.

Mandy throws the ball to Paul.

The ball flies past Paul. It goes into the street.

Paul runs to get the ball.

Mandy calls, "No, Paul! Don't get the ball!

Stay on the lawn!"

Mandy runs to stop Paul.

She grabs his arms. She sticks to him like glue!

Mandy makes Paul stop.

Mom and Dad run outside.

"Nice job, Mandy!" Mom says. "You saved Paul!"

"I always want Paul safe," Mandy says.

✓ What are Mandy and Paul doing?

✓ How does Mandy help Paul?

Name: _____ Date: _____

Mandy and Paul

6	Mandy always plays ball with Paul.
13	They like to play on the lawn.
20	Mandy is six and Paul is four.
26	Mandy throws the ball to Paul.
36	The ball flies past Paul. It goes into the street.
42	Paul runs to get the ball.
50	Mandy calls, "No, Paul! Don't get the ball!
54	Stay on the lawn!"
59	Mandy runs to stop Paul.
69	She grabs his arms. She sticks to him like glue!
73	Mandy makes Paul stop.
78	Mom and Dad run outside.
86	"Nice job, Mandy!" Mom says. "You saved Paul!"
93	"I always want Paul safe," Mandy says.

 What are Mandy and Paul doing?

 How does Mandy help Paul?

Words Read	-	Errors	=	WCPM

- ☐ **Fall (51 WCPM)**
- ☐ **Winter (72 WCPM)**
- ☐ **Spring (89 WCPM)**

WCPM	÷	Words Read	=	Accuracy %

PROSODY				
	L1	L2	L3	L4
Reading in Phrases	O	O	O	O
Pace	O	O	O	O
Syntax	O	O	O	O
Self-correction	O	O	O	O
Intonation	O	O	O	O

Firefighters

The firefighters wait in the station.

They are ready for a fire.

The alarm goes off! It is very loud.

The firefighters put on jackets.

The jackets will keep them safe.

Then they jump into the fire truck.

The lights on the truck turn on. The siren blasts.

It is loud so that other cars will clear the way.

The firefighters race to the fire.

Someone gave 911 the address.

The truck can get to the fire fast.

The firefighters work to stop the heat and fire.

They have a special hose. It puts the fire out.

Firefighters save lives.

✔ Why is the fire truck siren so loud?

✔ How do firefighters know there is a fire?

Name: _____ Date: _____

Firefighters

6	The firefighters wait in the station.
12	They are ready for a fire.
20	The alarm goes off! It is very loud.
25	The firefighters put on jackets.
31	The jackets will keep them safe.
38	Then they jump into the fire truck.
48	The lights on the truck turn on. The siren blasts.
59	It is loud so that other cars will clear the way.
65	The firefighters race to the fire.
70	Someone gave 911 the address.
78	The truck can get to the fire fast.
87	The firefighters work to stop the heat and fire.
97	They have a special hose. It puts the fire out.
100	Firefighters save lives.

✔ Why is the fire truck siren so loud?

✔ How do firefighters know there is a fire?

Words Read	-	Errors	=	WCPM

☐ **Fall (51 WCPM)**
☐ **Winter (72 WCPM)**
☐ **Spring (89 WCPM)**

WCPM	÷	Words Read	=	Accuracy %

PROSODY

	L1	L2	L3	L4
Reading in Phrases	O	O	O	O
Pace	O	O	O	O
Syntax	O	O	O	O
Self-correction	O	O	O	O
Intonation	O	O	O	O

Joan's Daydream

Joan did not want to play hopscotch.

But Maria said it would be fun.

Maria threw the first stone.

The stone landed on the first square.

Maria hopped over that square. Joan watched.

But Joan did not pay much attention.

She started to daydream.

Joan looked at squares. She watched Maria hop.

Wherever Maria hopped, flowers sprouted up!

Maria kept hopping. More flowers grew.

The flowers grew taller and taller.

Soon the hopscotch court was a jungle!

Joan heard a voice.

It came from deep in the jungle.

It was Maria's voice!

She was telling Joan that it was her turn.

✔ What are Joan and Maria playing?

✔ How can the reader tell that Joan is daydreaming?

Name: _____ Date: _____

Joan's Daydream

7	Joan did not want to play hopscotch.
14	But Maria said it would be fun.
19	Maria threw the first stone.
26	The stone landed on the first square.
33	Maria hopped over that square. Joan watched.
40	But Joan did not pay much attention.
44	She started to daydream.
52	Joan looked at squares. She watched Maria hop.
58	Wherever Maria hopped, flowers sprouted up!
64	Maria kept hopping. More flowers grew.
70	The flowers grew taller and taller.
77	Soon the hopscotch court was a jungle!
81	Joan heard a voice.
88	It came from deep in the jungle.
92	It was Maria's voice!
101	She was telling Joan that it was her turn.

✔ What are Joan and Maria playing?

✔ How can the reader tell that Joan is daydreaming?

Words Read	-	Errors	=	WCPM

☐ **Fall (51 WCPM)**
☐ **Winter (72 WCPM)**
☐ **Spring (89 WCPM)**

WCPM	÷	Words Read	=	Accuracy %

PROSODY

	L1	L2	L3	L4
Reading in Phrases	O	O	O	O
Pace	O	O	O	O
Syntax	O	O	O	O
Self-correction	O	O	O	O
Intonation	O	O	O	O

All Kinds of Holidays

Holidays are fun.

There are many different holidays.

One holiday, we give thanks for what we have.

Families share special meals.

What is this celebration called?

On another special day, there are parades.

There are lots of floats.

There are fireworks at night.

What is that holiday called?

Another holiday celebrates veterans.

People make speeches.

We remember veterans.

What is this day called?

Have you heard of a holiday called Arbor Day?

People plant new trees in dirt.

They try to help Earth.

What is your favorite holiday?

☑ Which holiday in the article is MOST LIKELY July 4th?

☑ What do people do on Arbor Day?

Name: _____   Date: _____

All Kinds of Holidays

3	Holidays are fun.
8	There are many different holidays.
17	One holiday, we give thanks for what we have.
21	Families share special meals.
26	What is this celebration called?
33	On another special day, there are parades.
38	There are lots of floats.
43	There are fireworks at night.
48	What is that holiday called?
52	Another holiday celebrates veterans.
55	People make speeches.
58	We remember veterans.
63	What is this day called?
72	Have you heard of a holiday called Arbor Day?
78	People plant new trees in dirt.
83	They try to help Earth.
88	What is your favorite holiday?

 Which holiday in the article is MOST LIKELY July 4th?

 What do people do on Arbor Day?

Words Read	-	Errors	=	WCPM

- ☐ **Fall (51 WCPM)**
- ☐ **Winter (72 WCPM)**
- ☐ **Spring (89 WCPM)**

WCPM	÷	Words Read	=	Accuracy %

PROSODY	L1	L2	L3	L4
Reading in Phrases	O	O	O	O
Pace	O	O	O	O
Syntax	O	O	O	O
Self-correction	O	O	O	O
Intonation	O	O	O	O

Carly in the Dark

My name is Carly.

I'm a smart kid, but I don't like the dark.

It doesn't matter if I am very tired.

As soon as Mom turns out the light, I'm awake.

Poor me! I pull my blanket up to my chin.

Then I look around my room.

Shapes seem to creep out of the walls.

I shout, "Mom!"

Mom says that the dark can play tricks.

"It's just car lights shining inside," she says.

Still, it's hard to sleep. So Mom has a plan.

She will get me a night-light. She's so smart!

Now I will sleep through the night.

✓ What is Carly's problem?

✓ How does Mom solve the problem?

Name: _____ Date: _____

Carly in the Dark

4	My name is Carly.
14	I'm a smart kid, but I don't like the dark.
22	It doesn't matter if I am very tired.
32	As soon as Mom turns out the light, I'm awake.
42	Poor me! I pull my blanket up to my chin.
48	Then I look around my room.
56	Shapes seem to creep out of the walls.
59	I shout, "Mom!"
67	Mom says that the dark can play tricks.
75	"It's just car lights shining inside," she says.
85	Still, it's hard to sleep. So Mom has a plan.
95	She will get me a night-light. She's so smart!
102	Now I will sleep through the night.

 What is Carly's problem?

 How does Mom solve the problem?

Words Read	-	Errors	=	WCPM

☐ Fall (51 WCPM)
☐ Winter (72 WCPM)
☐ Spring (89 WCPM)

WCPM	÷	Words Read	=	Accuracy %

PROSODY				
	L1	L2	L3	L4
Reading in Phrases	O	O	O	O
Pace	O	O	O	O
Syntax	O	O	O	O
Self-correction	O	O	O	O
Intonation	O	O	O	O

Elephants and Their Trunks

Baby elephants drink milk.

But soon they will find their own food.

Elephants have trunks. Trunks are like long noses.

A trunk grabs things. It picks them up.

Trunks are useful.

Trunks help elephants get food.

Baby elephants learn to use them.

Elephants eat leaves and fruit.

But these are high in the trees.

Trunks can help. They can reach high branches.

Elephants need water.

A trunk is helpful here, too.

Elephants suck water into their trunks.

They bring the trunks to their mouths.

They drink the water from their trunks.

✓ What do elephants eat?

✓ How do trunks help elephants?

Name: _____ Date: _____

Elephants and Their Trunks

4	Baby elephants drink milk.
12	But soon they will find their own food.
20	Elephants have trunks. Trunks are like long noses.
28	A trunk grabs things. It picks them up.
31	Trunks are useful.
36	Trunks help elephants get food.
42	Baby elephants learn to use them.
47	Elephants eat leaves and fruit.
54	But these are high in the trees.
62	Trunks can help. They can reach high branches.
65	Elephants need water.
71	A trunk is helpful here, too.
77	Elephants suck water into their trunks.
84	They bring the trunks to their mouths.
91	They drink the water from their trunks.

 What do elephants eat?

 How do trunks help elephants?

Words Read	-	Errors	=	WCPM

☐ **Fall (51 WCPM)**
☐ **Winter (72 WCPM)**
☐ **Spring (89 WCPM)**

WCPM	÷	Words Read	=	Accuracy %

PROSODY				
	L1	L2	L3	L4
Reading in Phrases	O	O	O	O
Pace	O	O	O	O
Syntax	O	O	O	O
Self-correction	O	O	O	O
Intonation	O	O	O	O

Lady and Spike

We have two pets. We have a cat and a dog.

Our dog's name is Lady. Her fur is white.

Our cat's name is Spike. His fur is black.

Lady likes to chase balls. She chases her tail.

Spike chases mice. Spike naps a lot.

People think dogs and cats are not friends.

That is not always true.

Lady and Spike are very good friends.

Sometimes they clean each other.

Spike licks Lady's ears.

Sometimes they play together.

Lady will roll a ball to Spike.

They like to nap together on the mat.

✔ What does Spike like to do?

✔ How are Spike and Lady different from other cats and dogs?

Name: _____   Date: _____

Lady and Spike

11	We have two pets. We have a cat and a dog.
20	Our dog's name is Lady. Her fur is white.
29	Our cat's name is Spike. His fur is black.
38	Lady likes to chase balls. She chases her tail.
45	Spike chases mice. Spike naps a lot.
53	People think dogs and cats are not friends.
58	That is not always true.
65	Lady and Spike are very good friends.
70	Sometimes they clean each other.
74	Spike licks Lady's ears.
78	Sometimes they play together.
85	Lady will roll a ball to Spike.
93	They like to nap together on the mat.

 What does Spike like to do?

 How are Spike and Lady different from other cats and dogs?

Words Read	-	Errors	=	WCPM

☐ **Fall (51 WCPM)**

☐ **Winter (72 WCPM)**

☐ **Spring (89 WCPM)**

WCPM	÷	Words Read	=	Accuracy %

PROSODY				
	L1	L2	L3	L4
Reading in Phrases	O	O	O	O
Pace	O	O	O	O
Syntax	O	O	O	O
Self-correction	O	O	O	O
Intonation	O	O	O	O

People Need Trees

Trees give people food to eat.

Fruits grow on trees. Apples come from trees.

Oranges and bananas do, too.

Trees give us wood. It is used for many things.

Wood makes good homes for people.

Some things in homes are made of wood.

Tables and chairs are made of wood.

Many toys are, too.

Trees also give us paper. Wood is cut into chips.

The wood chips are made into pulp.

Pulp is soft and wet. The pulp is pressed thin.

Then it dries into paper.

Trees are good for the air, too.

They keep the air clean. Trees are very helpful!

☑ Name two things for which wood is used.

☑ How is paper made?

Name: _____ Date: _____

People Need Trees

6	Trees give people food to eat.
14	Fruits grow on trees. Apples come from trees.
19	Oranges and bananas do, too.
29	Trees give us wood. It is used for many things.
35	Wood makes good homes for people.
43	Some things in homes are made of wood.
50	Tables and chairs are made of wood.
54	Many toys are, too.
64	Trees also give us paper. Wood is cut into chips.
71	The wood chips are made into pulp.
81	Pulp is soft and wet. The pulp is pressed thin.
86	Then it dries into paper.
93	Trees are good for the air, too.
102	They keep the air clean. Trees are very helpful!

 Name two things for which wood is used.

 How is paper made?

Words Read	-	Errors	=	WCPM

☐ **Fall (51 WCPM)**
☐ **Winter (72 WCPM)**
☐ **Spring (89 WCPM)**

WCPM	÷	Words Read	=	Accuracy %

PROSODY				
	L1	L2	L3	L4
Reading in Phrases	O	O	O	O
Pace	O	O	O	O
Syntax	O	O	O	O
Self-correction	O	O	O	O
Intonation	O	O	O	O

My Photo Album

I am looking at photos in my photo album.

This picture is from last spring.

I am standing with my mom and my dad.

We are about to get on an airplane.

We are going to see my grandparents.

This is my sister, Kim. Kim is five.

Here I am with Kim. We are standing by a lake.

The big, brown dog is Shaw.

In this picture, Shaw jumps into the lake.

He was soaked when he came out.

I had to dry him off.

There is more to see, but it is time for bed.

✔ When did the narrator take a plane ride?

✔ Who is Shaw?

Name: _____ Date: _____

My Photo Album

9	I am looking at photos in my photo album.
15	This picture is from last spring.
24	I am standing with my mom and my dad.
32	We are about to get on an airplane.
39	We are going to see my grandparents.
47	This is my sister, Kim. Kim is five.
58	Here I am with Kim. We are standing by a lake.
64	The big, brown dog is Shaw.
72	In this picture, Shaw jumps into the lake.
79	He was soaked when he came out.
85	I had to dry him off.
96	There is more to see, but it is time for bed.

✓ When did the narrator take a plane ride?

✓ Who is Shaw?

Words Read	-	Errors	=	WCPM

☐ **Fall (51 WCPM)**
☐ **Winter (72 WCPM)**
☐ **Spring (89 WCPM)**

WCPM	÷	Words Read	=	Accuracy %

PROSODY

	L1	L2	L3	L4
Reading in Phrases	O	O	O	O
Pace	O	O	O	O
Syntax	O	O	O	O
Self-correction	O	O	O	O
Intonation	O	O	O	O

A Family of Bears

Bears live in places called *dens*.

Baby bears are called *cubs*.

The cubs live with their mother.

The cubs are little.

They do not to go outside.

They run and play in the den.

The mother bear hunts for food.

Then she brings it to the den.

The cubs get bigger.

Their mother shows them how to hunt.

They look for mice and fish.

They search for nuts and ants.

They catch bugs called *grubs*.

They think that bugs are yummy!

✓ Why do cubs stay in dens?

✓ What do cubs eat?

Name: _____ Date: _____

A Family of Bears

6	Bears live in places called *dens*.
11	Baby bears are called *cubs*.
17	The cubs live with their mother.
21	The cubs are little.
27	They do not to go outside.
34	They run and play in the den.
40	The mother bear hunts for food.
47	Then she brings it to the den.
51	The cubs get bigger.
58	Their mother shows them how to hunt.
64	They look for mice and fish.
70	They search for nuts and ants.
75	They catch bugs called *grubs*.
81	They think that bugs are yummy!

 Why do cubs stay in dens?

 What do cubs eat?

Words Read	-	Errors	=	WCPM

☐ **Fall (51 WCPM)**
☐ **Winter (72 WCPM)**
☐ **Spring (89 WCPM)**

WCPM	÷	Words Read	=	Accuracy %

PROSODY

	L1	L2	L3	L4
Reading in Phrases	O	O	O	O
Pace	O	O	O	O
Syntax	O	O	O	O
Self-correction	O	O	O	O
Intonation	O	O	O	O

The Wright Brothers

The Wright brothers were inventors.

The both of them dreamed of flying.

They hoped to build a flying machine.

Both brothers were curious as children.

They liked to see how things worked.

As grownups, they worked in a bike shop.

The Wright brothers built a glider.

The glider was very light. It had two wings.

Each wing was covered with cloth.

They tested their glider. It flew like a kite.

After the test, one brother got on the glider.

He glided in the air.

The Wright brothers made many gliders.

They tested each one.

Their gliders got better with every test.

Each one stayed in the air longer and longer.

✓ What was the Wright brothers' dream?

✓ Where did the Wright brother work?

Name: _____ Date: _____

The Wright Brothers

5	The Wright brothers were inventors.
12	The both of them dreamed of flying.
19	They hoped to build a flying machine.
25	Both brothers were curious as children.
32	They liked to see how things worked.
40	As grownups, they worked in a bike shop.
46	The Wright brothers built a glider.
55	The glider was very light. It had two wings.
61	Each wing was covered with cloth.
70	They tested their glider. It flew like a kite.
79	After the test, one brother got on the glider.
84	He glided in the air.
90	The Wright brothers made many gliders.
94	They tested each one.
101	Their gliders got better with every test.
110	Each one stayed in the air longer and longer.

✎ What was the Wright brothers' dream?

✎ Where did the Wright brother work?

Words Read	-	Errors	=	WCPM

☐ **Fall (51 WCPM)**
☐ **Winter (72 WCPM)**
☐ **Spring (89 WCPM)**

WCPM	÷	Words Read	=	Accuracy %

PROSODY

	L1	L2	L3	L4
Reading in Phrases	O	O	O	O
Pace	O	O	O	O
Syntax	O	O	O	O
Self-correction	O	O	O	O
Intonation	O	O	O	O

The Pet Show

Last week, we put on a pet show.

It was at the Tate School in Ms. Hale's class.

Gale came with a fish, and Eric brought his dog.

Daniel came with a snake, and Jane had a frog.

"His name is Wade," said Jane. "He is the best!"

"Why?" Gale asked.

Then Wade jumped up.

Jane yelled, "Get Wade!"

We all helped, but Jane's frog got away.

Where did Wade end up?

We looked under desks; we looked in the hall.

Then we found him. He was inside the fish tank!

Ms. Hale located a net and scooped up Wade.

She said, "Everyone, hold on to your pets!"

✓ How can the reader tell that Jane likes Wade?

✓ Why is Wade hard to find?

Name: _____ Date: _____

The Pet Show

8	Last week, we put on a pet show.
18	It was at the Tate School in Ms. Hale's class.
28	Gale came with a fish, and Eric brought his dog.
38	Daniel came with a snake, and Jane had a frog.
48	"His name is Wade," said Jane. "He is the best!"
51	"Why?" Gale asked.
55	Then Wade jumped up.
59	Jane yelled, "Get Wade!"
67	We all helped, but Jane's frog got away.
72	Where did Wade end up?
81	We looked under desks; we looked in the hall.
91	Then we found him. He was inside the fish tank!
100	Ms. Hale located a net and scooped up Wade.
108	She said, "Everyone, hold on to your pets!"

 How can the reader tell that Jane likes Wade?

 Why is Wade hard to find?

Words Read	-	Errors	=	WCPM

☐ **Fall (51 WCPM)**
☐ **Winter (72 WCPM)**
☐ **Spring (89 WCPM)**

WCPM	÷	Words Read	=	Accuracy %

PROSODY				
	L1	L2	L3	L4
Reading in Phrases	O	O	O	O
Pace	O	O	O	O
Syntax	O	O	O	O
Self-correction	O	O	O	O
Intonation	O	O	O	O

Wildfires

Wildfires can ruin land.

These fires can damage homes.

They can hurt plants and animals.

Sometimes they hurt people, too.

These fires happen all around the world.

They show up in forests.

They appear in grasslands.

They tend to occur in hot, dry weather.

A wildfire starts like any fire.

It needs oxygen. Oxygen is a gas in the air.

A fire needs fuel. Fuel is something that burns.

Trees and grasses burn quickly. Fire spreads fast.

Wildfires need heat as well.

The heat might come from lightning.

It could come from striking a match.

That is why adults must take care with matches.

✔ What fuel do wildfires use?

✔ What is the MAIN idea of this article?

Name: _____   Date: _____

Wildfires

4	Wildfires can ruin land.
9	These fires can damage homes.
15	They can hurt plants and animals.
20	Sometimes they hurt people, too.
27	These fires happen all around the world.
32	They show up in forests.
36	They appear in grasslands.
44	They tend to occur in hot, dry weather.
50	A wildfire starts like any fire.
60	It needs oxygen. Oxygen is a gas in the air.
69	A fire needs fuel. Fuel is something that burns.
77	Tree and grasses burn quickly. Fire spreads fast.
82	Wildfires need heat as well.
88	The heat might come from lightning.
95	It could come from striking a match.
104	That is why adults must take care with matches.

 What fuel do wildfires use?

What is the MAIN idea of this article?

Words Read	-	Errors	=	WCPM

☐ **Fall (51 WCPM)**
☐ **Winter (72 WCPM)**
☐ **Spring (89 WCPM)**

WCPM	÷	Words Read	=	Accuracy %

PROSODY

	L1	L2	L3	L4
Reading in Phrases	O	O	O	O
Pace	O	O	O	O
Syntax	O	O	O	O
Self-correction	O	O	O	O
Intonation	O	O	O	O

Late for School

Jason sat up in bed and looked at the clock.

It was half past eight. "Oh, no!" he said.

"I overslept, and I will be late for school."

Jason brushed his teeth and got dressed.

He packed his books. His mom called upstairs.

"Come downstairs for your pancakes," she said.

"I can't eat pancakes today!" Jason cried.

"I am very late for school."

"You must eat three pancakes," she said.

"Breakfast is an important meal."

She put three pancakes on Jason's plate.

They were the size of saucers and delicious!

"Thanks, Mom," Jason said, racing out the door.

Then he ran all the way to school.

He sat in his seat just as the bell rang.

✔ What is Jason's problem at the beginning of the story?

✔ How big are the pancakes?

Name: _____ Date: _____

Late for School

10	Jason sat up in bed and looked at the clock.
19	It was half past eight. "Oh, no!" he said.
28	"I overslept, and I will be late for school."
35	Jason brushed his teeth and got dressed.
43	He packed his books. His mom called upstairs.
50	"Come downstairs for your pancakes," she said.
57	"I can't eat pancakes today!" Jason cried.
63	"I am very late for school."
70	"You must eat three pancakes," she said.
75	"Breakfast is an important meal."
82	She put three pancakes on Jason's plate.
90	They were the size of saucers and delicious!
98	"Thanks, Mom," Jason said, racing out the door.
106	Then he ran all the way to school.
116	He sat in his seat just as the bell rang.

 What is Jason's problem at the beginning of the story?

 How big are the pancakes?

Words Read	-	Errors	=	WCPM

☐ Fall (51 WCPM)
☐ Winter (72 WCPM)
☐ Spring (89 WCPM)

WCPM	÷	Words Read	=	Accuracy %

PROSODY				
	L1	L2	L3	L4
Reading in Phrases	O	O	O	O
Pace	O	O	O	O
Syntax	O	O	O	O
Self-correction	O	O	O	O
Intonation	O	O	O	O

Shoes from Long Ago

People have worn shoes for a long time.

Today, some shoes are worn as decoration.

The first shoes were not.

They were worn to protect. They kept feet safe.

Some people lived in cold places.

Their shoes looked like bags of fur.

They were made from the skins of animals.

Others lived in warm places.

They could wear sandals on their feet.

The sandals were made from grass or leather.

There have been many types of shoes.

Some of them were funny.

At one time, some men wore quite long shoes.

The front of the shoe had a chain.

It was attached to the man's knee.

Why? This kept him from tripping!

✔ What were the first cold weather shoes like?

✔ Why could people in warm places
wear sandals?

Name: _____ Date: _____

Shoes from Long Ago

8	People have worn shoes for a long time.
15	Today, some shoes are worn as decoration.
20	The first shoes were not.
29	They were worn to protect. They kept feet safe.
35	Some people lived in cold places.
42	Their shoes looked like bags of fur.
50	They were made from the skins of animals.
55	Others lived in warm places.
62	They could wear sandals on their feet.
70	The sandals were made from grass or leather.
77	There have been many types of shoes.
82	Some of them were funny.
91	At one time, some men wore quite long shoes.
99	The front of the shoe had a chain.
106	It was attached to the man's knee.
112	Why? This kept him from tripping!

 What were the first cold weather shoes like?

 Why could people in warm places wear sandals?

Words Read	-	Errors	=	WCPM

☐ **Fall (51 WCPM)**
☐ **Winter (72 WCPM)**
☐ **Spring (89 WCPM)**

WCPM	÷	Words Read	=	Accuracy %

PROSODY

	L1	L2	L3	L4
Reading in Phrases	O	O	O	O
Pace	O	O	O	O
Syntax	O	O	O	O
Self-correction	O	O	O	O
Intonation	O	O	O	O

Something Stinks

Carlos and Mark were in the yard after dark.

They were gazing up at the stars.

They had to draw a constellation for their class.

Carlos saw something. It darted across the yard.

"Did you see a black ball just now?" he asked.

Then Mark saw something move, too.

"Did you see that white streak?" he asked.

Carlos asked, "Do you smell something rotten?"

He held his nose as Mark replied, "I sure do."

Mark made a face. He held his nose as well.

They knew what they had seen. It was a skunk!

✓ Where are Carlos and Mark?

✓ How do Carlos and Mark know they saw
a skunk?

Name: _____ Date: _____

Something Stinks

9	Carlos and Mark were in the yard after dark.
16	They were gazing up at the stars.
25	They had to draw a constellation for their class.
33	Carlos saw something. It darted across the yard.
43	"Did you see a black ball just now?" he asked.
49	Then Mark saw something move, too.
57	"Did you see that white streak?" he asked.
64	Carlos asked, "Do you smell something rotten?"
74	He held his nose as Mark replied, "I sure do."
84	Mark made a face. He held his nose as well.
94	They knew what they had seen. It was a skunk!

 Where are Carlos and Mark?

 How do Carlos and Mark know they saw a skunk?

Words Read	-	Errors	=	WCPM

☐ **Fall (51 WCPM)**
☐ **Winter (72 WCPM)**
☐ **Spring (89 WCPM)**

WCPM	÷	Words Read	=	Accuracy %

PROSODY

	L1	L2	L3	L4
Reading in Phrases	O	O	O	O
Pace	O	O	O	O
Syntax	O	O	O	O
Self-correction	O	O	O	O
Intonation	O	O	O	O

Helicopters Help!

Helicopters are much different than airplanes.

They fly straight up or straight down.

They can fly backward and sideways.

They can even stay in one place.

Planes need a runway. Helicopters do not!

They can land in tight spaces.

Helicopters are used to do many things.

They can rescue people. A rope can be dropped.

Sometimes a big basket is tied to the rope.

This can pick up people below.

Helicopters can pull people from sinking ships.

They can save people from burning buildings.

Helicopters also are used to carry things.

They can carry food and medicine.

They take it to places that are hard to reach.

Helicopters help!

✔ How are helicopters different than airplanes?

✔ Name one thing helicopters are used for.

Name: _____   Date: _____

Helicopters Help!

6	Helicopters are much different than airplanes.
13	They fly straight up or straight down.
19	They can fly backward and sideways.
26	They can even stay in one place.
33	Planes need a runway. Helicopters do not!
39	They can land in tight spaces.
46	Helicopters are used to do many things.
55	They can rescue people. A rope can be dropped.
64	Sometimes a big basket is tied to the rope.
70	This can pick up people below.
77	Helicopters can pull people from sinking ships.
84	They can save people from burning buildings.
91	Helicopters also are used to carry things.
97	They can carry food and medicine.
107	They take it to places that are hard to reach.
109	Helicopters help!

✓ How are helicopters different than airplanes?

✓ Name one thing helicopters are used for.

Words Read	-	Errors	=	WCPM

☐ **Fall (51 WCPM)**
☐ **Winter (72 WCPM)**
☐ **Spring (89 WCPM)**

WCPM	÷	Words Read	=	Accuracy %

PROSODY

	L1	L2	L3	L4
Reading in Phrases	O	O	O	O
Pace	O	O	O	O
Syntax	O	O	O	O
Self-correction	O	O	O	O
Intonation	O	O	O	O

Fox and Grapes

One night, Fox had a good dream about grapes.

Fox woke up and thought about his dream.

It's late June, and the weather is hot and sunny.

The grapes are ripe, and I can find them.

Fox set off across the hill where he saw grapes.

They sat way up on vines on tree branches.

Fox went after the tasty grapes.

First, he ran to gain speed. Then he jumped up.

However, he couldn't reach. Fox rose on tiptoes.

But it was still no use; he just couldn't reach.

At last Fox gave up. "This is silly," Fox said.

"I don't want those grapes. They are not great."

✓ What is the moral of this story?

✓ What does Fox dream about?

Name: _____ Date: _____

Fox and Grapes

9	One night, Fox had a good dream about grapes.
17	Fox woke up and thought about his dream.
27	*It's late June, and the weather is hot and sunny.*
36	*The grapes are ripe, and I can find them.*
46	Fox set off across the hill where he saw grapes.
55	They sat way up on vines on tree branches.
61	Fox went after the tasty grapes.
71	First, he ran to gain speed. Then he jumped up.
79	However, he couldn't reach. Fox rose on tiptoes.
89	But it was still no use; he just couldn't reach.
99	At last Fox gave up. "This is silly," Fox said.
108	"I don't want those grapes. They are not great."

✔ What is the moral of this story?

✔ What does Fox dream about?

Words Read	-	Errors	=	WCPM

☐ **Fall (51 WCPM)**
☐ **Winter (72 WCPM)**
☐ **Spring (89 WCPM)**

WCPM	÷	Words Read	=	Accuracy %

PROSODY

	L1	L2	L3	L4
Reading in Phrases	O	O	O	O
Pace	O	O	O	O
Syntax	O	O	O	O
Self-correction	O	O	O	O
Intonation	O	O	O	O

Team Tryouts

Harry woke up. He rolled over and groaned. Getting up early was the worst part of training. The tryouts were only a day away. Harry had started last week. He'd been jogging every morning. His mom was a strong runner. Harry wanted to be one, too.

After school, Harry met his dad at the basketball courts. Harry's dad was a great basketball player. Harry was training for the basketball team, too. Harry and his dad played. Harry made a tough shot.

It was the night before the tryouts. Harry went to bed early. He stared at his uniform. He wondered if he could ever be a track star. Maybe he could become a basketball star too!

✔ Why is Harry training?

✔ How is Harry's work connected to his parents?

Name: _____ Date: _____

Team Tryouts

9	Harry woke up. He rolled over and groaned. Getting
19	up early was the worst part of training. The tryouts
29	were only a day away. Harry had started last week.
38	He'd been jogging every morning. His mom was a
46	strong runner. Harry wanted to be one, too.
55	After school, Harry met his dad at the basketball
67	courts. Harry's dad was a great basketball player.
76	Harry was training for the basketball team, too. Harry
85	and his dad played. Harry made a tough shot.
95	It was the night before the tryouts. Harry went to
106	bed early. He stared at his uniform. He wondered if he
117	could ever be a track star. Maybe he could become a
120	basketball star too!

 Why is Harry training?

 How is Harry's work connected to his parents?

Words Read	-	Errors	=	WCPM

☐ **Fall (71 WCPM)**
☐ **Winter (92 WCPM)**
☐ **Spring (107 WCPM)**

WCPM	÷	Words Read	=	Accuracy %

PROSODY				
	L1	L2	L3	L4
Reading in Phrases	O	O	O	O
Pace	O	O	O	O
Syntax	O	O	O	O
Self-correction	O	O	O	O
Intonation	O	O	O	O

Shipwrecks

Some people look for shipwrecks. Shipwrecks are ships that have sunk. These ships sank long ago. People look for treasures and objects from the past. They can find amazing things!

Some shipwrecks are easy to find. The ship sank in shallow water. It can be seen from the water's surface. Divers reach it easily.

But some ships sink in very deep water. They are hard to find. People spend a lot of time looking for them. They have to search vast areas of water.

First, searchers scan the water. They use special tools. They find where the ships sank. Then, divers go into the ocean. They take a closer look.

Submarines also help with the search. Searchers use cameras, videos, and radios. They record what they see.

✓ Which shipwrecks are most difficult to find?

✓ Why do people look for shipwrecks?

Name: _____ Date: _____

Shipwrecks

7	Some people look for shipwrecks. Shipwrecks are
16	ships that have sunk. These ships sank long ago.
25	People look for treasures and objects from the past.
30	They can find amazing things!
40	Some shipwrecks are easy to find. The ship sank in
50	shallow water. It can be seen from the water's surface.
54	Divers reach it easily.
64	But some ships sink in very deep water. They are
75	hard to find. People spend a lot of time looking for
84	them. They have to search vast areas of water.
93	First, searchers scan the water. They use special tools.
103	They find where the ships sank. Then, divers go into
110	the ocean. They take a closer look.
117	Submarines also help with the search. Searchers
125	use cameras, videos, and radios. They record what
127	they see.

 Which shipwrecks are most difficult to find?

✓ Why do people look for shipwrecks?

Words Read	-	Errors	=	WCPM

☐ **Fall (71 WCPM)**
☐ **Winter (92 WCPM)**
☐ **Spring (107 WCPM)**

WCPM	÷	Words Read	=	Accuracy %

PROSODY				
	L1	L2	L3	L4
Reading in Phrases	O	O	O	O
Pace	O	O	O	O
Syntax	O	O	O	O
Self-correction	O	O	O	O
Intonation	O	O	O	O

The Animal Rescue Center

"Catch him!" Lindy shouted.

The monkey jumped on top of the boxes. It tried to balance. But it could not. Crash! The boxes fell to the ground. The monkey landed safely.

It was another day in the animal rescue center. Lindy's mom picked up the monkey.

"It's good that he's jumping around," said Lindy's mom. "This means that his broken leg is healing. Soon we'll be able to take him back to the wild."

The animal rescue center was in the African grasslands. It was an hour away from the nearest town. Lindy's mom was a doctor for animals. They needed care all day and night. Lindy and her mom lived next to the center. Lindy loved it. She couldn't imagine living anywhere more fun.

✔ Why is it a good sign that the monkey is jumping around?

✔ What job does Lindy's mom have?

Name: _____ Date: _____

The Animal Rescue Center

4	"Catch him!" Lindy shouted.
15	The monkey jumped on top of the boxes. It tried to
26	balance. But it could not. Crash! The boxes fell to the
31	ground. The monkey landed safely.
40	It was another day in the animal rescue center.
46	Lindy's mom picked up the monkey.
54	"It's good that he's jumping around," said Lindy's
64	mom. "This means that his broken leg is healing. Soon
74	we'll be able to take him back to the wild."
82	The animal rescue center was in the African
92	grasslands. It was an hour away from the nearest town.
101	Lindy's mom was a doctor for animals. They needed
112	care all day and night. Lindy and her mom lived next
121	to the center. Lindy loved it. She couldn't imagine
125	living anywhere more fun.

 Why is it a good sign that the monkey is jumping around?

Why is it a good sign that the monkey is jumping around?

What job does Lindy's mom have?

Words Read	-	Errors	=	WCPM

- ☐ **Fall (71 WCPM)**
- ☐ **Winter (92 WCPM)**
- ☐ **Spring (107 WCPM)**

WCPM	÷	Words Read	=	Accuracy %

PROSODY				
	L1	L2	L3	L4
Reading in Phrases	O	O	O	O
Pace	O	O	O	O
Syntax	O	O	O	O
Self-correction	O	O	O	O
Intonation	O	O	O	O

The Telephone

Today we can talk to anyone in the world. We can use phones or computers. How did people send messages before these devices existed? People used the telegraph. They could send messages quickly; however, they could not talk to each other.

People wanted a way to talk to someone far away. Then Alexander Graham Bell invented the telephone. Bell taught deaf children. He knew a lot about how people speak. He knew how they hear. He used what he knew to invent a telephone.

Bell worked on his design for years. He made the first call in 1876. The call was to his helper, Thomas Watson. Watson was in the room next door. Watson heard Bell's voice. Bell said, "Mr. Watson, come here! I need you!"

✓ How did people send long-distance messages before the telephone was invented?

✓ Who received the first phone call?

Name: _____ Date: _____

The Telephone

11	Today we can talk to anyone in the world. We can
19	use phones or computers. How did people send
27	messages before these devices existed? People used the
34	telegraph. They could send messages quickly; however,
41	they could not talk to each other.
51	People wanted a way to talk to someone far away.
58	Then Alexander Graham Bell invented the telephone.
68	Bell taught deaf children. He knew a lot about how
78	people speak. He knew how they hear. He used what
84	he knew to invent a telephone.
94	Bell worked on his design for years. He made the
105	first call in 1876. The call was to his helper, Thomas
114	Watson. Watson was in the room next door. Watson
123	heard Bell's voice. Bell said, "Mr. Watson, come here!
126	I need you!"

 How did people send long-distance messages before the telephone was invented?

 Who received the first phone call?

Words Read	-	Errors	=	WCPM

☐ **Fall (71 WCPM)**
☐ **Winter (92 WCPM)**
☐ **Spring (107 WCPM)**

WCPM	÷	Words Read	=	Accuracy %

PROSODY				
	L1	L2	L3	L4
Reading in Phrases	O	O	O	O
Pace	O	O	O	O
Syntax	O	O	O	O
Self-correction	O	O	O	O
Intonation	O	O	O	O

Karl's Trip

Karl hugged his mom good–bye.

"Have fun!" she called.

The train moved out of the city. Karl was going to visit his grandmother in the mountains. The train climbed through a forest of fir trees. Heavy snowfall covered their branches.

Karl looked out his window. The snow in the city was dirty and melted quickly. It looked different in the mountains. It was clean and fresh.

Grandmother hugged Karl at the station. Back home, she looked concerned. She said, "You must be hungry." She had baked spicy biscuits and a sweet purple plum tart.

It tasted delicious after the long ride. "Thank you," Karl said. He could already tell this was going to be a good trip.

✓ Where is Karl going to at the beginning of the story?

✓ What makes Karl think his trip will be good?

Name: _____ Date: _____

Karl's Trip

6	Karl hugged his mom good–bye.
10	"Have fun!" she called.
21	The train moved out of the city. Karl was going to
29	visit his grandmother in the mountains. The train
38	climbed through a forest of fir trees. Heavy snowfall
41	covered their branches.
51	Karl looked out his window. The snow in the city
61	was dirty and melted quickly. It looked different in the
67	mountains. It was clean and fresh.
74	Grandmother hugged Karl at the station. Back
83	home, she looked concerned. She said, "You must be
94	hungry." She had baked spicy biscuits and a sweet
97	purple plum tart.
106	It tasted delicious after the long ride. "Thank you,"
118	Karl said. He could already tell this was going to be a
120	good trip.

✔ Where is Karl going to at the beginning of the story?

✔ What makes Karl think his trip will be good?

Words Read	-	Errors	=	WCPM

☐ **Fall (71 WCPM)**
☐ **Winter (92 WCPM)**
☐ **Spring (107 WCPM)**

WCPM	÷	Words Read	=	Accuracy %

PROSODY

	L1	L2	L3	L4
Reading in Phrases	O	O	O	O
Pace	O	O	O	O
Syntax	O	O	O	O
Self-correction	O	O	O	O
Intonation	O	O	O	O

Cats in History

Cats have been around for thousands of years. Today, we think of cats as house pets. Long ago, people thought they had special powers. Artists painted pictures of cats. They made sculptures. We can see these paintings and sculptures in museums today.

Cats were important in ancient Egypt. They were honored animals. The Egyptians loved cats. They even had a god with the head of a cat. People who hurt cats were punished. Cats were thought of as treasures.

The ancient Romans also liked cats. They thought cats were a symbol. They stood for being free. Cats could go in temples. No other animals could. There are still many cats in Rome even now. They are protected.

✔ How has thinking about cats changed over time?

✔ What did cats symbolize to the ancient Romans?

Name: _____ Date: _____

Cats in History

8	Cats have been around for thousands of years.
19	Today, we think of cats as house pets. Long ago, people
26	thought they had special powers. Artists painted
35	pictures of cats. They made sculptures. We can see
42	these paintings and sculptures in museums today.
50	Cats were important in ancient Egypt. They were
58	honored animals. The Egyptians loved cats. They even
71	had a god with the head of a cat. People who hurt cats
79	were punished. Cats were thought of as treasures.
87	The ancient Romans also liked cats. They thought
97	cats were a symbol. They stood for being free. Cats
107	could go in temples. No other animals could. There are
117	still many cats in Rome even now. They are protected.

✔ How has thinking about cats changed over time?

✔ What did cats symbolize to the ancient Romans?

Words Read	-	Errors	=	WCPM

☐ **Fall (71 WCPM)**

☐ **Winter (92 WCPM)**

☐ **Spring (107 WCPM)**

WCPM	÷	Words Read	=	Accuracy %

PROSODY

	L1	L2	L3	L4
Reading in Phrases	O	O	O	O
Pace	O	O	O	O
Syntax	O	O	O	O
Self-correction	O	O	O	O
Intonation	O	O	O	O

Marta and the Gray Wolf

Once there was a girl named Marta. She lived near a big forest. Every day, her mother told her to avoid the forest. She would say, "Do not go in there. If you do, the Gray Wolf might get you."

One day, Marta was walking in the grass. She saw some flowers growing at the edge of the woods. They were so pretty. She had to pick them. Deeper into the forest, she saw some more. She picked them, too. All the while, she sang a sweet song to herself.

Suddenly, up rose the Gray Wolf. He said, "Little girl, sing that song again!" Marta did as she was told. Soon the Gray Wolf fell fast asleep. Her lovely song had lulled the wolf.

Marta raced out of the forest. She promised she would listen to her mother. And she never went into the forest again.

✔ What is the moral of this story?

✔ How does Marta escape the Gray Wolf?

Name: _____ Date: _____

Marta and the Gray Wolf

11	Once there was a girl named Marta. She lived near a
22	big forest. Every day, her mother told her to avoid the
34	forest. She would say, "Do not go in there. If you do,
40	the Gray Wolf might get you."
50	One day, Marta was walking in the grass. She saw
60	some flowers growing at the edge of the woods. They
71	were so pretty. She had to pick them. Deeper into the
81	forest, she saw some more. She picked them, too. All
90	the while, she sang a sweet song to herself.
99	Suddenly, up rose the Gray Wolf. He said, "Little
110	girl, sing that song again!" Marta did as she was told.
120	Soon the Gray Wolf fell fast asleep. Her lovely song
124	had lulled the wolf.
133	Marta raced out of the forest. She promised she
143	would listen to her mother. And she never went into
146	the forest again.

 What is the moral of this story?

How does Marta escape the Gray Wolf?

Words Read	-	Errors	=	WCPM

☐ **Fall (71 WCPM)**
☐ **Winter (92 WCPM)**
☐ **Spring (107 WCPM)**

WCPM	÷	Words Read	=	Accuracy %

PROSODY				
	L1	L2	L3	L4
Reading in Phrases	O	O	O	O
Pace	O	O	O	O
Syntax	O	O	O	O
Self-correction	O	O	O	O
Intonation	O	O	O	O

Colors All Around Us

Colors help us understand the world around us.

Sunflowers have bright faces. They look like tiny suns. Their centers are filled with seeds. Yellow petals are around the seeds.

The artist Vincent van Gogh painted sunflowers. He was inspired by their colors. He made more than ten paintings of them. His paintings are treasures; you can find them in museums all over the world.

We often say the ocean is blue. However, water is colorless. Still, a clean ocean can look blue on a sunny day. Sometimes the ocean seems to change colors. Watch it on a stormy day. It may look gray. It may look green.

The color red can mean many things. Red can mean danger. Some animals are red for a reason. They are warning you. Their color shouts, "Stay away!"

✔ Who is Vincent van Gogh?

✔ What does the color red on some animals mean?

Name: _____ Date: _____

Colors All Around Us

8	Colors help us understand the world around us.
16	Sunflowers have bright faces. They look like tiny
25	suns. Their centers are filled with seeds. Yellow petals
29	are around the seeds.
37	The artist Vincent van Gogh painted sunflowers. He
47	was inspired by their colors. He made more than ten
56	paintings of them. His paintings are treasures; you can
64	find them in museums all over the world.
74	We often say the ocean is blue. However, water is
85	colorless. Still, a clean ocean can look blue on a sunny
93	day. Sometimes the ocean seems to change colors.
105	Watch it on a stormy day. It may look gray. It may
107	look green.
117	The color red can mean many things. Red can mean
127	danger. Some animals are red for a reason. They are
134	warning you. Their color shouts, "Stay away!"

✓ Who is Vincent van Gogh?

✓ What does the color red on some animals mean?

Words Read	-	Errors	=	WCPM

☐ **Fall (71 WCPM)**
☐ **Winter (92 WCPM)**
☐ **Spring (107 WCPM)**

WCPM	÷	Words Read	=	Accuracy %

PROSODY

	L1	L2	L3	L4
Reading in Phrases	O	O	O	O
Pace	O	O	O	O
Syntax	O	O	O	O
Self-correction	O	O	O	O
Intonation	O	O	O	O

Antarctica

Travel as far south as you can go. You will reach the South Pole. The South Pole is in Antarctica. Antarctica is a continent covered with ice and snow. It is the coldest place on Earth.

Strong winds blow across Antarctica. It does not rain. It does not even snow very much. A vast layer of ice covers the land. This layer is called an *ice cap*. It is more than a mile thick. The ice cap extends into the sea.

The temperature in Antarctica is very cold. It is well below zero degrees! Water freezes at this temperature. Ice and snow don't melt in Antarctica.

Very few animals live in Antarctica. But many animals live in the oceans around the ice cap. Whales, seals, and sharks live there for part of the year.

👆 Where is the South Pole located?

👆 What is the MAIN idea of this article?

Name: _____ Date: _____

Antarctica

12	Travel as far south as you can go. You will reach the
21	South Pole. The South Pole is in Antarctica. Antarctica
32	is a continent covered with ice and snow. It is the
36	coldest place on Earth.
44	Strong winds blow across Antarctica. It does not
56	rain. It does not even snow very much. A vast layer of
69	ice covers the land. This layer is called an *ice cap*. It is
81	more than a mile thick. The ice cap extends into the sea.
91	The temperature in Antarctica is very cold. It is well
99	below zero degrees! Water freezes at this temperature.
106	Ice and snow don't melt in Antarctica.
114	Very few animals live in Antarctica. But many
124	animals live in the oceans around the ice cap. Whales,
134	seals, and sharks live there for part of the year.

 Where is the South Pole located?

 What is the MAIN idea of this article?

Words Read	-	Errors	=	WCPM

☐ **Fall (71 WCPM)**
☐ **Winter (92 WCPM)**
☐ **Spring (107 WCPM)**

WCPM	÷	Words Read	=	Accuracy %

PROSODY				
	L1	L2	L3	L4
Reading in Phrases	O	O	O	O
Pace	O	O	O	O
Syntax	O	O	O	O
Self-correction	O	O	O	O
Intonation	O	O	O	O

Something Special

There was something that Edie wanted to buy. But she did not have the money. So she rushed around doing work. She hoped doing chores would help her get the money.

Edie cleaned the family's towels and hung them out to dry. Dad helped, but still he paid her a dollar. Edie washed her brother's car. Her dog Spot helped her. He could fetch the hose and the sponge for her. Her brother helped, too. When she could not reach the roof of the car, he picked her up. She got three dollars from him when she was done.

Then Edie babysat for her cousin, Ben. Her aunt was making jam. While it simmered on the stove, Edie helped make a sandwich for Ben. She made him laugh with a cute song.

At the end of the week, Edie had enough money. She had ten dollars. Edie couldn't wait to go to the bookstore!

How does Edie's dog help her with a job?

What is Edie MOST LIKELY going to buy?

Name: _____ Date: _____

Something Special

9	There was something that Edie wanted to buy. But
19	she did not have the money. So she rushed around
28	doing work. She hoped doing chores would help her
31	get the money.
40	Edie cleaned the family's towels and hung them out
52	to dry. Dad helped, but still he paid her a dollar. Edie
61	washed her brother's car. Her dog Spot helped her.
72	He could fetch the hose and the sponge for her. Her
82	brother helped, too. When she could not reach the roof
94	of the car, he picked her up. She got three dollars from
99	him when she was done.
108	Then Edie babysat for her cousin, Ben. Her aunt
118	was making jam. While it simmered on the stove, Edie
128	helped make a sandwich for Ben. She made him laugh
132	with a cute song.
142	At the end of the week, Edie had enough money.
152	She had ten dollars. Edie couldn't wait to go to
154	the bookstore!

✔ How does Edie's dog help her with a job?

✔ What is Edie MOST LIKELY going to buy?

Words Read	-	Errors	=	WCPM

☐ **Fall (71 WCPM)**
☐ **Winter (92 WCPM)**
☐ **Spring (107 WCPM)**

WCPM	÷	Words Read	=	Accuracy %

PROSODY				
	L1	L2	L3	L4
Reading in Phrases	O	O	O	O
Pace	O	O	O	O
Syntax	O	O	O	O
Self-correction	O	O	O	O
Intonation	O	O	O	O

An Interesting Career

What are illustrators? These are the men and women who create the art that goes with books. The art from a book can bring back memories. It can help a reader picture characters.

Art in books helps to tell the story. There are many books that would not be the same without the art. The story would not change. However, the books would feel "unfinished" in some way.

Being an illustrator may seem like fun. But it is a job. The work must be done with care. Illustrators have to learn how to draw well. They need to show different things. They must draw people and animals that seem real.

The same person can be a book's author and illustrator. But that is often not the case. Sometimes the author writes the story first. Then the illustrator comes in and creates the art.

✔ How does art help a book?

✔ What are the challenges in being an illustrator?

Name: _____   Date: _____

An Interesting Career

9	What are illustrators? These are the men and women
20	who create the art that goes with books. The art from
31	a book can bring back memories. It can help a reader
33	picture characters.
44	Art in books helps to tell the story. There are many
55	books that would not be the same without the art. The
63	story would not change. However, the books would
68	feel "unfinished" in some way.
80	Being an illustrator may seem like fun. But it is a job.
90	The work must be done with care. Illustrators have to
100	learn how to draw well. They need to show different
108	things. They must draw people and animals that
110	seem real.
119	The same person can be a book's author and
129	illustrator. But that is often not the case. Sometimes the
138	author writes the story first. Then the illustrator comes
143	in and creates the art.

 How does art help a book?

 What are the challenges in being an illustrator?

Words Read	-	Errors	=	WCPM

☐ **Fall (71 WCPM)**
☐ **Winter (92 WCPM)**
☐ **Spring (107 WCPM)**

WCPM	÷	Words Read	=	Accuracy %

PROSODY				
	L1	L2	L3	L4
Reading in Phrases	O	O	O	O
Pace	O	O	O	O
Syntax	O	O	O	O
Self-correction	O	O	O	O
Intonation	O	O	O	O

Pip the Penguin

Pip is an emperor penguin. He started life as an egg. His mother, Peggy, laid the egg just before she went away. It was a beautiful white egg. She was very proud of it.

All the females left together. They traveled across the ice. They had to find food. They walked toward the sea under a stormy sky.

Pip's father, Philip, watched as the females left. He balanced Peggy's egg on his feet to keep it warm. His feathers fluttered as the wind blew. All of the other fathers in the colony had an egg to look after, too. They knew it was a very important job.

The females returned soon after Pip hatched. His mother recognized them from his father's call. She brought a lot of food.

✔ Why does Pip's mother leave before he hatches?

✔ What job do the fathers have?

Name: _____   Date: _____

Pip the Penguin

11	Pip is an emperor penguin. He started life as an egg.
21	His mother, Peggy, laid the egg just before she went
32	away. It was a beautiful white egg. She was very proud
34	of it.
43	All the females left together. They traveled across the
54	ice. They had to find food. They walked toward the sea
58	under a stormy sky.
66	Pip's father, Philip, watched as the females left.
77	He balanced Peggy's egg on his feet to keep it warm.
88	His feathers fluttered as the wind blew. All of the other
99	fathers in the colony had an egg to look after, too.
107	They knew it was a very important job.
114	The females returned soon after Pip hatched.
122	His mother recognized them from his father's call.
128	She brought a lot of food.

✔ Why does Pip's mother leave before he hatches?

✔ What job do the fathers have?

Words Read	-	Errors	=	WCPM

☐ **Fall (71 WCPM)**
☐ **Winter (92 WCPM)**
☐ **Spring (107 WCPM)**

WCPM	÷	Words Read	=	Accuracy %

PROSODY				
	L1	L2	L3	L4
Reading in Phrases	O	O	O	O
Pace	O	O	O	O
Syntax	O	O	O	O
Self-correction	O	O	O	O
Intonation	O	O	O	O

Australia

Australia is one of the seven continents of the world. Of the seven, it is the driest. It has ten deserts.

All deserts are dry. They are hot during the day and cold at night. Still, many plants and animals live in the desert. People can live in the desert, too.

The red kangaroo lives in the Australian desert. A female can carry its young in a pouch on its stomach. A pouch is like a pocket. Animals that have this type of pouch are called *marsupials*. There are more than 200 kinds of these animals living in or near Australia. One example is the numbat. But it is different from the red kangaroo. How? It does not have a pouch.

✔ How are the red kangaroo and numbat different?

✔ What is the driest continent?

Name: _____ Date: _____

Australia

10	Australia is one of the seven continents of the world.
21	Of the seven, it is the driest. It has ten deserts.
32	All deserts are dry. They are hot during the day and
43	cold at night. Still, many plants and animals live in the
51	desert. People can live in the desert, too.
59	The red kangaroo lives in the Australian desert.
71	A female can carry its young in a pouch on its stomach.
82	A pouch is like a pocket. Animals that have this type
91	of pouch are called *marsupials*. There are more than
101	200 kinds of these animals living in or near Australia.
112	One example is the numbat. But it is different from the
121	red kangaroo. How? It does not have a pouch.

✔ How are the red kangaroo and numbat different?

✔ What is the driest continent?

Words Read	-	Errors	=	WCPM

☐ **Fall (71 WCPM)**
☐ **Winter (92 WCPM)**
☐ **Spring (107 WCPM)**

WCPM	÷	Words Read	=	Accuracy %

PROSODY

	L1	L2	L3	L4
Reading in Phrases	O	O	O	O
Pace	O	O	O	O
Syntax	O	O	O	O
Self-correction	O	O	O	O
Intonation	O	O	O	O

Liza's Ankle

A big storm left puddles everywhere. After school at soccer practice, Liza slipped in the mud. Ouch! Her ankle hurt. She couldn't get up. Coach Grimes put an ice pack on her ankle.

Liza's dad came. He drove her to the emergency room. "I hope you didn't break your ankle, honey," he said.

Liza felt like crying. She didn't want to miss the rest of the soccer season.

The doctor said Liza's ankle was sprained. It was not broken. He told Liza to stay off the soccer field for a few weeks until her ankle healed.

After a few weeks, Liza could play again. In her first game back, Liza scored the winning goal for her team.

"I feel as good as new. No, better than new!" she told her dad.

What causes Liza's injury?

What is most upsetting to Liza?

Name: _____   Date: _____

Liza's Ankle

8	A big storm left puddles everywhere. After school
18	at soccer practice, Liza slipped in the mud. Ouch! Her
28	ankle hurt. She couldn't get up. Coach Grimes put an
33	ice pack on her ankle.
42	Liza's dad came. He drove her to the emergency
51	room. "I hope you didn't break your ankle, honey,"
53	he said.
64	Liza felt like crying. She didn't want to miss the rest
68	of the soccer season.
78	The doctor said Liza's ankle was sprained. It was not
90	broken. He told Liza to stay off the soccer field for a
96	few weeks until her ankle healed.
107	After a few weeks, Liza could play again. In her first
117	game back, Liza scored the winning goal for her team.
129	"I feel as good as new. No, better than new!" she told
131	her dad.

 What causes Liza's injury?

 What is most upsetting to Liza?

Words Read	-	Errors	=	WCPM

☐ **Fall (71 WCPM)**
☐ **Winter (92 WCPM)**
☐ **Spring (107 WCPM)**

WCPM	÷	Words Read	=	Accuracy %

PROSODY

	L1	L2	L3	L4
Reading in Phrases	O	O	O	O
Pace	O	O	O	O
Syntax	O	O	O	O
Self-correction	O	O	O	O
Intonation	O	O	O	O

Hummingbirds

Hummingbirds do not actually hum. But they do beat their wings very fast. This makes a humming sound. If you see a hummingbird, stop and listen. You will hear a buzzing sound. That is the sound of the hummingbird's wings!

Hummingbirds are tiny. They are about the size of large bumblebees. Hummingbirds build small nests. They build the nests with moss, tree bark, leaves and feathers. The nests are very small. Most people don't even notice them because they are so small. The inside of the nest is soft. The mother hummingbird lays two eggs. Soon the baby hummingbirds hatch. When they hatch, the mother hummingbird needs to care for them. The father hummingbird does not share the work.

Hummingbirds have long bills to drink nectar from flowers. Nectar is a sweet juice. They must drink a lot of nectar. They need it to fly. It gives them energy.

✔ Why are hummingbird nests difficult to notice?

✔ Why do hummingbirds have long bills?

Name: _____ Date: _____

Hummingbirds

8	Hummingbirds do not actually hum. But they do
17	beat their wings very fast. This makes a humming
26	sound. If you see a hummingbird, stop and listen.
38	You will hear a buzzing sound. That is the sound of the
40	hummingbird's wings!
49	Hummingbirds are tiny. They are about the size of
55	large bumblebees. Hummingbirds build small nests.
65	They build the nests with moss, tree bark, leaves and
74	feathers. The nests are very small. Most people don't
84	even notice them because they are so small. The inside
94	of the nest is soft. The mother hummingbird lays two
102	eggs. Soon the baby hummingbirds hatch. When they
111	hatch, the mother hummingbird needs to care for them.
119	The father hummingbird does not share the work.
127	Hummingbirds have long bills to drink nectar from
138	flowers. Nectar is a sweet juice. They must drink a lot
149	of nectar. They need it to fly. It gives them energy.

Why are hummingbird nests difficult to notice?

Why do hummingbirds have long bills?

Words Read	-	Errors	=	WCPM

☐ **Fall (71 WCPM)**
☐ **Winter (92 WCPM)**
☐ **Spring (107 WCPM)**

WCPM	÷	Words Read	=	Accuracy %

PROSODY

	L1	L2	L3	L4
Reading in Phrases	O	O	O	O
Pace	O	O	O	O
Syntax	O	O	O	O
Self-correction	O	O	O	O
Intonation	O	O	O	O

Mouse, Rat, and Owl

Mouse and Rat were playing outside. Then they heard someone shout, "Go away! You are too loud." They looked all around, but they could not see who was talking. Then the voice said, "Look up here in the tree."

Mouse and Rat looked up and saw a brown owl. Owl said, "You are making too much noise. I am trying to sleep now."

"But it's light out," said Mouse.

"Yes, I know. Owls sleep in the day. We hunt at night," said Owl.

Mouse and Rat were surprised. They thought everyone slept at night.

Owl startled them out of their thoughts. "Now go away!" he shouted. "And be quiet down there, or I will hunt for you tonight!" Mouse and Rat ran away so that Owl would not be able to find them later.

✔ Why is Owl upset?

✔ What surprises Mouse and Rat?

Name: _____ Date: _____

Mouse, Rat, and Owl

8	Mouse and Rat were playing outside. Then they
17	heard someone shout, "Go away! You are too loud."
27	They looked all around, but they could not see who
37	was talking. Then the voice said, "Look up here in
39	the tree."
50	Mouse and Rat looked up and saw a brown owl. Owl
61	said, "You are making too much noise. I am trying to
63	sleep now."
69	"But it's light out," said Mouse.
80	"Yes, I know. Owls sleep in the day. We hunt at
83	night," said Owl.
90	Mouse and Rat were surprised. They thought
94	everyone slept at night.
103	Owl startled them out of their thoughts. "Now go
114	away!" he shouted. "And be quiet down there, or I will
125	hunt for you tonight!" Mouse and Rat ran away so that
134	Owl would not be able to find them later.

 Why is Owl upset?

 What surprises Mouse and Rat?

Words Read	-	Errors	=	WCPM

☐ **Fall (71 WCPM)**
☐ **Winter (92 WCPM)**
☐ **Spring (107 WCPM)**

WCPM	÷	Words Read	=	Accuracy %

PROSODY

	L1	L2	L3	L4
Reading in Phrases	O	O	O	O
Pace	O	O	O	O
Syntax	O	O	O	O
Self-correction	O	O	O	O
Intonation	O	O	O	O

Lin's Painting

"You're doing very well, class," said Ms. Tallant.

The second graders were working on a mural. It was a picture of their town, Greenville.

Each group was painting a panel. Each panel was put up on the wall as it was finished. Their town had spread across the walls of their classroom!

Lin was working hard on her part of the panel. She carefully painted the park, her favorite part of town. She put herself in the picture with her dog, Gus.

The bell rang. Everyone except Lin packed up for recess.

"It is recess time, Lin," said Ms. Tallant. "You need to get some fresh air."

"Yes, Ms. Tallant," Lin sighed. She put down her paint brush, put away her paints, and put on her coat. She didn't really want to play outside with her classmates. She would rather play in her own park with Gus.

✔ What is Ms. Tallant's class creating?

✔ Why is Lin not excited about recess?

Name: _____ Date: _____

Lin's Painting

8	"You're doing very well, class," said Ms. Tallant.
18	The second graders were working on a mural. It was
24	a picture of their town, Greenville.
33	Each group was painting a panel. Each panel was
45	put up on the wall as it was finished. Their town had
52	spread across the walls of their classroom!
63	Lin was working hard on her part of the panel. She
72	carefully painted the park, her favorite part of town.
82	She put herself in the picture with her dog, Gus.
90	The bell rang. Everyone except Lin packed up
92	for recess.
102	"It is recess time, Lin," said Ms. Tallant. "You need
107	to get some fresh air."
116	"Yes, Ms. Tallant," Lin sighed. She put down her
126	paint brush, put away her paints, and put on her
135	coat. She didn't really want to play outside with
144	her classmates. She would rather play in her own
147	park with Gus.

 What is Ms. Tallant's class creating?

✔ Why is Lin not excited about recess?

Words Read	-	Errors	=	WCPM

☐ **Fall (71 WCPM)**
☐ **Winter (92 WCPM)**
☐ **Spring (107 WCPM)**

WCPM	÷	Words Read	=	Accuracy %

PROSODY				
	L1	L2	L3	L4
Reading in Phrases	O	O	O	O
Pace	O	O	O	O
Syntax	O	O	O	O
Self-correction	O	O	O	O
Intonation	O	O	O	O

The Talking Glove

People who cannot hear have other ways of talking. For instance, many deaf people sign with their hands. But some people do not understand signing. How can deaf people who sign talk with these people?

Scientists are working on solutions. For example, a scientist invented a special glove. A computer in the glove translates sign language. Here's how it works. First, a person puts on the glove. This person signs with his or her hands. Then the glove translates the hand motions into words. It displays these words on a screen. It reads the words through a speaker, too. People nearby may not understand signing. But they can read and hear what the glove says.

Right now this special glove only works in English. But soon it will work in other languages. Deaf and hearing people from many cultures will be able to "talk" to each other.

How is the talking glove a solution to a problem?

How does the talking glove work?

Name: _____ Date: _____

The Talking Glove

9	People who cannot hear have other ways of talking.
18	For instance, many deaf people sign with their hands.
27	But some people do not understand signing. How can
35	deaf people who sign talk with these people?
43	Scientists are working on solutions. For example, a
52	scientist invented a special glove. A computer in the
60	glove translates sign language. Here's how it works.
70	First, a person puts on the glove. This person signs
80	with his or her hands. Then the glove translates the
89	hand motions into words. It displays these words on
99	a screen. It reads the words through a speaker, too.
107	People nearby may not understand signing. But they
115	can read and hear what the glove says.
124	Right now this special glove only works in English.
134	But soon it will work in other languages. Deaf and
143	hearing people from many cultures will be able to
147	"talk" to each other.

 How is the talking glove a solution to a problem?

✔ How does the talking glove work?

Words Read	-	Errors	=	WCPM

☐ **Fall (71 WCPM)**
☐ **Winter (92 WCPM)**
☐ **Spring (107 WCPM)**

WCPM	÷	Words Read	=	Accuracy %

PROSODY				
	L1	L2	L3	L4
Reading in Phrases	O	O	O	O
Pace	O	O	O	O
Syntax	O	O	O	O
Self-correction	O	O	O	O
Intonation	O	O	O	O

The Dirty Creek

"This creek is really dirty," said Marcella.

Mark frowned. "Look at how the reeds are thinning," he said. "I bet that's because the litter is getting in the way of the plants. If this doesn't get cleaned up, all the plants will die. The animals living here will lose their home."

"Yes," said Marcella. "Someone should clean it up."

"Then what are we waiting for?" asked Mark.

Marcella and Mark borrowed a garden rake, large plastic bags, and a box of plastic gloves from their mother. Then they began to clear the litter from the creek bed. Next, they scooped up bottles and cans from the water. Then they picked up garbage from among the reeds. They were so busy that at first they didn't notice they were being watched. Marcella looked up.

"We have company," she said to Mark.

They both smiled as their mom walked over to them, ready to help.

✔ Why are Mark and Marcella concerned?

✔ What do Mark and Marcella decide to do?

Name: _____ Date: _____

The Dirty Creek

7	"This creek is really dirty," said Marcella.
16	Mark frowned. "Look at how the reeds are thinning,"
28	he said. "I bet that's because the litter is getting in the
39	way of the plants. If this doesn't get cleaned up, all
49	the plants will die. The animals living here will lose
51	their home."
59	"Yes," said Marcella. "Someone should clean it up."
67	"Then what are we waiting for?" asked Mark.
75	Marcella and Mark borrowed a garden rake, large
85	plastic bags, and a box of plastic gloves from their
95	mother. Then they began to clear the litter from the
105	creek bed. Next, they scooped up bottles and cans from
114	the water. Then they picked up garbage from among
125	the reeds. They were so busy that at first they didn't
133	notice they were being watched. Marcella looked up.
140	"We have company," she said to Mark.
150	They both smiled as their mom walked over to them,
153	ready to help.

✔ Why are Mark and Marcella concerned?

✔ What do Mark and Marcella decide to do?

Words Read	-	Errors	=	WCPM

☐ **Fall (71 WCPM)**
☐ **Winter (92 WCPM)**
☐ **Spring (107 WCPM)**

WCPM	÷	Words Read	=	Accuracy %

PROSODY

	L1	L2	L3	L4
Reading in Phrases	O	O	O	O
Pace	O	O	O	O
Syntax	O	O	O	O
Self-correction	O	O	O	O
Intonation	O	O	O	O

Boat Safety

Boat rides are a great way to be on the water without getting wet. A boat ride can be a fast way to get to places. Many people like to fish from a boat. There are rules to follow so you can stay safe while boating.

First, never go on a boat without an adult. Always check the weather before you leave, and don't get in a boat if a storm is coming.

When you are in the boat, you must wear a life jacket. Be careful when you get in and out of a boat. It is easy to slip and fall. Don't jump in a boat. The boat can tip over. And ask an adult before jumping or diving from a boat. You need to watch out. Rocks or other sharp objects can be under the water.

What do you do if there is an issue when you are out at sea? Reach the U.S. Coast Guard. The Coast Guard watches over the coastline and seas of America.

✔ What must you always wear on a boat?

✔ Why can diving from a boat be risky?

Name: _____   Date: _____

Boat Safety

12	Boat rides are a great way to be on the water without
25	getting wet. A boat ride can be a fast way to get to
36	places. Many people like to fish from a boat. There are
46	rules to follow so you can stay safe while boating.
56	First, never go on a boat without an adult. Always
67	check the weather before you leave, and don't get in a
73	boat if a storm is coming.
84	When you are in the boat, you must wear a life
96	jacket. Be careful when you get in and out of a boat.
109	It is easy to slip and fall. Don't jump in a boat. The
120	boat can tip over. And ask an adult before jumping or
131	diving from a boat. You need to watch out. Rocks or
139	other sharp objects can be under the water.
152	What do you do if there is an issue when you are out
162	at sea? Reach the U.S. Coast Guard. The Coast Guard
170	watches over the coastline and seas of America.

✔ What must you always wear on a boat?

✔ Why can diving from a boat be risky?

Words Read	-	Errors	=	WCPM

☐ **Fall (71 WCPM)**
☐ **Winter (92 WCPM)**
☐ **Spring (107 WCPM)**

WCPM	÷	Words Read	=	Accuracy %

PROSODY				
	L1	L2	L3	L4
Reading in Phrases	O	O	O	O
Pace	O	O	O	O
Syntax	O	O	O	O
Self-correction	O	O	O	O
Intonation	O	O	O	O

Football Tryouts

Bindi and Amy were practicing for touch football tryouts, but Amy was having trouble throwing the ball straight.

"Come on, Amy," shouted Bindi. "Throw the football to me!"

Amy threw the football, but it dropped as soon as it left her hands and tumbled slowly along the ground. She walked away and sat down on a bench. Amy didn't like touch football tryouts. Everyone threw better than she did. Plus, Amy had stayed home sick from school the last two weeks. She still felt weak and not totally healthy.

Bindi ran over. "Come on, Amy," he said. "We're not going to be on the same team if you don't try harder."

Amy shook her head. "I just want to sit and watch right now," she explained.

"I know it's hard, Amy," said Bindi. "But if we work together, I know you'll get better. I promise! The team won't feel the same to me if you are not on it."

✔ What is Bindi's promise?

✔ What text evidence supports the idea that Bindi and Amy are friends?

Name: _____   Date: _____

Football Tryouts

8	Bindi and Amy were practicing for touch football
16	tryouts, but Amy was having trouble throwing the
18	ball straight.
26	"Come on, Amy," shouted Bindi. "Throw the football
28	to me!"
39	Amy threw the football, but it dropped as soon as it
48	left her hands and tumbled slowly along the ground.
58	She walked away and sat down on a bench. Amy
65	didn't like touch football tryouts. Everyone threw
75	better than she did. Plus, Amy had stayed home sick
86	from school the last two weeks. She still felt weak and
89	not totally healthy.
99	Bindi ran over. "Come on, Amy," he said. "We're not
111	going to be on the same team if you don't try harder."
122	Amy shook her head. "I just want to sit and watch
126	right now," she explained.
137	"I know it's hard, Amy," said Bindi. "But if we work
147	together, I know you'll get better. I promise! The team
159	won't feel the same to me if you are not on it."

 What is Bindi's promise?

 What text evidence supports the idea that Bindi and Amy are friends?

Words Read	-	Errors	=	WCPM

☐ **Fall (71 WCPM)**
☐ **Winter (92 WCPM)**
☐ **Spring (107 WCPM)**

WCPM	÷	Words Read	=	Accuracy %

PROSODY	L1	L2	L3	L4
Reading in Phrases	O	O	O	O
Pace	O	O	O	O
Syntax	O	O	O	O
Self-correction	O	O	O	O
Intonation	O	O	O	O

The Discovery of Troy

Around 3,000 years ago, Greece and Troy were at war. Troy was an ancient city. It lay on the coast of what is now Turkey.

According to legend, 10,000 Greek ships sailed to Troy. Greece and Troy fought for ten years. The war ended when some Greek soldiers came up with a plan. They built a huge wooden horse and hid inside. The people of Troy thought the horse was a gift. They pulled it inside the city walls. At night, the Greek soldiers climbed out. Then they attacked the city.

Years later, many people thought Troy was just a legend. But a German archaeologist changed their minds. In 1871, he went to the coast of Turkey. He began digging at a small hill. Inside the hill, he found the remains of nine ancient cities. One city had large stone walls. He thought he had found the walls of Troy.

✔ How did the Greek soldiers trick the people of Troy?

✔ Where was Troy located?

Name: _____   Date: _____

The Discovery of Troy

9	Around 3,000 years ago, Greece and Troy were at
21	war. Troy was an ancient city. It lay on the coast of
25	what is now Turkey.
33	According to legend, 10,000 Greek ships sailed to
43	Troy. Greece and Troy fought for ten years. The war
52	ended when some Greek soldiers came up with a
62	plan. They built a huge wooden horse and hid inside.
73	The people of Troy thought the horse was a gift. They
83	pulled it inside the city walls. At night, the Greek
91	soldiers climbed out. Then they attacked the city.
100	Years later, many people thought Troy was just a
107	legend. But a German archaeologist changed their
118	minds. In 1871, he went to the coast of Turkey. He
129	began digging at a small hill. Inside the hill, he found
139	the remains of nine ancient cities. One city had large
150	stone walls. He thought he had found the walls of Troy.

 How did the Greek soldiers trick the people of Troy?

✔ Where was Troy located?

Words Read	-	Errors	=	WCPM

☐ **Fall (71 WCPM)**
☐ **Winter (92 WCPM)**
☐ **Spring (107 WCPM)**

WCPM	÷	Words Read	=	Accuracy %

PROSODY

	L1	L2	L3	L4
Reading in Phrases	O	O	O	O
Pace	O	O	O	O
Syntax	O	O	O	O
Self-correction	O	O	O	O
Intonation	O	O	O	O

Mrs. Bailey's Store

Mrs. Bailey's country store stood at the end of Cherry Blossom Lane. It was famous for its beautiful knitted goods. If you looked around the store, you were sure to see Mrs. Bailey. She was always knitting or cleaning.

One morning, Mrs. Bailey was dusting and fussing even more than usual. Her new helper was about to arrive.

Clip-clop-trip-trop went the sound of the hooves up the pebbled path.

"She's here!" Mrs. Bailey said excitedly. She hung up her duster and ran to the front door. She flung open the door and bounced down the path. She passed the vegetable garden and the flower garden. She passed the old oak tree that shaded the yard. Finally, she reached the front gate. It swung open with a creak.

"Welcome, Sarah," Mrs. Bailey called out eagerly. "Follow me inside, and let's get started!"

✔ Why is Mrs. Bailey cleaning up at the start of the story?

✔ Who is Sarah?

Name: _____ Date: _____

Mrs. Bailey's Store

10	Mrs. Bailey's country store stood at the end of Cherry
19	Blossom Lane. It was famous for its beautiful knitted
30	goods. If you looked around the store, you were sure to
39	see Mrs. Bailey. She was always knitting or cleaning.
47	One morning, Mrs. Bailey was dusting and fussing
56	even more than usual. Her new helper was about
58	to arrive.
69	*Clip-clop-trip-trop* went the sound of the hooves up
72	the pebbled path.
80	"She's here!" Mrs. Bailey said excitedly. She hung
92	up her duster and ran to the front door. She flung open
102	the door and bounced down the path. She passed the
110	vegetable garden and the flower garden. She passed
120	the old oak tree that shaded the yard. Finally, she
130	reached the front gate. It swung open with a creak.
137	"Welcome, Sarah," Mrs. Bailey called out eagerly.
144	"Follow me inside, and let's get started!"

 Why is Mrs. Bailey cleaning up at the start of the story?

 Who is Sarah?

Words Read	-	Errors	=	WCPM

- ☐ **Fall (71 WCPM)**
- ☐ **Winter (92 WCPM)**
- ☐ **Spring (107 WCPM)**

WCPM	÷	Words Read	=	Accuracy %

PROSODY

	L1	L2	L3	L4
Reading in Phrases	O	O	O	O
Pace	O	O	O	O
Syntax	O	O	O	O
Self-correction	O	O	O	O
Intonation	O	O	O	O

Henry Ford's Assembly Line

In the 1880s, two German inventors built the first modern cars. These cars were a lot like cars today. But another important change came in 1913. This change affected how cars were made.

The first cars were very expensive. Many people could not buy them. Henry Ford changed that. Ford was an American car maker. He started making cars on an assembly line. On an assembly line, each worker only does one job. This is a much faster way of working. It is also much cheaper. Today, many cars are made this way in factories.

Before assembly lines, Ford's workers built a single car in 12 hours. After, it only took 90 minutes. By the 1920s, Ford made one car every 43 seconds! Ford cars were cheap to make. As a result, they were also cheap to buy. More people were able to own cars.

✔ What change did Ford bring to making cars?

✔ How did Ford's idea result in more people owning cars?